Braid of Feathers

Braid of Feathers

American Indian Law and
Contemporary Tribal Life

Frank Pommersheim

UNIVERSITY OF CALIFORNIA PRESS
Berkeley · *Los Angeles* · *London*

University of California Press
Berkeley and Los Angeles, California

University of California Press, Ltd.
London, England

Earlier versions of some of these chapters have been published separately, in somewhat different form, in the following journals, which have granted permission to reprint here. Parts of chapter 3 appeared in 18 NEW MEXICO LAW REVIEW 49 (1988) and 31 ARIZONA LAW REVIEW 329 (1989); parts of chapter 4 appeared in 1992 WISCONSIN LAW REVIEW 411 (1992) and 27 GONZAGA LAW REVIEW 393 (1991/92); parts of chapter 6 appeared in 12 AMERICAN INDIAN LAW REVIEW 195 (1984); and a small part of the Conclusion appeared in 69 NORTH DAKOTA LAW REVIEW 337 (1993).

First Paperback Printing 1997

Library of Congress Cataloging-in-Publication Data

Pommersheim, Frank.
    Braid of feathers : American Indian law and contemporary tribal life / Frank Pommersheim.
        p. cm.
    Includes bibliographical references and index.
    ISBN 0-520-20894-3 (alk. paper)
    1. Indians of North America—Legal status, laws, etc. 2. Tribal government—United States. I. Title.
KF8205.P6   1995
973'.0497—dc20   94-4846

Printed in the United States of America

10   09   08   07   06   05   04
12   11   10   9   8   7   6   5   4   3

The paper used in this publication meets the minimum requirements of ANSI/NISO Z39.48-1992 (R 1997) (Permanence of Paper). ∞

For Stanley Red Bird (1917–87) and
Tillie Black Bear:
mentors, friends, relatives

Contents

Acknowledgments

Somewhat unexpectedly, I have been at work for many years on this book, even when I didn't think I was working on it. Many pieces came together to make the whole, and many individuals assisted in bringing this process to fruition. To all of them I owe a substantial debt of gratitude. They include the many thoughtful (and supportive) scholars in the field of Indian law, namely, Milner Ball, Bob Clinton, Vine Deloria, Jr., Phil Frickey, David Getches, Nell Newton, Rennard Strickland, Charles Wilkinson, and Rob Williams; esteemed colleagues (past and present) on both the Rosebud Sioux and Cheyenne River Sioux Tribal Courts of Appeal, namely, Justices Tony Rivers, Everett Dupris, Mario Gonzalez, Jim Abourezk, and Bob Clinton at Cheyenne River and Mary Wynne, Ramon Roubideaux, Mike Swallow, Robert Grey Eagle, Marvin Amiotte, Cheryl Three Stars Valandra, Pat Lee, Leroy Greaves, and Diane Zephyier Byrd at Rosebud, as well as Chief Trial Judges Rochelle Ducheneaux at Cheyenne River and Sherman Marshall at Rosebud; leading and dedicated practitioners of Indian law in South Dakota, namely, Terry Pechota, General Counsel, of the Rosebud Sioux Tribe and Steve Emery, Tim Joranko, and Mark Van Norman of the Cheyenne River Sioux Tribe's Attorney General's office; and, finally, helpful friends and former colleagues at Sinte Gleska University on the Rosebud Sioux Reservation including Cheryl Crazy Bull, Victor Douville, Archie Beauvais, Ron Goodman, Jerry Mohatt, and Beth Windsor.

I also owe a debt of gratitude to the support staff at the Rosebud Sioux Tribal Court, particularly Carmen Hicks and Denita Marshall, and at the Cheyenne River Sioux Tribal Court, especially Murphy Herrera.

No project of consequence can easily move forward without institutional encouragement and support. At the University of South Dakota School of Law, I have worked for three cordial and collegial deans: Walt Reed, Mike Driscoll, and Barry Vickrey. I thank them, as well as being grateful for the financial support of the H. Lauren Lewis Faculty Research Fellowship of the University of South Dakota Law School Foundation.

And yes, special thanks to those wonderful typists at the University of South Dakota School of Law who have translated chicken scratch into literate copy, including Carol Hanson, Linda Broderson, Elayne Lande, Lois Gregoire, and Gayle Bliss. I am not worthy. Also, I thank my faithful and indefatigable research assistants, including Jenny Fyten, Mike Loos, Okorie Ngwuta, Tal Weizorek, and Jean Pendleton, and the gems of the University of South Dakota's School of Law, law librarians Delores Jorgensen and Candice Spurlin.

My deepest gratitude to Barb Sokolow for her fine illustrations and cover art.

And finally, my family—Anne Dunham and our children, Nicholas, Kate, and Hannah. Without them, nothing is possible.

Introduction:
Why Indian Tribes and
Indian Law Matter

If history is simply the propaganda of the victors, as suggested by the influential writer Simone Weil, then much dominant legal history concerning Native Americans and Indian tribes is inherently suspect. This history is not necessarily false or erroneous; rather, it is simply something worthy of close scrutiny, intense reflection, and energetic dialogue. Although much has been written about Indian history and law, little of what has been written concerning Indian law carefully scrutinizes the assumptions that support the historical and contemporary ratification of federal dominance and the parallel limits on tribal sovereignty and self-government. In addition, almost none of what has been written reflects the indigenous, localized tribal perspective.

Indeed, most Indian law[1] writing focuses on the pervasive role of Congress and the Supreme Court and their enduring dominance, whether for good or ill. In general, federal hegemony in Indian law and Indian affairs is extensive, but if we do not acknowledge the counterweight of tribal sovereignty and authority, the federal presence seems more dominant than it really is. Most scholarship in this area tends to relegate, even if inadvertently, important tribal institutions like tribal courts to a continuing role of passivity and marginality, dependent on federal jurisprudential largesse. If tribal courts are not seen as a vital force in the development of Indian law, their important and instructive struggles will remain largely unknown—consigned to the corridors of (dominant) legal history. This concedes far too much power to the laws and courts of the conqueror.

Much of what is happening in tribal law and tribal courts is exciting and important, and these events provide an enviable window through which to observe the development of several themes significant at both the tribal and national—the indigenous and dominant—levels of American and global society. These themes include (1) an examination of the dominant society's historical, legal, and cultural commitment to diversity and pluralism; (2) an analytical perspective from a unique minority viewpoint that does *not* seek assimilation or greater access to the dominant society but seeks rather to preserve a historically based "measured separatism"; (3) a view of the dominant society's rule of law in an indigenous, colonized, and developing society; (4) an opportunity to observe the development of the foundational concept of tribal sovereignty at the local, reservation level; and (5) a chance to ascertain the relationship of law—both federal and tribal—to the quality of contemporary tribal life as one critical element of the braid of feathers that makes up tribal culture and society.

The view of this book, then, is more of an inside-out view from the grassroots, reservation level rather than the traditional top-down view that permeates most Indian law writing. According to this inside-out view, a pivotal ingredient in realizing tribal sovereignty within such a national pluralistic republic as the United States is the understanding and implementation of the indigenous vision that develops in its localized institutional settings. For example, in this view we should examine tribal court jurisprudence with reference to the tribal perception of its struggle to render justice and fair play within Indian country. This analysis does not ignore federal constraints but seeks rather to place them in a more limited (albeit forceful) context that achieves a better balance and equilibrium from which to view emerging tribal court development. Without this angle of vision, the field of Indian law becomes relentlessly monolithic and self-referential. If tribal courts exist only to mimic the majoritarian legal system, the work of colonization and assimilation is complete. Thus, one important goal of tribal court jurisprudence is to produce a creative body of law that synthesizes the best of the dominant legal system with the legal imperatives of tribal history and culture, while at the same time avoiding dominant pressures that would render such a synthesis irrelevant or contrary to the national interest. In addition, emerging tribal court jurisprudence provides a valuable perspective on the meaning and use of language, the importance of narrative and story, and the meaning of justice from the indigenous point of view.

The reservation perspective also allows ample opportunity to elucidate the theme of "difference" that is inherent in any consideration of Indian law matters, as well as directing our attention to the *values* that tribal legal systems seek to actualize as significant aspects of contemporary tribal life. On the relatively rare occasions when commentators examine tribal courts and judicial systems, they limit their examination to a comparison with state and federal systems, focusing narrowly on resources and procedural competence without any understanding of or reference to the values these systems are trying to realize. This view, which lacks any sense of culture or context, deprives tribal courts of their legitimate aspirations toward relative independence and cultural integrity. More explicit concerns include how much power tribal courts have or ought to have and what federal limitations, constitutional or otherwise, constrain the judicial authority of tribal courts.

Indian tribes and their institutions also play a significant role in the life of the West and are key players within the region both politically and economically. The West has always been a source of valuable national assets such as land, water, timber, coal, and uranium. A good deal of these resources in the West are owned and controlled by Indian tribes, and therefore much of the future vitality of Indian tribes is bound up with their role in the region and the outlook for the region as a whole. These tribal and regional concerns in turn raise hard questions about economic development, the integrity of the landscape, and cultural continuity. How tribes decide to deal with local development and regional issues will powerfully determine the future identity not only of the tribes but of the entire region as well.

The material well-being of tribes—in other words, their economic sovereignty—will in turn have a direct bearing on their political and legal sovereignty. If tribes remain materially impoverished, especially within a national capitalist-welfare state, their political sovereignty and aspirations will be continually undermined. In this republic, political and economic well-being often go hand in hand. The democratic ideals of freedom and liberty flourish best within an economic framework of growth, progress, and stability. Such economic well-being need not be limited, however, to individual accumulation that is antithetical to group or collective tribal well-being. This interweaving of economic and political concerns raises serious questions for tribes in the context of their commitment to cultural fidelity and continuity with the past.

The regional landscape of the West also provides a valuable locus for an examination of tribes' interactions with their most immediate physical neighbors, the state and local governments. Despite the pervasive role of the federal government in Indian law and affairs, the most prominent day-to-day reality in the life of many tribes is the quotidian presence of and interaction with non-Indians and the states. It is here that tribes often confront the reality of racial animus and the fiercest competition for resources and jurisdiction. Thoughtful consideration of the issues of economic development, tribal-state relations, and regional identity provides a valuable complement to the federal-tribal perspective that so often holds sway in Indian law writing.

The ability of tribes to realize important cultural and economic values is severely tested at the state and local level. Nevertheless, there are many examples of, and opportunities for, cooperative and creative ventures that can advance mutual self-interests, particularly in light of the historical, political, and economic dominance of the entire region by outside interests. In many cases the state and regional issues have too often been eclipsed by the federal presence in Indian affairs and its determinative role throughout the West. But that presence too must yield if there is to be hope for the future in Indian country and throughout the region.

In much of the analysis presented here, I attempt to identify several angles of vision—including those of the reservation and the region—that help to reveal the situation confronting Indian tribes as they continue their quest to define and to effectuate a meaningful agenda of sovereignty in the latter part of the twentieth century. These angles of vision suggest that there may be greater possibilities for self-determination than conventional top-down, federally saturated views usually permit. In addition, such views minimize (without ignoring) dependence in favor of an optimal explanation identifying the widest possible area of self-defining autonomy. Possibilities for change are, in part, a function of perceptions about social and cultural reality; the analysis here seeks to enhance social and cultural perceptions that make potential liberating change more likely than not.

The inside-out view is grounded, in part, in a commitment to dialogue and praxis as critical elements for developing a strategy of change. This means encouraging talk within and across tribal (and nontribal) communities about what is desirable and what is possible. It means using the gifts of culture and education and the tools of analysis and action both to describe and to transform the inimical pressures of oppressive historical and contemporary circumstance in order to advance a flourishing tribal way of life.

All of this, of course, poses trenchant questions for the dominant society, particularly regarding its legacy of prejudice and exploitation as well as its ideals of freedom and democratic pluralism. The point, as suggested by Vine Deloria, Jr., a leading Sioux intellectual, is not to excoriate the "white man" once again to come to his senses but to look to a more humane and morally coherent era that is based in the core values of respect and dignity:

> The lesson which seems so hard to learn is that of dignity and respect. Some of the voices contained herein may appear to be complaining about the loss of land, the loss of a way of life, or the continuing propensity of the white man to change the terms of the debate to favor himself. But deep down these are cries about dignity, complaints about the lack of respect. "It is not necessary," Sitting Bull said, "that eagles should be crows." [2]

Inevitably, I have a personal point of view. It is neither detached nor neutral but engaged and committed. I lived and worked on the Rosebud Sioux Reservation in South Dakota for ten years and continue to serve on the appellate courts of both the Rosebud Sioux Tribe and the Cheyenne River Sioux Tribe. It was and continues to be an important personal and professional experience for me and my family. It was and continues to be an opportunity to see (dominant) injustice up close, as well as to experience the richness and reverence of Lakota culture. This experience has also deepened my awareness of many of the problems addressed in this book and sharpened my understanding of their etiology; perhaps more important, it has helped me identify possibilities for effective change.

My point of view is also grounded in the particular western landscape of Indian country in South Dakota and the specifics of a treaty-based indigenous jurisprudence. This reality is not necessarily identical with the rest of Indian country, which often varies dramatically as it runs from east to west across this country. Yet despite this diversity, the central unity of Indian country is the essential commitment to survive and to flourish within a tribal context. Within this larger unity, I believe, the analytical and narrative motifs of this book will be equally resonant and familiar even to distant friends. Ultimately, of course, readers must evaluate for themselves the validity and worth of these claims and assessments.

PART ONE

Different Roots, Different Branches

The Cultural and Legal Setting

A rich diversity of landscapes, cultures, histories, and people exists throughout Indian country. This country includes, for example, 278 federal reservations, ranging from that of the Navajo Tribe, with 160,000 members and fifteen million acres located in parts of Arizona, New Mexico, and Utah, to a few California rancherias that consist of only one or two families living on less than fifty acres. Economic conditions vary significantly, but poverty is extensive, with conservative estimates placing at least one-third and perhaps two-thirds of the 800,000 persons living on reservations across the country below the poverty level. Reservation unemployment rates often climb as high as 60 to 70 percent. Health conditions are also consistently below the national standard, with life expectancy below normal and infant mortality above. Educational accomplishment also consistently falls below national averages, with high dropout rates particularly at the high school level.[1]

Despite these generally dismal numbers, two interrelated features stand out. First, the statistics relevant to education, health care, and unemployment are generally improving; and second, there is a firm, almost fervent commitment to the reservation as the centerpiece of contemporary Indian life. Chapter 1, on the reservation as place, seeks to detail the historical, legal, and cultural elements embedded in this commitment to particularized landscapes that are often erroneously described as unattractive.

These descriptions are drawn primarily from my twenty years of experience in and around Indian country in South Dakota. Here I seek to develop a sense of context—cultural, spiritual, and physical—to help explain why Indian people are committed to reservation life and why non-Indians need to honor and respect that commitment. For it is this commitment to the reservation as place that undergirds all the central legal struggles in Indian country about land, water, natural resources, and jurisdiction. Unless we understand this context, there is little chance that we can forge a commitment to eradicate the stigma of invidious difference while at the same time preserving an enduring pride of difference. Without the human and cultural specifics, the field of Indian law is hopelessly abstract and disconnected from the reality and aspiration of contemporary tribal life. The thick description of the reservation as place provides a context for caring as well as a firm grounding for understanding the pain and promise of law in contemporary Indian life.

Chapter 2 changes focus to provide a national perspective on the development of foundational Indian law principles that set the dominant framework for analyzing the status and aspiration of Indian tribes within this republic from its very beginnings in the 1700s through the last decade of the twentieth century and beyond. These materials demonstrate a variegated admixture of attitudes and doctrines, including constitutional shortcomings, a poverty of coherent theory, consistent exploitation, and only intermittent concern for human rights. Not surprisingly, a pattern of both theoretical and practical inconsistency emerges.

This early work was largely undertaken and accomplished by the U.S. Supreme Court under the leadership of Chief Justice John Marshall, particularly in the seminal trilogy of cases including *Johnson v. McIntosh,*[2] *Cherokee Nation v. Georgia,*[3] and *Worcester v. Georgia.*[4] These foundational cases are replete with their own paradoxes of racial animus, false anthropology, sincere engagement, and modest humanitarian concern. These early efforts also reflected a basic recognition of some kind of tribal sovereignty and self-government as part of the nascent doctrinal patchwork of treaties, the trust relationship, and the plenary authority of Congress. The metaphor of a conqueror with a conscience is a relatively accurate description of these early efforts.

Federal Indian law has yet to resolve these paradoxes, develop coherent theory, and establish a reliable conceptual and human framework within which to engage modern Indian law issues and tribal aspirations. The legacy of this colonized context persists, and until it is understood and transformed, there can be little hope for a national legal reality that meaningfully integrates tribal sovereignty within its fabric of permanence and legitimacy. Mastery and appreciation of this background is essential in order to understand the federal legal reality that tribes confront in their continuing efforts to establish tribal sovereignty and advance the flourishing of tribal life.

CHAPTER ONE

The Reservation as Place

From the Indians we learned a toughness and a
    strength; and we gained
A freedom: by taking theirs: but a real freedom:
    born
From the wild and open land our grandfathers
    heroically stole.
But we took a wound at Indian hands: a part of
    our soul scabbed over.

           Thomas McGrath, Letter to an
                      Imaginary Friend

Indian reservations are often described as islands of poverty and despair torn from the continent of national progress.[1] Less often, they are extolled as places luckily isolated from the predations of the twentieth century.[2] Each of these descriptions invokes, in part, the complex field of Indian law as a touchstone of both the past and future, as either the wedge that will break up the Indians' natural resources, land, and culture[3] or as a countervailing force of restraint that promises cultural renewal.[4] Hidden in this web of description and claims lies the important notion of the reservation as place: a physical, human, legal, and spiritual reality that embodies the history, dreams, and aspirations of Indian people, their communities, and their tribes. It is a place that marks the endurance of Indian communities against the onslaught of a marauding European society; it is also a place that holds the promise of fulfillment. As Lakota[5] people say, "*Hecel lena Oyate nipikte*" (That these people may live). The reservation constitutes an abiding place full of quotidian vitality and pressing dilemmas that continue to define modern Indian life.

There is little doubt that the states of the West, and South Dakota in particular, have often resisted the notion that the reservations possess any positive significance for the individual states or the region.[6] The history of litigious animosity is long and bitter, with continuous and ongoing disputes about reservation boundaries,[7] water rights,[8] the Black Hills,[9] and state authority on the reservation,[10] to name only the most prominent. Yet at this juncture it may be worthwhile to suggest another angle of vision which might, in turn, suggest an angle of repose[11]—a vision infused by mutual understanding and common interest.

This chapter centers on the continuing process of cultural self-scrutiny and intercultural contact between Indians and non-Indians and between Indian tribes and the state and federal governments. This "contact,"[12] which began with the arrival of the first Europeans, is continuous. The process should not, of course, be understood in terms of the ethnocentric concepts of manifest destiny, progress, and cultural superiority; rather, we must examine the forces at play in the "contact" and the rubric of *choices* that emerges in the process. Choice, whether conscious or not, has very real implications for individuals, communities, and tribes. Choice is not always apparent, and the failure to be aware of it often results in loss and forfeited opportunity. It is therefore important to highlight and clarify these choices as they emerge from the consideration of the reservation as place and eternal center. These choices are not merely grounded in considerations of efficiency but are also located in the larger space of culture and meaning.[13]

There are no "answers," and the imposition of "answers" in the past—answers such as cultural assimilation, religious conversion, and the concept of individual property—resulted in substantial cultural loss and the severe erosion of political and personal autonomy. These were answers to the wrong questions, for the questions were framed against the desires and beliefs of a European, expansionary society, not against the needs and values of tribal communities. Sovereignty and freedom have no meaning apart from the ability to make informed choices. My intention here is to elucidate the contours of some of the right questions about the reservation—their texture, their import, and the options they suggest. Doing so honors my obligation that flows from my friendship with people and communities who have done so much, with lasting good humor, to highlight the issues and enhance the choices in my own life and those of my family.[14]

More broadly, I write from two overarching assumptions. One is that, despite grinding poverty and widespread despair, there is nevertheless a flame of hope and a broadening range of choices in almost all aspects of reservation life. If the most observable and detrimental aspect of the dominance of the majority society in Indian country has been the presence of substantial constraints and a reduced flexibility of choice,[15] this situation has been successfully reversed. Despite the difficult and often inimical conditions, renaissance and struggle at the grassroots level have accomplished important changes in options for growth and fulfillment.

The second assumption is that, whatever the conditions, tribal members have been committed to remaining indelibly Indian, proudly defining themselves as a people apart and resisting full incorporation into the dominant society around them.[16] Yet Indians and their tribes must encounter and transform modern social, economic, and political conditions in order to achieve a meaningful and flourishing future; the encounter and transformation must be governed by wise choice and mediated through deeply held cultural values.

A new understanding and willingness by the non-Indian community to listen to and to engage in dialogue and discussion with the Indian community may also help accomplish this formidable task of transformation. Such mutual efforts may, in turn, redefine and redirect the political, legal, and social relationships between Indians and non-Indians and the tribes and the state. Yet the realization of any of these aspirations must rest on a firm understanding of the role of the reservation as the irreducible touchstone of tribal posterity and well-being.

FIGURES ON MOTHER EARTH

Land is basic to Indian people: they are part of it and it is part of them; it is their Mother. Nor is this just a romantic commonplace. For most Indian groups, including the Lakota people, land is a cultural centerpiece with wide-ranging implications for any attempt to understand contemporary reservation life.

The importance of the land is severalfold. Beyond the obvious fact that land provides subsistence, it is the source of spiritual origins and sustaining myth, which in turn provide a landscape of cultural and emotional meaning. The land often determines the values of the human landscape.[17] The harsh lands of the prairie helped to make Lakota tribal communities austere and generous, places where giving and sharing were first principles.[18] The people needed the land and each other too much to permit wanton accumulation and ecological impairment to the living source of nourishment.[19] Much of this is, of course, antithetical to European history and culture. As Frederick Turner suggests, the Western ethos reflects a commitment

> to *take* possession without being possessed: to take secure hold on the lands beyond and yet hold them at a rigidly maintained spiritual distance. It was never to merge, to mingle, to marry. To do so was to become an apostate from Christian history and so be kept in an eternal wilderness.[20]

Such differing conceptions between Indians and non-Indians about the nature of land only added tinder to the flame of adversity and misunderstanding. And sure enough, one of the results of over three centuries of contact has been the nearly complete severing of this cultural taproot connecting Indian people to the land. Impaired but not eradicated, this root is being rediscovered and tended with renewed vigor and stewardship. In fact, this is so prevalent that it has been noted as a recurrent theme in contemporary Indian literature. The theme involves the loss of the old guardian spirits of place and the process by which they might be made to speak again—how the land may become numinous once more and speak to its dwellers.[21]

This then is one pull of the land, the source of vital myth and cultural well-being. But there is also the complementary notion of a homeland where generations and generations of relatives have lived out their lives and destiny—that it is, after all, one's home, one's community, one's reservation in Indian country.

Many reservations may seem rural and isolated, and indeed they are; but many, like the Rosebud Sioux Reservation in South Dakota, are quite beautiful, captivating in the way the subtle canvas of the prairie often is. The Rosebud Reservation and others like it do not possess (fortunately) the grandeur that attracts tourists, but a long stay makes lasting impressions on one's psyche. This notion of homeland is not, of course, unique to Indians, and despite the obvious irony, it is valued by many non-Indians, including non-Indian residents of the reservation.

These attractions and connections do not prevent people from leaving the reservation, but they do make leaving hard. People do depart, most often for greater economic opportunity, and sometimes to escape violence and perceptions about inferior schools. But most who leave return. Maybe Robert Logterman, a long-time non-Indian rancher on the Rosebud Reservation, said it best: "[T]hey ought to send someone from the reservation into outer space because then they would be sure that they would return safely." [22] Even the federal government learned this lesson and abandoned its program of "relocation," [23] which attempted to take people from the reservation and resettle them in major urban areas with greater economic opportunities. Few participated, and most of those who did refused to stay long on the fringes of urban ghettos.

The reservation is home. It is a place where the land lives and stalks people; a place where the land looks after people and makes them live right; [24] a place where the earth provides solace and nurture. Yet, paradoxically, it is also a place where the land has been wounded; a place where the sacred hoop has been broken; a place stained with violence and suffering. And this painful truth also stalks the people and their Mother.

THE GENESIS OF RESERVATIONS

Any attempt to understand contemporary reservation life also requires an understanding of what reservations are and how they came to be. What have been the federal policies and expectations concerning reservations, and how have they harmonized or clashed with tribal objectives? Without an understanding of the legal and cultural roots involved in the formation of reservations, we cannot comprehend much of the current social reality and political atmosphere that dominates individual and institutional life in Indian country. The particular history of any given reservation can augment this general understanding. Particulars include such things as whether the reservation is located within a tribe's aboriginal homeland,[25] whether more than one tribe is "confederated"[26] there, and the degree of permanent non-Indian presence. All of these elements intensify expectations and affect the course of life on the reservation. Much of how the people live and what colors their aspirations and struggles is the modern refraction of old promises and commitments—the covenant with the past.

The concept of an Indian reservation is best defined as the concrete manifestation of a guarantee of a "measured separatism"[27] to Indian people as the result of negotiated treaties[28] and settlements reached between Indian tribes and the federal government. Most of these treaties between mutual sovereigns were agreed upon in the nineteenth century through negotiations which represented political and legal adjustments between an expansionary, westward-marching American society and established, staunchly resistant tribal societies.

The treaties that established reservations had extensive effects. They helped create the enduring and special legal and moral relationship that exists between the federal government and Indian tribes.[29] Treaties also reflect a set of sovereign promises and expectations that continue to define the modern contours of this relationship. It is therefore instructive to explore the roots of these interactions and legal exchanges because they affect so much of what continues today in this dynamic though often misunderstood relationship.

The meetings of tribes and representatives of the federal government brought together people with very different languages, cultures, and worldviews.[30] These often extreme divergences must have gravely affected emotions and understandings. Perhaps only under these circumstances, where raw, historical necessity brought one sovereign power face to face with another, could these disparate human configurations have come together. Yet

they did. And the treaties represent the documents of that unprec-
edented exchange where, in part, each side cast its future on the
integrity and goodwill of the other side. Yet the dominant culture
has not always honored its part of the bargain.[31]

Treaties represent a bargained-for exchange, and it is important to understand what the exchange was. The Indians usually agreed to make peace and cede land—often vast amounts
of it—to the federal government in exchange for a cessation of
hostilities, the provision of some services, and, most important,
the establishment and recognition of a homeland free from the
incursion of both the state and non-Indian settlers.

The quality of these exchanges varied significantly. Many
tribes were forced to agree to small reservations in regions removed from their aboriginal territories because the federal government had the strong military upper hand.[32] Yet in other
cases—particularly involving the Lakota of the Great Sioux Nation in South Dakota—there was a virtual military standoff, and
the reservations were established in the heart of the traditional
Sioux homeland in the Dakota Territory.[33]

Much of the negotiations surrounding the treaties focused on
guarantees to protect tribes from the swelling tide of western settlement. For example, the Chippewas, Ottawas, and Potawatomies were told that

> the Great Spirit has ordained that your Great Father and Congress
> should be to the Red Man, as Guardians and Fathers. . . . [S]oon . . .
> you shall be at a permanent home from which there will be no danger
> of your moving again, you will receive their full benefit.[34]

The need for reservations was the one point on which both the
tribes and federal government could readily agree. Such entities
met important policy objectives for each side. The United States
wanted to regulate and reduce the contact of Indians with future
settlers in order to minimize violence. This federal policy was
consistent from the beginning of the republic. Non-Indians could
not live harmoniously with Indians; hence, the federal government early on regulated contact between the two groups. Non-
Indians (including the states) could not purchase lands from
individual Indians or tribes without the approval of the federal

government. The federal government also regulated trade, forbade the sale of liquor, and maintained jurisdiction over most criminal activity in Indian country.[35]

This nonintercourse policy was complemented by a policy of removal. When non-Indians continually pressed on Indian lands and settlements, Indians were often "removed" from their aboriginal homelands and relocated west of the Mississippi River. The most notorious example of this policy resulted in the Trail of Tears, when President Andrew Jackson in 1831, under the conditions imposed in the Treaty of Dancing Rabbit Creek, removed the Cherokees, Creeks, Choctaws, Chickasaws, and Seminoles to their new "homes" in the Oklahoma Territory.[36] In the West, removal was less often an option since the continent ended at the not-so-distant west coast and since many tribes, including the Lakota of the Great Sioux Nation, were not sufficiently "subdued" to have such conditions imposed on them.

The tribes, for their part, wanted to be left alone. For instance, the Fort Laramie Treaty of 1868[37] provided that reservations were to be

> set apart for the absolute and undisturbed use and occupation of the Indians herein named . . . and the United States now solemnly agrees that no person except those herein designated and authorized so to do, . . . shall ever be permitted to pass over, settle upon, or reside in the territory described in the article.[38]

Much of what federal negotiators said and did, ultimately, was a mixture of grandiloquence and ash. For the Indians, a great deal was at stake. They were concerned not simply with having a place to live but with preserving the land, which was critical for cultural survival and spiritual succor. Despite these contrasting needs and expectations, the notion was born at this time that reservations were to exist as islands of Indianness within an ever-expanding, encroaching society.[39] Whatever their shortcomings—and there are many—reservations continue to provide the opportunity to strengthen and fulfill the national commitment to a vital, pluralistic society and to preserve the promise of a measured separatism.

Despite this history of bargained-for exchange, treaties and reservations are often misconstrued as unilateral, revocable acts of federal largesse. Tribes gave up much for what they received in return—homelands, often reduced in size, with the right to govern their own affairs. If this mutuality had been preserved and legally vouchsafed, perhaps the original purpose of reservations might have been achieved and maintained. Yet these treaty-based promises were often quickly eroded and the "strong fences" of federal protection torn down.

"MEASURED SEPARATISM" UNDER ASSAULT

The pressure of western expansion did not abate with the signing of treaties, and the federal policy of measured separatism soon gave way to a policy of vigorous assimilation, which had dire consequences for reservations as islands of Indianness. The homelands were cut open. The bright line separating Indians and non-Indians was obliterated. Much land was lost as many non-Indian settlers came into Indian country. Cultural ways were strained, and traditional tribal institutions were undermined and weakened. For many, this was the most devastating historical blow to tribalism and Indian life.[40]

The linchpin of this policy was the Dawes Severalty Act, also known as the General Allotment Act of 1887.[41] President Theodore Roosevelt most forcefully described this Act as "a mighty pulverizing engine to break up the tribal mass. It acts directly upon the family and the individual."[42] The General Allotment Act authorized the Bureau of Indian Affairs (BIA) to allot 160 acres of tribal land to each head of household and forty acres to each minor. Allotments were originally to remain in trust for twenty-five years; they would be immune from sale and local property taxes during the period of transition from being a tribally owned communal resource to an individually owned piece of land managed and used like surrounding non-Indian farms and ranches. This twenty-five-year trust period was undermined by the Burke Act of 1906,[43] which allowed the transfer of a fee patent to "competent" Indians prior to the expiration of the trust period. Competency commissions were quickly established to determine whether individual Indians were "competent" to receive fee patents, which would remove restrictions against alienation and tax obligations. These commissions often made competency determinations based on the most perfunctory of findings, including whether the individual was one-half degree Indian blood or less.[44] In addition to authorizing allotments, the Act permitted the opening of so-called surplus reservation lands for non-Indian homesteading.[45]

The allotment policy was imposed from the top down without tribal input and consent. It was grossly undercapitalized, sometimes providing less than ten dollars per allottee for implements, seeds, and instruction; it was insensitive to the hunting and food-gathering traditions of nonagricultural tribes; and it was devoid of any cultural understanding of the roles of the *tiyospaye* (the extended family of the Lakota), often assigning to individuals allotments outside their home communities and beyond their familial landscape. Seen from this perspective, the allotment policy was apparently formulated to fail.

The results were truly devastating. The national Indian land estate was reduced from 138 million acres in 1887 to 52 million acres in 1934. More than 26 million acres of allotted land were transferred from the tribe to individual Indian allottees and then to non-Indians through purchase, fraud, mortgage foreclosures, and tax sales.[46]

Sixty million of the eighty-six million acres lost by Indians during the allotment era were lost because of the "surplus" land provisions of the Act. According to the historian Father Francis Prucha, thirty-eight million acres of unallotted tribal lands were declared "surplus" to Indian needs and were ceded to the federal government for sale to non-Indians. The federal government opened to homesteading another twenty-two million acres of "surplus" tribal land.[47] The ravages of the allotment policy were halted only by the Indian Reorganization Act of 1934,[48] which permanently extended the trust status of all existing allotments and halted the issuance of any new allotments.

These ravages had equally scarring collateral effects. For the first time the reservations became checkerboards of tribal, individual Indian, individual non-Indian, and corporate properties. Individual Indian allotments quickly fractionated within several generations, often split among dozens or even hundreds of heirs. In addition, land that remained in trust was more often leased to non-Indians than used by the allottees.[49]

More difficult to assess is the direct effect of the allotment process on tribal government and tribal institutions. Some commentators[50] have argued that when the reservations were opened, true traditional governments were essentially doomed in most tribes, and the authority of any form of tribal government was undermined. The great influx of non-Indian settlers, coupled with the loss of communal lands and the attendant yoke of federal support of these policies, simply eradicated much of the tribes' ability to govern. In the resulting void, the Bureau of Indian Affairs and Christian missionaries became the true power brokers and the de facto governing forces.

The missionaries in particular wreaked havoc with their religious and educational programs, particularly the boarding school program which took Indian children away from their families for substantial periods of time and specifically forbade the speaking of tribal languages in school.[51] It is not difficult to perceive the strain and pressure placed on traditional culture under these circumstances. This is even more apparent when these policies were joined to BIA directives outlawing traditional religious practices such as the Sun Dance.[52] As a result, the core of the culture was driven underground into a shadow existence.

Many people on the reservation vividly recall these times. Albert White Hat, an instructor of Lakota thought and philosophy at Sinte Gleska University on the Rosebud Sioux Reservation, speaks of the many instances in which he and his classmates at St. Francis Indian School had their mouths washed out with soap for speaking Lakota in school. As Mr. White Hat eloquently summarizes without rancor: "You gave us the Bible, but stole our land. You taught us English only so we could take orders, not so that we might dream."[53]

The point is not to assign blame—an essentially fruitless exercise—but rather to comprehend more deeply the forces at work on the reservation. The governmental and religious policies of

assimilation were, at least in hindsight, clearly erroneous; but
they were, at least in part, driven by worthy motives. The more
sinister motives of greed, ethnocentrism, and religious exclusivity
are clear, even glaring, but it is also true that many well-meaning
individuals and groups clearly identified as Indian supporters believed that the policies of allotment and assimilation were the
only way to stave off complete obliteration at the hands of the
forces of manifest destiny. As the leading historian of the allotment era, D. S. Otis, has written:

> That the leading proponents of allotment were inspired by the high-
> est motives seems conclusively true. A member of Congress, speaking
> on the Dawes bill in 1886 said, "It has ... the endorsement of the
> Indian rights associations throughout the country, and of the best
> sentiment of the land." [54]

A minority of Congressional opponents saw it more unsparingly.
In 1880 the minority report of the House Indian Affairs Committee stated:

> The real aim of this bill is to get at the Indian lands and open them
> up to settlement. The provisions for the apparent benefit of the In-
> dian are but the pretext to get at the lands and occupy them. . . . If
> this were done in the name of greed it would be bad enough; but to
> do it in the name of humanity, and under the cloak of an ardent
> desire to promote the Indian's welfare by making him like ourselves
> whether he will or not is infinitely worse. [55]

With all this imposed slash and burn, cultural and institutional
loss was inevitable.

Federal government endorsement of these policies was reversed with the Indian Reorganization Act of 1934 (IRA), which
ended the allotment process and supported the development of
tribal self-government. [56] The reforms of the IRA, including explicit authorization and assistance in the adoption of tribal constitutions, sought to engender recovery from stultification. Yet
the "new" opportunity held out in the IRA has long been perceived on the reservation as further evisceration of traditional
tribal government, since the "modern" tribal governments rely
on the "white man's way" of elections, the use of English, and the
written word. For some, the apparatus of IRA tribal governments

further disturbed and unsettled the cultural balance necessary to support traditional forms of self-rule often associated with tribal governance in force when the treaties were made. As a result, IRA-elected tribal governments often remain controversial and occasionally have a hint of illegitimacy about them.[57]

The dismal effects of allotment and assimilation have been halted and the thrust of self-rule reworked and reinvigorated. But the scars of the severe loss of land and the reminders of social weakening verify the inextricable bond among the people, the culture, and the land.

THE SOUTH DAKOTA EXPERIENCE

All reservations in South Dakota have felt the battering of the allotment and assimilation process.[58] Some reservations, such as the Sisseton-Wahpeton Reservation[59] and the Yankton Sioux Reservation,[60] were completely allotted, with the remainder ceded to the federal government and subsequently made available to non-Indian homesteaders. On both these reservations the portions allotted to tribal members comprise only 15 to 20 percent of the original reservation territory. No longer is any land held in common by these tribes. In other instances, such as Pine Ridge[61] and Rosebud,[62] the tribes were able to retain approximately one-third of the reservation land base under tribal ownership, with approximately one-third held by individually allotted Indians and one-third by non-Indians.

Coordinate with the allotment and assimilation process was the related process of diminishment, which often reduced the boundaries of a reservation. The diminishment issue addresses the question not of who *owns* the land but more precisely of whether the process through which the federal government obtained "surplus" unallotted tribal lands for non-Indian homesteading resulted in a corresponding reduction of the reservation's boundaries. At issue is the size of the reservation, not the composition of land ownership patterns within it. Therefore, the question of diminishment focuses most directly on the potential territorial scope of tribal governmental authority.

The principal legal issue in diminishment cases has been whether Congress, in "opening" unallotted portions of reservations for non-Indian settlement, intended to reduce the size and boundaries of the reservation or whether it simply intended to allow non-Indians to settle on the reservation.[63] The authority to do either is within the scope of Congress's plenary authority in Indian affairs,[64] but since Congress never directly addressed the issue in any of the acts which encouraged non-Indian settlement in Indian country, the question has tended to center on congressional intent. That Congress never directly addressed the issue seems wholly remarkable given the potentially serious consequences attendant on its actions.

The Supreme Court has itself noted the incongruity. As Justice Marshall pointed out in his dissent in *Rosebud Sioux Tribe v. Kneip*:[65]

> Congress manifested an "almost complete lack of . . . concern with the boundary issue." This issue was of no great importance in the early 1900s as it was commonly assumed that all reservations would be abolished when the trust period on allotted lands expired. There was no pressure on Congress to accelerate this timetable, so long as settlers could acquire unused land. Accordingly, Congress did not focus on the boundary question. . . . For the Court to find in this confusion and indifference a "clear" congressional intent to disestablish its reservation is incomprehensible.[66]

The test for determining Congressional intent in diminishment cases finds its most recent elucidation in *Solem v. Bartlett*.[67] Justice Marshall, writing for a unanimous Court, held that a 1908 act[68] of Congress opening part of the Cheyenne River Sioux Reservation to non-Indian settlement did *not* evince any Congressional intent to diminish the boundaries of the reservation.[69] The Court stated that diminishment will not be lightly inferred and that the examination of surplus land acts requires that Congress clearly evince an "intent" to change "boundaries" before diminishment will be found.[70] Pertinent indicia of congressional intent include the statutory language used to open the Indian lands, regarded by the Court as "most probative,"[71] as well as surrounding circumstances—particularly the manner in which the transaction was negotiated with the tribes involved and the tenor of legislative reports of Congress.[72] "To a lesser extent," the

Court has "looked to events that occurred after the passage of a surplus land act to decipher Congress's intentions."[73] And finally, "on a more pragmatic level, [the Court] recognized that who actually moved into open reservation lands is also relevant to deciding whether a surplus land act diminished a reservation."[74]

Four reservations in South Dakota have been diminished under the *Solem* analysis. These are the Sisseton-Wahpeton,[75] Yankton,[76] Rosebud,[77] and Pine Ridge.[78] The result in each instance was to reduce the boundaries of the reservation and in effect to contract the size of the "homeland." Diminishment can also have the anomalous effect of placing substantial numbers of Indian people and their communities *outside* the reservation. For example, one of the results of the Supreme Court's decision in *Rosebud Sioux Tribe v. Kneip,* which upheld the diminishment of the Rosebud Sioux Reservation, was to place two thousand tribal members and seven recognized tribal communities outside the official reservation boundaries.[79] The social, cultural, and psychological—not to mention the obvious legal—impact of such decisions exacerbates the burden of maintaining individual and tribal well-being and integrity.

This wrenching epoch of allotment and diminishment was not the last of its kind in South Dakota. Another round of federal "takings" of Indian lands in South Dakota occurred in the 1940s as part of the Pick-Sloan project. The Pick-Sloan Plan consisted of a joint water development project designed by the Army Corps of Engineers and the Bureau of Reclamation in 1944 for the Missouri River Basin.[80] As finally adopted by Congress, the Pick-Sloan Plan—officially labeled the Missouri River Basin Development Program—included a total of 107 dams, 13 of which had previously been authorized. The five Corps of Engineers dams on the Missouri provided the key structures. They included Garrison Dam in North Dakota and the Oahe, Big Bend, Fort Randall, and Gavins Point dams in South Dakota.[81] The primary goals of the project were flood control, irrigation, and hydroelectric power.

These five main stem dams destroyed over 550 square miles of tribal land in North and South Dakota and dislocated more than nine hundred Indian families. Most of the damage was sustained

by five Sioux reservations in South Dakota: Standing Rock and
Cheyenne River, reduced by the Oahe project; Yankton, affected
by Fort Randall Dam; and Crow Creek and Lower Brule, dam-
aged by both the Fort Randall and Big Bend projects.[82] Army
Corps of Engineers dams on the Missouri inundated another
200,000 acres of Sioux land and uprooted an additional 580
families.[83] The results of this destruction are summarized by Michael Lawson, a leading chronicler of the Pick-Sloan project:

> [Sioux families were] uprooted and forced to move from rich shel-
> tered bottomlands to empty prairies. Their best homesites, their fin-
> est pastures, croplands and hay meadows, and most of their valuable
> timber, wildlife, and vegetation were flooded. Relocation of the
> agency headquarters on the Cheyenne River, Lower Brule, and Crow
> Creek reservations seriously disrupted governmental, medical, and
> educational services and facilities and dismantled the largest Indian
> communities on these reservations. Removal of churches and com-
> munity centers, cemeteries, and shrines impaired social and religious
> life on all five reservations. Loss not only of primary fuel, food, and
> water resources but also of prime grazing land effectively destroyed
> the Indians' economic base. The thought of having to give up their
> ancestral land, to which they were so closely wedded, caused severe
> psychological stress. The result was extreme confusion and hardship
> for tribal members.[84]

The Sioux knew little of the Pick-Sloan project until long after
it had been passed by Congress. Despite treaty rights that provided that land could not be taken without their consent, none
of the tribes were consulted prior to the program's enactment.
The Bureau of Indian Affairs was fully informed, but it made no
objections to Congress and did not inform tribes of their im-
pending loss until 1947—three years after the project was approved by Congress![85] Financial settlements, generally regarded
as grossly inadequate, were not achieved until the period between
1954 and 1957.[86]

Vine Deloria, Jr., a leading Sioux intellectual, has noted that
this flooding of ancestral lands ruthlessly took away old memories and led to material and spiritual impoverishment. He has
characterized the Pick-Sloan Plan as "the single most destructive
act ever perpetrated on any tribe by the United States."[87] Yet
this legacy of loss has not reduced but rather has extended and

deepened the emotional and cultural commitment of Lakota people to the land as the enduring repository of their ultimate well-being. Without the land, there is no center to resist the historical pressures created by the dominant society.

THE AMERICAN WEST AS LIVING SPACE

Despite the pervasive conflict between tribes and the state and federal governments, and between Indians and non-Indians, other more unitive factors point to similarities in situation that are often not perceived and occasionally even ignored.[88] One such fact is the unique geographical situation of living in the West[89]—a West that constitutes a unique environmental and ecological system that exacts a premium for successful living. The key attributes of this habitat are space and aridity.

Wallace Stegner, a leading western novelist and critic, aptly describes this West of living space:

In the West it is impossible to be unconscious of or indifferent to space. At every city's edge it confronts us as federal lands kept open by aridity and the custodial bureaus; out in the boondocks it engulfs us. And it does contribute to individualism, if only because in that much emptiness people have the dignity of rareness and must do much of what they do without help, and because self-reliance becomes a social imperative, part of a code. . . .

. . . It encourages a fatal carelessness and destructiveness because it seems so limitless and because what is everybody's is nobody's responsibility. It also encourages, in some, an impassioned protectiveness: the battlegrounds of the environment movement lie in the western public lands. Finally, it promotes certain needs, tastes, attitudes, skills. It is those tastes, attitudes, and skills, as well as the prevailing destructiveness and its corrective, love of the land, that relate real Westerners to the myth.[90]

The complement to the space of the West is aridity, a physical and often brutal fact that is also a determinant of the social fabric:

Aridity and aridity alone makes the various Wests one. The distinctive western plants and animals, the hard clarity (before power plants and metropolitan traffic altered it) of the western air, the look and location of western towns, the empty spaces that separate them, the way farms and ranches are either densely concentrated where water is plentiful or widely scattered where it is scarce, the pervasive presence of the federal government as land owner and land manager, the even more noticeable presence as dam builder and water broker, the snarling state's-rights and antifederal feeling whose burden Bernard DeVoto once characterized in a sentence—"Get out and give us more money"—those are all consequences, and by no means all the consequences of aridity.[91]

The facts of aridity and space have combined to establish a unique environment in which a sharp sense of independence is often pitted against the encroaching tentacles of federal authority. Despite the vastness of geography and the mythic claims of western individualism and tribal sovereignty, there is significant and seemingly intractable dependence on, and resentment of, the federal presence. This bleak history is keenly summarized: "Take for granted federal assistance, but damn federal control. Your presence as absentee landlord offends us, Uncle. Get out, and give us more money."[92]

This description contains the necessary tools to cultivate a renewed examination of the role that federal money and the federal government play in Indian country and throughout the West. Although Indian tribes are often casually described as too dependent on the federal government,[93] it is less often noted that many of their non-Indian "rugged individualist" neighbors are equally dependent on federal largesse, through federal farm subsidies and below-cost access to and use of the public domain for water, natural resources, and grazing rights.[94] This knot of common dependency must be examined in order to determine whether there are sufficient common interests on which Indians and non-Indians, tribes and states might be able to define a clearer, more productive, and more satisfying relationship with the federal government.

This is not an easy matter. Tribal dependency on the federal government is grounded in the unique "trust relationship"[95] that exists between the federal government and Indian tribes; this relationship is grounded in turn in the mutual covenants of the treaty relationship. The object therefore is not, or should not be, to end this important relationship but rather to redefine its contours in such a way as to make the relationship less asymmetrical and more mutual. There also needs to be a concomitant reduction of the dependence of western farmers, ranchers, and loggers on federal subsidies and profligate use of the public domain. No doubt there is the potential for exacerbated state and tribal conflict here, but that risk must be taken if the people who actually call the West home are serious about realigning their interests.

This federal dependence also has its nongovernmental analogue in the western suspicion and distrust of outsiders and do-gooders and the resultant insularity of vision.

> The history of the West, from the fur trader to tomorrow, is a history of colonialism, both material and cultural. Is it any wonder we are so deeply xenophobic, and regard anything east of us as suspect? The money and power always came from the East, took what it wanted, and left us, white or Indian, with our traditions dismantled and our territory filled with holes in the ground.[96]

This insularity, at least in South Dakota, remains more prominent in the non-Indian than in the Indian community. Tribes increasingly look to and find more congenial support for their efforts outside rather than inside the state; witness the Black Hills controversy.[97] Yet it remains true for both communities that difficulty and exploitation have often come from outsiders. This aggravated insularity needs to be set aside, with an eye toward allowing each group to assay and to rethink the potential coalition *against* real outside exploiters and support *for* outsiders who have genuine empathy and commitment to both the Indian and non-Indian communities. Outsiders to be opposed might include the corporate disposers of nuclear and other toxic waste who want to dump in South Dakota and Indian country; outsiders to support might include those planners and businesses who, of course, seek profit, but who are willing to pay fair wages and help enhance rural life.

Implicit in such a process of clarifying relationships with both governmental and nongovernmental "external" forces is the opportunity to improve "internal" relations between Indians and non-Indians, between tribes and the states. Such improvement will not be easy given the historical animosity. Yet it is necessary if there is to be any unity on the issues central to the existence and reinvigoration of Indian and non-Indian rural communities, which often share the common attributes of being underdeveloped, isolated, and easily ignored by the powers that be. A good example might be, on the one hand, to prevent the corporate purchase and control of agricultural lands within the state and to prevent the massive leasing and development of tribal lands and, on the other hand, to explore the potential for joint agricultural or tourism ventures by Indians and non-Indians, by the tribes and the state.

The import of these suggestions is that Indians and non-Indians have more in common than they might think. Despite a history of conflict, their future is inextricably linked. There cannot be well-being for some if not for all. Many of the dominant forces—such as the scarcity of capital, the shortage of human resources, the increased reliance on technology, and a disappearance of markets that threatens to, and in many cases already does, impinge on the integrity of rural communities—devastate Indian and non-Indian communities equally.

Each side must, however, accede to a condition before any of the mutual agenda can be addressed. Each side—and each group—must recognize the permanence and legitimacy of the other. Neither the states nor the tribe, neither Indians nor non-Indians, will disappear, so they should try to see how they might join in preserving the best of what they already have. To use another parallel, this is not unlike the situation of the Israelis and Palestinians in the Middle East. Neither the Israelis nor the Palestinians are going to disappear, and both have legitimate claims to a homeland in the area.[98] Without this threshold admission, the disputants can look forward only to more of the violence and bloodshed that has so far defined their interaction. The tragedy of that controversy ought to be instructive for all sides in South Dakota.

What both sides already have is space and aridity, but what is most important is a sense of place to meet the deep human need of belonging, particularly in our complex and riven society—a sense of place that provides silence, space, and solitude for the healing of our raw spirits.[99] Yet it is unlikely that we can achieve such a sense without painful introspection, particularly in the

non-Indian community. The mythology of the non-Indian West
is grounded in conquest and possession, and it no longer works.
As William Kittredge has suggested in an incisive essay:

> [A]ll over the West, as in all of America, the old folkway of property
> as an absolute right is dying. Our mythology doesn't work anymore.
>
> We find ourselves weathering a rough winter of discontent, snared
> in the uncertainties of a transitional time and urgently yearning to
> inhabit a story that might bring sensible order to our lives—even as
> we know such a story can only evolve through an almost literally
> infinite series of recognitions of what, individually, we hold sacred.
> The liberties our people came seeking are more and more con-
> strained, and here in the West, as everywhere, we hate it.
>
> Simple as that. And we have to live with it. There is no more
> running away to territory. This is it, for most of us. We have no
> choice but to live in community. If we're lucky we may discover a
> story that teaches us to abhor our old romance with conquest and
> possession.[100]

This outworn mythology has also been fueled by the excesses of
individualism which have hindered the development of communities and traditions. It has robbed much of the non-Indian community of the gods who make places holy. American individualism, much celebrated and cherished, has developed without its
essential corrective, which is *belonging.*[101]

In South Dakota, particularly in the rural areas on or near
Indian country, this sense of belonging in the non-Indian community may not be so sharply attenuated, which again suggests the
potential for a coming together on these issues. Yet the key, it
seems to me, to generating a long-term coming together is the
development of a *story* or an *ethic.* There are complex issues
aplenty—for instance, those concerning the use of the Missouri
River and the Oglala Aquifer and the status of the Black Hills—
to bring Indians and non-Indians together, but the development
of a greater ethic or story, beyond the particulars of any issue, is
needed to hold us together. Of course, no one knows exactly how
to do this, yet important work has begun in this area:

> We need to develop an ethic of place. It respects equally the people
> of a region and the land, animals, vegetation, water, and air. An ethic
> of place recognizes that Western people revere the physical surround-
> ings and that they need and deserve a stable, productive economy

that is accessible to those of modest incomes. An ethic of place ought to be a shared community value and ought to manifest itself in a dogged determination of the society at large to treat the environment and its people as equals, to recognize both as sacred, and to insure that all members of the community not just search for, but insist upon, solutions that fulfill the ethic.[102]

And within this ethic of place we need to recognize that Indians

possess individuality as people and self-rule as governments, but they are also an inseparable part of the larger community, a proud and valuable constituent group that must be extended the full measure of respect mandated by an ethic of place.[103]

The emergence of such a story and ethic remains critical to the viability of the West, if it is to join its spacious physical terrain to the geography of hope.[104]

There are some vital signs of sharing and coming together. These examples are found most often in the area of education, and specifically in the experience of the Indian-controlled colleges located on several reservations throughout Indian country. Sinte Gleska University at Rosebud and Oglala Lakota College at Pine Ridge are the two fastest-growing colleges in the state of South Dakota.[105] These colleges, both founded in the early 1970s, represent successful acts of self-determination by local tribal leaders to meet the higher education needs of tribal people through accredited tribal institutions.[106] Yet in meeting these tribal needs, the reservation colleges were also made available to non-Indians living on or near the reservation.

Non-Indians make up a sizable minority (10 to 15 percent) of students and staff at these institutions, and they receive quality educations which prepare them to be teachers, nurses, and counselors. The more extraordinary aspect of this experience is that the colleges have provided—simply by existing and not being racially exclusive—rare forums in which Indians and non-Indians come together in and out of the classroom. These opportunities for face-to-face communication and exchange foster increased personal, cultural, and political respect and understanding.

During the time I taught at Sinte Gleska University,[107] I was repeatedly struck by the transformative nature of these exchanges, particularly as they affected non-Indians. Non-Indians reacted most favorably in three areas: (1) to the rigor and quality of education they were receiving; (2) to the fact that they were welcomed and not discriminated against; and (3) to the opportunity to meet Indians and their cultures in a nonthreatening, non-stereotyped situation.

The most striking attributes of these exchanges are legitimacy and humanity: legitimacy in the sense that most non-Indians begin to recognize and appreciate the legal and ethical thrust of Indian people to develop and to improve their institutions and government; and humanity in the sense that they begin to appreciate the human faces behind these exertions. Non-Indians gain a perception that, despite differences in culture and historical circumstances, a common thread of effort binds both sides to the task of improving the quality of opportunity and life in one's family and community. This alone, of course, does not solve difficult questions, but it is important in shaping discussions concerning such pressing issues as the alleviation of discrimination, the Black Hills controversy, and the recognition of authentic tribal government permanence in Indian country. The education process, which has often held so much promise for fulfillment in the dominant community, holds equal sway in tribal communities. Yet there is also the added potential for the emergence of a precious ethic of common understanding and respect.

The questions of the land have profound implications. They suggest the primary role of the land as the mediator of unity and wholeness, the central intercessor for a people. The bond to the land was almost completely severed by the grievous loss of so much of it through enforced assimilation and changed land tenure patterns and by almost total eradication of an economic relation to it as a material provider of sustenance. As Gerald Clifford, an Oglala and Chairman of the Black Hills Steering Committee, has said, "Our relationships to one another as Lakota are defined by our relationship to the earth. Until we get back on track in our relationship to the earth, we cannot straighten out any of our relationships to ourselves, to other people."[108] The difficult question is *how* to get back on track in the relationship to the earth. There are no easy or simple answers.

For many on the reservation, the relationship to the land has become more passive than active. The land does not provide economic livelihood for very many, and the dominant society often invades the landscape, marring the land with modern detritus. Discussions about Indians and their relationship to the land often conjure disturbing utopic visions that endlessly romanticize the people and the land.[109] Wendell Berry's bracing observations about a visit to a reservation in the Southwest are salutary:

> I was . . . impressed by the amount of junk on the reservation—the usual modern American assortment of cars and bottles, plastic jugs, old cars, blowing paper, etc. The junk surprised me, most people who write or talk about Indians, I think, try to see or imagine them apart from the worst—or at least the most unsightly—influence of white society. But of course one should not be surprised. When junk is everywhere—better hidden in some places than others—why should one not expect to find it here?[110]

The rupture in the relationship of the people to the land has also had adverse social effects. Ronnie Lupe, former chairman of the White Mountain Apache Tribe in New Mexico, vividly articulates this view. "Our children are losing the land. It doesn't work on them anymore. They don't know the story about what happened to these places. That's why some get into trouble."[111] At Rosebud and other reservations in South Dakota, problems of teenage alcoholism and juvenile crime provide dispiriting confirmation of this observation. Yet as Stanley Red Bird, a cherished friend and founder and former chairman of the Board of Directors at Sinte Gleska University of the Rosebud Reservation, has observed, "You white people got a lot of our land and a lot of our heart, but we know you were wrong and now with the help of the Great Spirit, and the new warriors of education, we will live again."[112]

The land needs to be retained, restored, and redefined. Its economic role—long dormant—must be resuscitated. Its spiritual role—long atrophied—must be revivified. Its healing role—long obscured—must be revitalized. The land must hold the people, and give direction to their aspirations and yearnings. In this way of looking at the reservation as place, the land may be seen as part of the "sacred text"[113] of Lakota religion and culture.

As part of the sacred text, the land—like sacred texts in other traditions—is *not* primarily a book of answers but rather a principal symbol of—perhaps *the* principal symbol of and thus a central occasion of recalling and heeding—the fundamental aspirations of the tradition.[114] It summons the heart and the spirit to difficult labor. In this sense, the sacred text constantly *disturbs:* it serves a prophetic function in the life of the community.[115] The land constantly evokes the fundamental Lakota aspirations to live in harmony with Mother Earth and to embody the traditional virtues of wisdom, courage, generosity, and fortitude. The "sacred text" itself guarantees nothing, but it does hold the necessary potential to mediate the past of the tradition with its present predicament.

The vindication of any tradition—including Lakota tradition—cannot be assumed. Yet the potential for the vindication and the flowering of the tradition is contingent, in part, on the commitment and exertions of the tradition's followers. This process is richly described by Jaroslav Pelikan, a leading commentator within the Christian community:

> Ultimately, however, tradition will be vindicated for us as an individual and for us as communities, by how it manages to accord with our own deepest intuitions and highest aspirations.... Those intuitions and aspirations tell us that there must be a way of holding together what the vicissitudes of our experience have driven apart— a realism about a fallen world and our hope for what the world may still become, our private integrity and our public duty, our hunger for community and our yearning for personal fulfillment, what Pascal called "the grandeur and the misery" of our common humanity.[116]

This concept of a sacred text and its tradition not only illuminates the commitment and struggle of Indian people in South Dakota and throughout the West but also challenges non-Indians to examine their own traditions. For many in South Dakota and the West in general, this would include a review of the Christian tradition and whether its aspirations include solidarity with the struggles of others for justice and self-realization. Non-Indians also need to consider the deeper quandary of their Indian neighbors' commitment to a sacred text so often assaulted by Western history. Within the legal profession itself, such consideration might include an examination of the aspirations of our constitutional "faith." [117]

The breath of despair once so prevalent in Indian country seems to be yielding to the air of hope. The answers to these troubling questions about the land and its economic, cultural, and spiritual roles do not readily reveal themselves, but the questions are increasingly recognized and energetically posed. Nor are these questions confined to Indians and reservations. They also pierce with unerring aim the larger society's assumptions about cultural diversity and the use and exploitation of the earth to sustain economic prodigality and waste. The questions inevitably challenge all of us—Indian and non-Indian, tribes and states alike—to summon the honor and wisdom of ourselves, our communities, and our traditions and to apply them to these relentless and provocative issues.

CHAPTER TWO

The Colonized Context

Federal Indian Law and
Tribal Aspiration

THE LEGACY OF EXPLOITATION

From the very beginning of this republic, the federal government has sought economic and political advantage in its dealings with Indian tribes. In addition to the economic and political exploitation of colonialism, there is a legacy of impoverished legal theory concerning the nature of tribal legal authority and sovereignty.

The origins of the ruthless pursuit of advantage can be seen in the colonial fur trade. This burgeoning commercial activity often developed on terms initially quite favorable to Indian tribes. After all, tribes possessed the expert knowledge of the resource. For a time, the economics of this trade were also critical to the survival of many of the colonies, providing them with resources to eradicate financial deficits and establish a favorable balance of payments.[1]

As in any lengthy period of "contact,"[2] however, substantial change occurred on both sides. For most Indians in early contact with Europeans, the fur trade alone defined Indian–non-Indian relations.[3] Economic results were uneven, but in the long run these contacts were instrumental in establishing a tribal pattern of growing dependency on foreign goods and nonindigenous, exogenous economic structures of exchange and consumption.

In addition to the economic consequences of the fur trade, perhaps more pertinent were its extensive political ramifications.

Early political interaction took place between relative equals, but over time the political balance tilted toward the non-Indians. Increasing economic diversification in Europe and the colonies led non-Indians to depend on the fur trade less and less while Indians came to depend on it more and more.[4] As Steven Cornell notes, the consequence was that "the power of the Europeans grew while the power of the natives, like the trade itself, slowly slipped away."[5]

Following the exhaustion of the fur trade, the focus of Indian–non-Indian exchanges shifted to the land itself. Yet the underlying trend of this relationship had already been established, a trend characterized by continued decline in Indian political autonomy and economic self-sufficiency and a concomitant increase in constraints imposed by growing non-Indian political and economic power.[6] The growth in American economic power during the nineteenth century was fueled by Indian land. The resulting disposition of Indian lands and cultures reduced Indian economic self-sufficiency and led to much underdevelopment in Indian country.[7]

As noted in chapter 1, the pressure of western expansion did not abate with the signing of treaties. Measured separatism soon gave way to a federal policy of vigorous assimilation, with dire consequences for the concept of reservations as islands of Indianness. Homelands were cut open, and the bright line separating Indians and non-Indians was obliterated. As a result, much land was lost as many non-Indian settlers came into Indian country, and cultural ways were strained and traditional tribal institutions were undermined and weakened. For many, these inroads into Indian culture and institutions were the most debilitating historical blow to tribalism and Indian life.[8]

THE ROOTS OF THE FEDERAL-TRIBAL RELATIONSHIP

It was in this soil of expansion and exploitation that federal Indian law developed and took root. This was a soil without constitutional loam, but it nevertheless included elements of a developing federalism, a commitment to the rule of law, religious missionary zeal, and merely residual concern for human and civil rights.[9]

Because of the extraordinarily dominant role that the federal government has played and continues to play in Indian affairs generally and Indian law particularly,[10] any description of Indian law must include a discussion of the conceptual underpinnings of the federal-tribal relationship. In examining this relationship, one is struck almost immediately by the absence of any true constitutional benchmark to orient the federal-tribal discourse on sovereignty. Tribes and Indians are mentioned only sporadically in the Constitution: in Article I, Section 2 (as not being taxed),[11] in the Indian Commerce Clause,[12] and implicitly in the treaty-making clause.[13]

In the absence of any specific federal-tribal constitutional benchmark, the federal-state comparison is fruitful. In that relationship, the Tenth Amendment is pivotal in structuring the discourse on federal-state sovereignty. That amendment provides, in part, that "the powers not delegated to the United States by the Constitution, nor prohibited by it to the States, are reserved to the States respectively, or to the people."[14] Certainly, many scholars and commentators[15] have noted that there have been substantial changes in the allocation of authority as the federal government and the attendant federalism have become even more ascendant. Yet there remains a constitutional baseline for that discourse, and that is the Tenth Amendment and the Constitution as a whole.

Outside of Indian affairs, a central tenet of federal courts' jurisprudence is that the Constitution is the beginning of the analysis for the exercise of all powers of the federal government, and that, by constitutional interpretation, federal powers are limited and constrained.[16] No such guidance is available in demarcating the relationship of Indian tribes to the federal government. That relationship is arguably, in part, preconstitutional and, in part, extraconstitutional.[17] Further, the relationship is grounded in three separate, overlapping, and somewhat incompatible doctrines, including treaties,[18] the trust relationship,[19] and the plenary power of Congress[20] in Indian affairs. These doctrines find their earliest statement in the seminal cases of *Johnson v. McIntosh*,[21] *Cherokee Nation v. Georgia*,[22] and *Worcester v. Georgia*,[23] which are often referred to as the Marshall trilogy because Chief Justice John Marshall wrote the central opinion in each.

TREATIES

Treaties entered into between the federal government and Indian tribes provide the primary doctrinal grounding for the recognition of tribal sovereignty.[24] These agreements between mutual sovereigns provide the foundation for the recognition of a government-to-government relationship. Not only do treaties provide the legal cornerstone for the tribal-federal government-to-government relationship, but as a result they become the closest thing to a (federal) constitutional benchmark from which to engage in legal discourse about the nature of tribal sovereignty within a constitutional democracy. Treaties are, or ought to be, the cornerstone for the federal-tribal government-to-government relationship; but more broadly, treaties recognize and embody tribal sovereignty as the basis for a government-to-government relationship with other sovereigns, including states.

Treaties have not, however, been consistently accorded this constitution-like status within the U.S. legal system. Despite the historical fact that treaties are grounded in the federal recognition of tribal nationhood and sovereignty, they have often been altered, ignored, or displaced in the service of the pernicious "plenary power"[25] doctrine. For example, the U.S. Supreme Court has ruled that Indian treaty rights are not to be ordinarily disregarded, but they are nevertheless subject to unilateral abrogation by Congress if such abrogation is consistent with the national interest[26] In this sense, the plenary power doctrine, which often limits the sovereignty implicit in treaties, is extraconstitutional in that it finds no justification or authorization within the specific confines of the Constitution. This doctrine embodies the classic notions that "might makes right" and that the simple declaration and repetition that a concept is legal and constitutional can convert the mantra into a doctrine, even if there is no legal or constitutional grounding for it in the first instance.

The legal significance of treaties is properly denominated in another sense as preconstitutional in that treaties made by the federal government and other European colonial powers with Indian tribes were often entered into prior to the adoption of the U.S. Constitution in 1789. These early treaties were based on the political, military, and cultural "contacts"[27] between these mutual sovereigns as they evolved during the period of European invasion and settlement of the Americas. These treaties, as well as others entered into by the U.S. government, are enshrined in the supremacy clause of the Constitution as the "supreme law of the land."[28]

These conflicting doctrinal interpretations on the nature of treaties continue to hinder the mutual identification of the appropriate outlines of the relationship between federal and tribal sovereignty. This legal inconsistency about the nature of treaty law and the attendant commitments also reflects an ethical failure and moral shortcoming that has tainted tribal-federal relations from their inception. This conflict is further coarsened when leavened with the competing and in some ways contrary concepts of the trust relationship and the plenary power doctrine.

Treaties play an additional and complicating role in Indian affairs. Treaties not only recognized tribal sovereignty but in many cases also contained *affirmative* obligations on the part of the U.S. government to provide specific services—usually in the areas of health, education, and social services—to Indian tribes.[29] These affirmative duties, which were usually not of a fixed duration, help to form part of the basis for a unique continuing federal legal duty to provide health, education, and social services to Indians. This is not a question of federal largesse but rather one of a federal *legal obligation*. These treaty-based duties are not readily acknowledged by the federal government and are often erroneously subsumed under the trust relationship.

THE TRUST RELATIONSHIP

The trust relationship between the federal government and Indian tribes, which is also a significant component of the federal-tribal relationship, emerges from early Supreme Court cases, particularly the trilogy of cases in which Chief Justice Marshall authored the primary opinions.[30] These cases include *Johnson*,[31] *Cherokee Nation*,[32] and *Worcester*.[33] In these cases certain legendary phrases and concepts in Indian law were first articulated. They include the doctrine of discovery,[34] the guardian-ward relationship,[35] and the description of Indian tribes as "domestic dependent nations"[36] and "distinct independent political communities."[37] These doctrines and phrases ultimately coalesced into the notion of the trust relationship, in which the federal government has a unique fiduciary and managerial responsibility to Indian land and natural resources[38] as well as ongoing responsibility to provide health, education, and social services.[39]

In these cases, with minimal guidance from the text of the Constitution,[40] Justice Marshall articulated a vision of tribes as possessing a unique position as "domestic dependent nations" and "distinct, independent political communities" within an emerging national federalism.[41] This position was grounded in a recognition of tribal sovereignty that was largely independent of state aggression and interference.[42] These nascent doctrines were not grounded in precedent because there was none. Rather, they were fashioned from a combination of political-legal expediency and historical urgency. These views have been increasingly attenuated over the years, but they have not been overruled or completely abandoned.[43]

Much of the discussion in Chief Justice Marshall's opinions is taken up with the task of assessing the nature of Indian people and tribes. He does not see much that is encouraging or worthy of respect. For example, in *Johnson v. McIntosh*, which involved the question of the nature of tribal property rights, he noted that it was the "character and religion of [the Indian] inhabitants" which "afforded an apology for considering them as a people over whom the superior genius of Europe might claim ascendancy."[44] Indians "were fierce savages," and to leave them in possession of their land was "to leave the country a wilderness."[45] These assertions bristle with a colonizing arrogance and are without anthropological support and moral justification.

Nevertheless, Chief Justice Marshall also seemed to realize that there was something wrong with these claims and descriptions. He acknowledged, for example, that the principle of discovery and conquest was an "extravagant pretension" and likely "opposed to natural right and . . . the usages of civilized nations."[46] Yet the principle was "indispensable to [the] system under which [America] had been settled" and a response to "the actual condition of the two people."[47] In the end, however, the rights of the colonizer are ascendant while those of the colonized are minimized.

The *Cherokee Nation* case involved the question of whether the Cherokee Nation was a "foreign state" under Article III, Section 2 of the U.S. Constitution. Chief Justice Marshall evinced genuine concern for the nature of the intercourse between the U.S. and the Cherokee Nation. Marshall stated:

> If courts were permitted to indulge their sympathies, a case better calculated to excite them can scarcely be imagined. A people once numerous, powerful, and truly independent, found by our ancestors in the quiet and uncontrolled possession of an ample domain, gradually sinking beneath our superior policy, our arts and our arms, have yielded their lands by successive treaties, each of which contains a solemn guarantee of the residue, until they retain no more of their formerly extensive territory than is deemed necessary to their comfortable subsistence.[48]

The *Worcester* case involved the question of whether Georgia might extend and enforce its law in Cherokee Nation territory. *Worcester* illustrates the bifurcated notion of tribes as "domestic dependent nations" with authority to prohibit state intrusions on the reservation, but there is also the "guardian-ward" notion of dependence on the federal government. It has been said that Chief Justice Marshall "was genuinely touched by the plight of Indian tribes in America,"[49] yet he was whipsawed by his belief in the superiority of "white republican policy" and the recognition of the role of the dominant society in the "sinking" of Indians.[50] Indians remained the distant "other," and in the 160 years since these seminal cases, it remains to be seen if Indians have become any less "other."

These early cases also framed a despotic imperialism and racism to justify federal title to Indian land and attendant federal hegemony in Indian affairs. This is most apparent in *Johnson v.*

McIntosh, which rested almost entirely on the spurious and self-serving "doctrine of discovery." [51] This federal hegemony developed without constitutional safeguard or limits and ultimately spawned the astounding doctrine of congressional "plenary power" in Indian affairs. [52] This inconsistent, if not fully schizophrenic, approach to tribal sovereignty as either extensive and enduring or marginal and fleeting has further complicated the field of Indian law. This federal inconsistency has been exacerbated by the tendency of the federal courts and Congress to approach Indian tribes as little more than legislative and judicial objects rather than free-standing constitutional subjects.

Despite their flaws and inconsistencies, these foundational cases and their attendant historical gloss serve to identify the primary elements and aspects of the trust relationship. The federal government must act as a fiduciary in managing Indian property. [53] A principal task then becomes delineation of the particular constitutive elements of the trust relationship. This relationship includes such issues as what constitutes reasonable rates of return on the investment of tribal trust funds; whether the trustee federal government may *sell* tribal property or resources under the rubric of increasing acculturation and easing the Indians' move into the dominant culture; and whether the preservation of land and natural resources as part of the trust corpus is itself a critical value. [54] Most important, the issue arises as to what input, if any, tribes have or should have in any of this. [55]

Many treaties between these mutual sovereigns make reference to the federal government's responsibility to provide teachers, [56] doctors, [57] and annuities in the form of food and supplies. [58] These commitments, largely administered through the Bureau of Indian Affairs and the Indian Health Service, were also not generally of fixed duration and therefore continue as an integral part of the treaty and trust relationships. A central issue here is the problem of developing contemporary qualitative and quantitative equivalents for the treaty-based and statutory commitments in the areas of health, education, and welfare. This "valuation" problem is essentially resolved pragmatically, if not ethically, by what Congress appropriates—its own self-defining and self-serving solution.

The theory of the trust relationship with the U.S. government as the owner and trustee of Indian land, natural resources, and (trust) provider of many services is in direct conflict with any meaningful theory of tribal sovereignty. The trust relationship places the federal government in the role of all-knowing trustee while placing tribes in the role of largely voiceless beneficiaries with little or no input in determining the parameters of this relationship. This dependency is at odds with any coherent notion of sovereignty that posits an authentic government-to-government relationship.

The trust relationship needs to be reconceptualized both theoretically and operationally in order to establish more clearly the relationship between the federal trustee and tribal beneficiary as a relationship between equals. In fact, what may be needed is a mutually agreeable plan ending the trust relationship as it currently exists. Tribes may well continue to need federal expertise and resources, but they do not need the debilitating distortions that currently characterize the relationship. The dilemma here involves developing reforms that do not throw the baby out with the bathwater. The federal government must affirmatively perform and discharge its responsibilities in regard to land, natural resources, and social services in such a way that provides significant tribal input, meaningful judicial accountability, and transition to tribal control and delivery of these responsibilities and services. However, the trust relationship should not promptly terminate, absolving the federal government of its legal and moral responsibilities. One practical problem is the perception, common in Indian country, that any reform of the Bureau of Indian Affairs may be a prelude to federal termination[59] of the legal existence of many tribes and the end of the special government-to-government relationship (however skewed it might be) that exists between federal authorities and tribes. Therefore, any program of reform will probably need to rest on a federally enacted statute that ensures against termination and guarantees the government-to-government relationship.

In many ways the trust relationship is a classical colonizing doctrine that seeks, advertently or inadvertently, to enshrine a relationship of superiority and inferiority. It wears a mask of benevolence, but ultimately it represents a doctrine of hierarchy and control. The options for tribal delivery of BIA services that exist in the Indian Self-Determination and Education Assistance Act of 1975[60]—popularly known as 638 contracts—are a step in the right direction, but they are only a step, not the final resting place. Much additional creative and precise work needs to be done to avoid the pitfalls of the past and the inconsistencies of the present in order to achieve a mutually beneficial equilibrium.

These early cases and doctrines may be seen as an attempt to mediate between the Constitution and complete colonization. Neither the Constitution nor the fragile Court itself[61] could apparently stop the historical momentum of the early republic and its process of colonization. These early cases—particularly in Chief Justice Marshall's opinions—attempt to doctrinally curb the most likely excesses, such as tribes having no property rights or no insulation from the intrusion of state authority on the reservation. This process of seeking to blunt the assault of colonization was in many ways successful, particularly if viewed from the perspective of preserving the rights of tribes to exist and to have some measure of sovereign authority. Yet the extent of that authority has never been adequately measured, much less constitutionalized, and has bedeviled Indian law jurisprudence from the very beginning. It may be fairly said that we have made little or no progress from Chief Justice Marshall's pathbreaking yet ultimately cautious and ambivalent efforts in this regard.[62]

THE PLENARY POWER DOCTRINE

The plenary power doctrine, in its sweeping and pristine form, is awesome.[63] As noted by Professor Nell Newton, "The mystique of plenary power has pervaded federal regulation of Indian affairs from the beginning."[64] This extravagant concept was originally expounded by the U.S. Supreme Court in *Lone Wolf v. Hitchcock*.[65] In *Lone Wolf*, which involved the construction of a treaty between the Kiowa and Comanche tribes and the federal government, the Court held that Congress could *unilaterally* abrogate a treaty, in particular the requirement of approval of three-fourths of the adult male population for future land cessions.[66] Specifically, the Court opined that this was so because "*[p]lenary authority* over the tribal relations of the Indians has been exercised by Congress from the beginning, and the power has always been deemed a political one, not subject to be controlled by the judicial department of the government."[67]

This concept of congressional power in the field of Indian affairs is quite extraordinary in at least two important aspects. First, the power is denominated as one *without limitation,* and second, the authority is beyond judicial review. Such *absolute* notions of power are contrary to any understanding of a constitutional republic grounded in specified and limited powers. It is noteworthy that the Court in *Lone Wolf* did not cite (nor could it cite) any authority for this astounding proposition. The Court simply converted its perception of *congressional practice* into a valid *constitutional doctrine* without any legal support or analysis.

The plenary power doctrine opened the way for a wide-ranging and unchecked exercise of congressional authority in Indian affairs, including the continued unilateral abrogation of treaties[68] as well as the termination of the federal-tribal relationship of more than three hundred tribes.[69] Nevertheless, this plenary power doctrine, and particularly its "political question" component, has been slightly eroded by recent cases. Both the *Delaware Tribal Business Committee*[70] and the *Sioux Nation*[71] cases indicate that acts of Congress in Indian affairs are subject to judicial review in accordance with the rational basis test.[72] Yet it remains true that no act of Congress concerning Indian affairs, with two minor exceptions,[73] has ever been set aside or ruled unconstitutional by the Supreme Court. Given the fact that an entire volume of the United States Code deals with Indian legislation, this is no mean feat. The plenary power doctrine has extra-constitutional roots with only a limited accountability that has not been fully recognized or adequately addressed. This doctrine, in turn, has the potential to eclipse any meaningful examination of tribal-federal and tribal-state relations.

Despite their importance, these seminal doctrines and policies have had no real constitutional value in framing progressive or enduring federal-tribal discourse about the nature of tribal sovereignty. Treaties offer that potential, for they clearly possess the moral and legal foundations to play the benchmark role. Yet Congress and the federal courts have been unable, or unwilling, to see the vital role of treaties in their true constitutional dimension.

THE POVERTY OF LEGAL THEORY

One of the legacies of the colonization process is the fact that Indian tribes, which began their interaction with the federal government as sovereign entities largely *outside* the republic, became absorbed more and more into the republic, eventually becoming internal sovereigns of a *limited kind*. This process is most accurately characterized as one of involuntary annexation. Throughout the eighteenth and nineteenth centuries and continuing well into the early twentieth century, Indian people were neither federal nor state citizens. Their incorporation was not justified by any coherent legal theory and is, arguably, directly at odds with several key legal and political premises embedded in the U.S. Constitution. These premises, drawn heavily from the work of the political philosopher John Locke, include the principles of limited governmental sovereignty and the consent of the governed. As suggested by Professor Robert Clinton: "In Lockean social compact terms, Indian tribes never entered into or consented to any constitutional contract by which they agreed to be governed by federal or state authority, rather than by tribal sovereignty." [74]

The principle set out by Professor Clinton is, in fact, the essential holding in the early seminal cases of *Cherokee Nation* [75] and *Worcester*. [76] Describing Indian tribes as "domestic dependent nations" and "distinct independent political communities" respectively, Chief Justice Marshall's opinions in these cases placed tribes outside the state and national polities. Like so much in federal Indian law, the tides of history, if not compelling legal analysis, have nearly drowned these holdings. Subsequent cases in the late nineteenth and early twentieth centuries, particularly *Kagama v. United States* [77] and *Lone Wolf v. Hitchcock*, [78] fully incorporated tribes into the federal system and declared them subject to the "plenary power" of Congress. Despite its lack of constitutional roots, this power nevertheless proclaims extensive—even limitless—power over tribes in blatant contradiction of the Lockean notion of limited government sovereignty. The plenary power doctrine appears to be extraconstitutional in its origins and extravagant in its placement of unlimited authority in the hands of the federal government at the expense of the tribal sovereignty.[79]

This vast expansion of federal authority in Indian affairs has concomitantly, and almost brutally, constrained the parameters of tribal sovereignty. For example, as Justice Stewart wrote in *United States v. Wheeler*,[80] "[T]he sovereignty that the Indian tribes retain is of a unique and limited character. It exists only at the sufferance of Congress and is subject to complete defeasance." This bald colonizing language suggests that tribal sovereignty is really nonexistent. Within a national jurisprudence that recognizes the primacy of order, limits, and predictability within the legal system,[81] such pronouncements seem especially crabbed and destabilizing. This is particularly true for tribes attempting to build and to advance their vision of sovereignty. These unjustifiable constraints pose a constant and paralyzing threat to the efforts of tribes and tribal courts to move forward. This poverty of theory concerning tribal sovereignty—which reduces the tribal pursuit of self-determination to dependence on federal, particularly congressional, sufferance—contrasts sharply with the constitutional and theoretical solidity that governs the interaction of the federal and state sovereigns. The Tenth Amendment to the U.S. Constitution is the cornerstone of this dynamic relationship with its declaration that "[t]he powers not delegated to the United States by the Constitution, nor prohibited by it to the States, are reserved to the states respectively, or to the people."[82] The Tenth Amendment provides a clear constitutional marker for discussions of federal-state sovereignty,[83] while discussions of tribal sovereignty, when they are held at all, occur largely at the fringe of constitutional theory and analysis. Perhaps this is not surprising, but rather a common result for indigenous people and cultures whiplashed by the process of colonization.[84]

Yet if this were the full extent of such discussions, tribal sovereignty and tribal courts might not even exist, or they might have been confined to the dustbin of tribal and national history. Despite this vein of oppressive legal history, more encouraging Supreme Court declarations about the nature and potential of tribal sovereignty have also emerged. This is especially true in the Court's declaration of tribal courts' significance.

In both the *National Farmers Union*[85] and *Iowa Mutual*[86] cases, the Court ringingly endorsed the importance of tribal courts as the primary forums in which to resolve civil disputes arising on the reservation. As Justice Thurgood Marshall wrote in *Iowa Mutual,* "Tribal courts play a vital role in tribal self-government . . . and the Federal Government has consistently encouraged their development."[87] It is the force of these most recent cases, joined with the residual vitality of foundational cases such as *Cherokee Nation* and *Worcester,* that provides the necessary support, if not adequate legal and constitutional theory, for tribes and tribal courts to identify and explore the proper parameters of tribal sovereignty. These cases guarantee no affirmation of the *results*—practical or theoretical—of tribal court jurisprudence.[88] Tribal courts remain threatened by the dark shadow of federal plenary authority and the general incoherence of contemporary federal Indian law.[89] Nevertheless, tribal courts must use the available light to find their way in and around the corners of the shadow.

FORMULATIONS OF TRIBAL SOVEREIGNTY: AN ASSESSMENT

Tribal sovereignty is certainly a foundational concept in Indian law, but it has proved rather elusive in practice. Given the essential incompatibility of the treaty, trust relationship, and plenary power doctrines, the doctrine of tribal sovereignty often appears less than substantial, almost evanescent before federal dominance. The early cases and the resulting foundational doctrines are majestically ambiguous. The glass is half full or half empty. Tribal rights often exist, but not always. Tribes are entitled to some recognition, but not too much. Tribes have sovereignty, but not inconsistent with their dependent status. In light of this paradoxical inclusion and exclusion, parity and hierarchy, theoretical incoherence and destabilizing results predominate. Modern Indian law jurisprudence, especially in the last two decades, has intensified rather than ameliorated these difficulties. This is particularly true in light of Supreme Court ambivalence (and general non-Indian and state animus) in the face of tribal assertions of authority on the reservation in such diverse matters as taxing, hunting and fishing, and zoning rights. Therefore, it is revealing to review the discussions and formulations of sovereignty by leading scholars in the field.

In this regard, it is necessary to acknowledge the huge debt that practitioners and scholars of Indian law owe to the late Felix Cohen. The Herculean efforts of Professor Cohen in researching, synthesizing, and writing his seminal 1942 *Handbook of Federal Indian Law* cannot be praised enough. Indeed, it can be fairly claimed that his treatise literally created the field of Indian law as a discrete and recognizable area of study and practice that required special expertise and unique attention.

Two aspects of Cohen's work are particularly ripe for review and critical assessment. The first is his ethical injunction that "[l]ike the miner's canary, the Indian marks the shift from fresh air to poison gas in our political atmosphere; and our treatment of Indians, even more than our treatment of other minorities, reflects the rise and fall of our democratic faith." [90] Cohen's metaphor remains powerful, although the present ratio of fresh air to poison gas is not necessarily encouraging. Not only is that ratio discouraging, but there is no basic doctrinal stability or national moral commitment to ensure that the fresh air will not dissipate further. In fact, this book is an attempt to explore ways to improve the ratio and to identify and to shore up the practical and theoretical timbers of Indian law.

The second aspect, Cohen's definition of tribal sovereignty, may be briefly stated as the adherence to three fundamental principles: (1) An Indian tribe possesses, in the first instance, all the powers of a sovereign state. (2) Conquest renders the tribe subject to the legislative power of the United States and in substance terminates the tribe's external sovereignty, for example, its power to enter into treaties with foreign nations, but does not by itself affect the tribe's internal sovereignty, that is, its powers of local self-government. (3) These powers are subject to qualification by treaties and express legislation of Congress, but, save those expressly qualified, full powers of internal sovereignty are vested in the Indian tribe and in their duly constituted organs of government.[91]

The first component of Cohen's definition is doctrinally clear. Before contact with European explorers and invaders, tribes possessed all the powers of self-government, including the right to carry on foreign affairs—for example, the right to enter into treaties with European nations and the United States. In a phrase, tribes possessed complete sovereignty within the family of nations.

The second of Cohen's principles seems largely accurate as a statement of dominant history and jurisprudence. That is, as a result of being "conquered," tribes were stripped of certain powers such as the ability to carry on foreign affairs. While this is largely true as a statement of doctrine, it is not completely accurate as a summary statement of historical reality. Many tribes (including, for example, the Sioux Nation, as the Fort Laramie Treaty of 1868 amply attests to) never militarily capitulated to the U.S. government. Many tribes were not conquered; more accurately, they were annexed and absorbed within the national republic without any doctrinal coherence or justification.[92]

As to the final definitional element that tribes retain all powers not expressly extinguished by Congress, this principle cuts both ways. It is accurate and helpful from a tribal point of view because it recognizes inherent and reserved tribal powers that do not devolve from any federal delegation and in many cases predate the U.S. Constitution. Unfortunately, Cohen's doctrinal formulation may also severely limit tribal sovereignty because it recognizes the ability of Congress to extinguish tribal powers, apparently in accordance with the plenary power doctrine, which is itself without limitation or constitutional justification. This principle essentially reflects the image of the benevolent colonizer, and it is doctrinally insufficient to establish a more stable and enduring conception of tribal sovereignty. Cohen's formulation of tribal sovereignty nevertheless played a vital role in countering a growing federal perception of the decline of the viability of tribal autonomy and self-government.

Cohen's efforts to formulate a doctrinal benchmark for thinking about tribal sovereignty was an extraordinary achievement. By culling the strongest interpretations from the Marshall trilogy, as well as exercising his own scholarly heft, Cohen established a theoretical solidity that a certain line of Supreme Court cases such as *Kagama*,[93] *Lone Wolf*,[94] and *U.S. v. McBratney*[95] seemed to depart from with their explicit or implicit rationales "that Indian tribes had withered away under the weight of non-Indian society and that courts should acknowledge the decline of tribes and doctrines such as tribal sovereignty."[96]

It should be noted that Cohen's work is best seen in light of attempts to establish a foothold for tribal sovereignty in the context of the federal jurisdictional assault on tribes, as the above line of cases indicates. Even cases in the same historical period that were much more hospitable to tribal sovereignty, such as *Ex parte Crow Dog*[97] and *Talton v. Mayes*,[98] followed in the same federal-tribal vein, envisioning the federal government as the aggressor asserting its authority over the tribes, often without specific congressional enactments authorizing the controverted action.

The locus of contemporary sovereignty disputes is, for the most part, quite different. Most sovereignty issues today involve state-tribal disputes about "civil" jurisdictional authority over non-Indians and their property on the reservation in such diverse areas as taxation, hunting and fishing, and zoning. In these instances, the tribes are often defending against "renewed" state incursions while also reasserting long-dormant tribal authority.

It is in this context of the dramatic change in the playing field of Indian law that Cohen's concept of tribal sovereignty now seems inadequate. As tribes continue to move forward in their assertions of authority over non-Indians and their property with a complementary resistance to renewed state incursions on the reservation, tribal sovereignty, constricted by Congress's extensive plenary power, is constantly at risk. This is particularly true in the matter of tribal authority over non-Indians, an issue not addressed by Cohen. Tribal sovereignty may be broadly divided into two halves: (1) self-government over tribal members and tribal land within the reservation; and (2) self-government over nontribal members (non-Indians and nonmember Indians) and their land within the reservation. Cohen's work focuses almost solely on the first half, with little attention to the second half, which involves the searing jurisdictional controversies of today.

Cohen's *Handbook* says little about civil jurisdiction, particularly in the context of tribal authority over non-Indians, and says almost nothing about tribal courts.[99] This is not surprising given tribal inactivity in these arenas at the time Cohen wrote. But today this is where the action is in Indian law, and Cohen's writing is not adequate in these contexts. Therefore, those of us who write in his shadow need to bring light to these widespread areas.

The current judicial doctrine of "sovereignty as sufferance" is, in essence, theoretically incoherent within a constitutional democracy that is premised on a central government of limited and enumerated powers. The U.S. Constitution does not specify any "plenary authority" in Congress to unilaterally circumscribe or extinguish tribal authority. Such a doctrine is devastating in its implications, and many tribes have suffered from its unbridled exercise.

If one defines "sovereignty" (outside the context of foreign affairs) as the ability to govern all individuals and property found within one's borders, then it is clear that tribes do not possess complete sovereignty. States possess complete sovereignty subject only to the explicit limitations in the U.S. Constitution, limitations that are relatively specific within the context of the Tenth Amendment. Tribes possess residual sovereignty, meaning sovereignty not diminished by Congress or the courts. The problem here is that there is no clear constitutional or doctrinal limitation on the erosions or limitations permitted by Congress. This is a destabilized sovereignty, sovereignty that is, to paraphrase Justice Stewart, of a limited and unique kind, subject to complete defeasance by Congress.[100] A sovereignty of sufferance strikes many as literally oxymoronic and at odds with a national jurisprudence of integrity and stability. This crabbed view of tribal sovereignty needs critical exegesis, doctrinal extension, and, finally, permanent incorporation within our constitutional jurisprudence.

Professor Charles Wilkinson, in his influential work *American Indians, Time, and the Law,*[101] seeks to avoid this pitfall by placing confidence in the judicial branch, particularly the U.S. Supreme Court, to honor the treaties that are the bedrock of the field of Indian law and to hew "to a kind of morality profoundly rare in our jurisprudence."[102] He looks to the potential of treaties[103] when he suggests that the "organic governmental side of Indian treaties should be construed in the same manner as constitutional provisions,"[104] provisions whose goal was creating and preserving a "measured separatism." In particular, Professor Wilkinson envisions substantial change:

> Viewed in this light, the Court's recognition of rules providing for insulation against time, a tribal right to change, and special Indian law canons of construction is appropriate, indeed necessary; these doctrines allow principled growth of those organic governmental documents in much the same way as the Constitution evolves.[105]

Yet this enticing formalism is also presently inadequate because it has no widely recognized doctrinal footing and is largely unrecognized and unknown within the web of beliefs of the national legal, including the judicial, community. This "morality" has recently given us, for example, the slippery slope of the *Oliphant,*[106] *Montana,*[107] and *Brendale*[108] cases. In all of these cases, the Supreme Court sharply curtailed, with little hesitation, tribal authority over non-Indians in Indian country.

Even "good" judges need to be relieved of their current judicial burden, which lacks workable, coherent doctrine, by the formulation of enduring legal principles and laws that recognize and vouchsafe tribal sovereignty. "Morality" is an important human and social quality, but it is not in itself a reliable legal doctrine for guaranteeing tribal survival and the opportunity to flourish.

In the end, the work of Felix Cohen and others on tribal sovereignty cannot be seen as the final statement; as with any foundational doctrine, it needs to be revised and extended in light of contemporary circumstances. Cohen's work should be neither re-

ified nor deified but theoretically and practically emended. Without such an effort, the light of Cohen's work may cast a dark
and ironic shadow over the concept of tribal sovereignty. Tribal
sovereignty needs to be (re)conceptualized on the plane of the
federal Constitution and even international law to provide an
enduring theoretical base from which to work out its contours
and implications within late twentieth century American jurisprudence. Some of these possibilities are discussed in more detail
in chapter 4.

PART TWO

Justice, Liberation, and Struggle

Tribal Courts and Tribal Sovereignty

Tribal courts constitute the frontline tribal institutions that most often confront issues of self-determination and sovereignty, while at the same time they are charged with providing reliable and equitable adjudication in the many and increasingly diverse matters that come before them. In addition, they constitute a key tribal entity for advancing and protecting the rights of self-government. This is especially true in the wake of their development as a means by which many would assess the current status of tribal self-determination and reservation well-being in general.

Tribal courts are of growing significance throughout Indian country. This is especially true in light of the Supreme Court decisions in *National Farmers Union Insurance Cos. v. Crow Tribe of Indians*[1] and *Iowa Mutual Insurance Co. v. LaPlante*,[2] which hold that tribal courts are the primary forums for adjudicating civil disputes on the reservation. As Justice Marshall wrote in the *Iowa Mutual* case, "Tribal courts play a vital role in tribal self-government . . . and the Federal Government has consistently encouraged their development."[3] As a result of this continued and growing recognition, tribal courts have become the premier tribal institutions that struggle to analyze and to identify the range and scope of tribal jurisdiction and sovereignty.

Both the history and contemporary setting of tribal courts raise important questions about their structure, legitimacy, competency, and ability to define and render justice. The issue of contextual legitimacy—that is, the social, historical, and cultural setting of judicial adjudication rather than, for example, the simple logical application of rules of law in order to measure the systemic vitality and appropriateness of judicial decision making—is of particular significance in the tribal court setting. Closely related to the issue of contextual legitimacy is the question of whether the tribal bar functions as a significant interpretive community that provides a reliable framework to help identify tribal legal values and to define the parameters of legal advocacy and judicial decision making within tribal court systems. Taken together, these perspectives provide a valuable complement to the central problem of analyzing issues of tribal jurisdiction.

Tribal courts have never been analyzed from such a conceptual vantage point. However, these key elements are arguably the cardinal principles in determining the viability of tribal courts to advance important tribal values as well as to render case-by-case justice reliably and fairly. Such a view has nothing to do with the adoption of non-Indian, statelike standards (whatever they might be); rather, it has its roots in a commitment to understand how justice and judicial self-realization are achieved in any legal system and how such worthy aspirations may be furthered.

Tribal courts and their jurisprudence are involved in a period of rapid growth and development. As part of the process of significant change, tribal courts need to build an indigenous jurisprudence of vision and cultural integrity. This endeavor includes the necessity to transcend the legacy of colonization, to overcome the absence of effective theory concerning tribal sovereignty, and to solve the "dilemma of difference." In other words, tribal courts must strive to respond competently and creatively to both federal pressures and cultural values and imperatives. Some of the tools for this undertaking include language, narrative and story, and innovative conceptions about the meaning of justice. In addition, it is necessary to place these efforts within the horizons of constitutional and international law.

This part of the book—chapters 3 and 4—develops these themes within the context of the history of tribal courts, the realities of federal hegemony, and the often confusing jurisdictional backdrop, as well as the attendant challenge to the judicial administration of tribal law. This is a challenge that must be met in order to realize an enduring tribal jurisprudence that maintains cultural fidelity to the past and achieves current aspiration. Such potential achievements ultimately rest on the dreams and efforts of the committed individuals who work and practice within the tribal court setting.

When I sit as an appellate justice at either the Rosebud Sioux or Cheyenne River Sioux Reservation, I find the experience both moving and unique. Regardless of the dimensions and issues of the cases, these events represent tribal sovereignty in action. An important and significant tribal institution adjudicates particular cases and in the process enacts a critical judicial and cultural discourse on the meaning of law, justice, and tribal sovereignty within a localized reservation perspective. It is this incremental process that weaves piece by piece the sturdy and vital fabric of tribal sovereignty. My attitude toward this process is, I believe, shared by all local people who work within tribal courts, whether they are judges, prosecutors, public defenders, clerks, or administrators. A basic unity of important purpose dominates the daily workings of the tribal courts. It is this unity and commitment that demonstrates both the tenacity and the hope that underpin the struggle to flourish. All of this takes place in small tribal courthouses on the edge of the prairie and in other out-of-the-way places throughout Indian country, as local reservation people interact with the law in an ongoing effort to construct an enduring future.

The Crucible
of Sovereignty

*Tribal Courts, Legitimacy, and the
Jurisdictional Backdrop*

BACKGROUND AND HISTORY OF TRIBAL COURTS

Tribal courts in Indian country do not find their origins in any specific statutory authorization but rather in the early administrative practice of the Bureau of Indian Affairs and in the subsequent and implicit authorization suggested by the Indian Reorganization Act of 1934.[1] This view, of course, does not consider the existence of tribal adjudicatory mechanisms[2] that may have preexisted or existed in tandem with formally identified tribal courts. Such concerns are, however, often critical in examining the issue of legitimacy and are discussed later in this chapter.

The "need" for some sort of tribal court system emanated from the perception of local and national non-Indian administrators in Indian country that some formal device was necessary to regulate law and order on the reservation.[3] Prior to the authorization by the Secretary of the Interior in 1883 to establish Courts of Indian Offenses,[4] local Indian agents on the reservations resorted to a variety of expedients. The most common solution was for the agent himself to act as judge or to delegate the duty to one of his other subordinates or to a "trusted" Indian. This practice, though not statutorily authorized, was in line with the course of action suggested several times by earlier Commissioners of Indian Affairs and Secretaries of the Interior, who envisioned the local agents as justices of the peace.[5]

Despite these ad hoc practices throughout Indian country, the specific impetus for Courts of Indian Offenses seemed to come from the reform impulse of Secretary of the Interior H. M. Teller, who was appointed in 1882.[6] Indian Affairs Commissioner Hiram Price compiled a set of rules for Courts of Indian Offenses, which were approved on April 10, 1883, by Secretary Teller and circulated to the agents.[7] These rules provided guidelines for court organization and procedure and an abbreviated criminal and civil code.[8] The only express qualification for prospective jurists was that they not be polygamists.[9] The range of jurisdictional authority was thought to be modeled after that of a justice of the peace in the state or territory where such a court was located.[10]

It was recognized from the first that there was, at best, a shaky legal foundation for these tribunals.[11] There was no federal statutory authorization for the establishment of such courts, only the generally acknowledged authority of the Department of the Interior to supervise Indian affairs.[12] Because no authorizing legislation defined the jurisdiction of the Courts of Indian Offenses, the courts and police were often challenged. The usual reaction of the Commissioner of Indian Affairs in the face of a jurisdictional challenge was to try to avoid a showdown.[13] In this regard, there was unblemished success: no successful legal challenges were brought against the Courts of Indian Offenses.[14] Tribal courts remained fragile and potentially volatile forums for all concerned.

The tasks of the Courts of Indian Offenses became vastly more complicated when the ravages of the allotment process[15] and the sale of "surplus"[16] tribal lands brought substantial numbers of non-Indians as permanent residents to the reservation. The bright line that had separated white and Indian communities was obliterated; jurisdictional dilemmas became apparent. Various questions arose: What courts had (or would accept) jurisdiction over non-Indians, over Indian allottees, over mixed bloods? How would these courts be financed? These dilemmas are still not fully resolved today, more than one hundred years later.[17] Despite the principal claim that the Courts of Indian Offenses were necessary to maintain law and order on the reservation, other motives were at work. For example, the 1892 revision provided that "if an Indian refuses or neglects to adopt habits of industry, or to engage in civilized pursuits or employments, but habitually spends his time in idleness and loafing, he shall be deemed a vagrant" and punished accordingly.[18] The "need" for law and order often meant a "need" for acculturation and assimilation. This notion of reform often sought to impose or instill "proper virtues" in Indians; it was particularly characteristic of federal policy during the period 1871–1928.[19]

Courts of Indian Offenses were established when the Indian agent on a particular reservation and the Commissioner of Indian Affairs concluded they were practicable and desirable; thus, such courts were established for all Indians with the exception of the Five Civilized Tribes, the Indians of New York, the Osage, the Pueblos, and the eastern Cherokees, all of which had recognized tribal governments and courts. The peak of their activity was reached around 1900, when about two-thirds of the agencies had their own courts.[20] Some agencies never established a court, and others experimented with them only briefly.[21] Congress's penurious appropriations for the courts limited the number that could function at any time. The Commissioner of Indian Affairs determined where the courts would be located. In 1891 an Acting Commissioner expressed this selection process and its unbounded discretion by noting that courts would be established "as it may appear the good of the Indian Service requires."[22] Today only about twenty-five Courts of Indian Offenses continue to function. They are popularly referred to as "CFR" courts because most of their governing regulations are found in volume 25 of the Code of Federal Regulations. Most other tribes have established tribal courts pursuant to their tribal constitutions.

Finally, the wheels of reform began to turn in Indian country. The late 1920s saw renewed public concern for the conditions on Indian reservations. Reports appeared that criticized white-controlled land tenure patterns, growing poverty, and administrative abuse in Indian country.[23] The 1928 Meriam Report[24] initiated by Secretary of the Interior Hubert Work is the best known of these, but it made no recommendations on the subject of law and tribal courts. The situation, the report argued, varied too greatly from tribe to tribe.[25]

The Indian Reorganization Act of 1934[26] was the culmination of this reform movement. One of the sweeping changes it sought to accomplish was in the matter of law and order on Indian reservations. John Collier, Commissioner of Indian Affairs, proposed a sweeping reform bill that dealt with four major areas: self-government, special education for Indians, Indian lands, and a Court of Indian Affairs.[27] The Collier proposal envisioned a dual system of tribal courts. The first level was to be organized under the self-government title of the proposed act.[28] Tribes would be able to retain their local courts either as Courts of Indian Offenses or as tribal courts created through specific authorization in the tribe's constitution adopted pursuant to the Indian Reorganization Act.[29]

At the same time, a national Court of Indian Affairs would be staffed with seven judges appointed by the President and subject to confirmation by the Senate. The court would always be in session and would be held in a number of different circuits. Each judge would be responsible for a particular region.[30]

The jurisdiction of this special Court of Indian Affairs was set out in section 3 of the proposed legislation.[31] The court would assume responsibility over the following matters: major criminal cases; cases where an Indian tribe or community was a party; cases involving questions of commerce where one litigant was an Indian and the other a non-Indian; civil and criminal cases involving a tribal ordinance where a party was not a member of the Indian community; questions involving Indian allotments where the rights of an Indian were involved; and cases involving the determination of heirs and the settlement of such things as estates, land partitions, and guardianships.[32]

According to some commentators, a number of provisions in the Court of Indian Affairs title would have changed the traditional concept of Indian justice rather significantly.[33] All federal guarantees to criminal defendants and the federal rules of evidence would apply. In essence, the court would duplicate the system of procedure and appeal that prevailed in the federal court system.[34] Of course, no Indian thinking or input was considered in the drafting of the bill.[35] If things were not going well on the reservation,[36] improvement lay in ratcheting up of applicable federal standards.[37]

Despite these familiar difficulties, the Collier Bill did go a long way in attempting to improve the system of justice in Indian country. In addition to the powers already discussed, the proposed court could have removed cases from tribal and state courts and heard appeals from local tribal courts.[38] The Secretary of the Interior was also authorized to appoint ten special attorneys to provide legal advice and representation to both tribes and individual Indians before the court.[39] Not unexpectedly, as with much of the proposed Collier Bill, this title generated a great deal of controversy during the legislative hearings.[40] The final enactment of the bill, which became known as the Indian Reorganization Act of 1934, or the Wheeler-Howard Act, bore faint resemblance to the original proposal.[41] The title dealing with the Court of Indian Offenses disappeared entirely.

Under the IRA, tribes were to draft their own constitutions, adopt their own laws, and set up their own court systems.[42] Regardless of the statutory provisions, most tribal constitutions were drafted by the Bureau of Indian Affairs without tribal input and consequently reflected little, if any, direct local concern.[43] As a result, there was no opportunity to formally reinstitute traditional law on the reservation,[44] even if it existed at the time.

These BIA constitutions did not provide for any separation of powers and did not specifically create any court system. Most constitutions, rather facilely, it seems, recognized a power in the tribal council—the elected legislative body—to "promulgate and enforce ordinances providing for the maintenance of law and order and the administration of justice by establishing a reservation court and defining its duties and powers."[45] Most tribal legislation also required the approval of the Bureau of Indian Affairs.[46] In recent years a number of tribes have amended their constitutions to remove the Bureau of Indian Affairs approval power.[47] It is important to note, however, that the exercise of these tribal constitutional powers (whether by an IRA tribe or not) is not to be considered the exercise of federally delegated powers but rather the exercise of a tribal sovereign authority which predates the United States Constitution.[48]

Most current tribal codes which serve to elucidate the framework of tribal court activity are a combination of unique tribal law and adapted state and federal law principles. Apparent in the newer codes is a decided commitment to develop increased tribal statutory, including customary, law and an organized and reported body of tribal decisional law.

THE CONTEXTUAL LEGITIMACY OF ADJUDICATION IN TRIBAL COURTS

Once established, tribal courts face two critical issues. The first is related to the issue of legitimacy, and the second is related to the scope of their authority or jurisdiction. Together, these interrelated issues form the cornerstone concerns relative to the viability and importance of tribal courts. Two critical terms, "contextual legitimacy" and "interpretive community," are key concepts in understanding the nature and quality of adjudication in tribal courts. Each term will first be defined and examined and then brought to bear in the tribal court context.

The concept of contextual legitimacy represents a particular gloss on the fundamental concept of formal legitimacy. In the U.S. legal system, this demand for (formal) legitimacy has traditionally rested on the pristine view that judges should decide cases in accordance with the law. Most conventionally and simply stated, this has meant that any judicial decision must logically follow from the authoritative legal rule or rules and not, for example, from personal or other values which are not validated by the law.[49] This classic formulation has been seriously criticized as inadequate to explain the relationship of judicial adjudication to the larger legal and political system of which it is a part. Further criticism argues that the legal and political system cannot be adequately understood apart from its social, historical, and cultural context.[50]

The notion of contextual legitimacy looks to the social, historical, and cultural setting of judicial adjudication that provides a most fruitful framework for examining tribal courts and tribal court adjudication. Tribal courts need to be viewed within this wide area to better understand what social and cultural values are actually becoming embedded in these relatively young judicial systems. This is necessary to avoid a sterile analysis of the application of rules of law unhinged from the larger concerns of tribal integrity and culture.

In the postformalist concept of contextual legitimacy, the meaning of legitimacy shifts from a concern for antecedent legitimating foundations, such as the logical application of rules of law, to a demand for a legal and political system which on the whole enjoys and merits the allegiance of the people. The propriety and integrity of adjudication therefore depends on the people's contribution to the legitimacy of the legal and political system in its social, historical, and cultural context.[51]

Contextual legitimacy in this view has two interrelated components, (1) the obligation and (2) the desire to abide by the law within a legal and political system that merits fidelity and affirmation. Whether this obligation is generally recognized by the people is a question of social fact. Whether the desire exists to abide by the law is more a normative question. Yet neither aspect, taken alone, is sufficient to establish contextual legitimacy, and the two together imply a tension between the search for a more orderly and just society and the requirements of a constitutional democracy.[52]

Although much of this may sound arcane, I believe it has significant import in an examination of tribal court systems. One of the dilemmas that permeates tribal courts is the whole notion of legitimacy. Identifiable segments of most tribes have at times refused to consider tribal courts legitimate. In this regard, many tribal courts are vilified as "white men's" creations flowing from the IRA and an entire federal history directed to assimilation. The courts are seen as instruments of outside forces and values that are not traditional and therefore not legitimate.

By contrast, some segments of most tribal populations (and local non-Indian populations) view tribal courts as illegitimate because they fall, or appear to fall, far below recognized state and federal standards in such matters ranging from the institutional separation of powers to the provision of civil due process and enforcement of judgments. These combined forces often threaten the viability of tribal courts as legitimate justice-rendering institutions. Regardless of competence and commitment, legitimacy becomes illegitimacy when large numbers of people in fact cease to recognize an obligation to abide by laws or judicial decisions with which they disagree. This problem is further aggravated in the tribal context when the tribal government itself may refuse to abide by tribal court decisions or submit to tribal court jurisdiction.[53] Needless to say, claims of illegitimacy have been made throughout U.S. legal history, ranging from the colonial claim of the illegitimacy of the rule of the British crown to the large-scale civil disobedience of segregationist laws in the South during the 1960s. Nevertheless, these wrenching challenges to the legal system have been met by significant modification and reform.

It has been suggested that the normative aspect of contextual legitimacy depends on whether the system as a whole adequately contributes to a more orderly and just society in light of contemporary circumstances and evolving notions of justice.[54] Such a view does not deny the importance of change and reform but holds that such claims must not challenge the legitimacy of the system as a whole.[55] It is here, I believe, that tribal courts find themselves most delicately placed. The increase in the bona fide legitimacy of tribal courts is (and has been) inextricably bound to their amenability to change and reform. This adaptability serves to increase the perception in both the Indian and non-Indian community of the development of a more orderly and just system and society. This enhanced perception has actively drawn from both streams—traditional and progressive—of discontent.

What then, one might ask, are some examples of this growing legitimacy of tribal courts? Some of the numerous examples include the increase of law-trained Indian people within many systems, tribal and constitutional code revision, the nascent development of traditional and customary law, and the continued recognition of tribal courts by the U.S. Supreme Court[56] as viable and important forums for resolution of reservation-based claims involving both Indians and non-Indians.

A recent example vividly demonstrates the growth and development of legitimacy. Chief Trial Judge Sherman Marshall, who is a law-trained, bilingual member of the Rosebud Sioux Tribe, addressed students of my Indian law class during our visit to the Rosebud Sioux Tribal Court. In the course of his presentation, Chief Judge Marshall stated several times that he believed it was part of his job (but obviously not in his job description) to travel to the twenty tribal communities scattered over the most rural parts of the reservation to discuss what the tribal court was and what it was doing.[57] Chief Judge Marshall understood full well that the success and legitimacy of the court depends, in significant part, on the understanding and support of community people—many of whom know little about the tribal court or have had negative and dispiriting experiences with it. Legitimacy, at the grassroots level, is not a given; rather, it is the result of much necessary but unappreciated toil. It is not only the message but also the messenger. It is important to note that a young, law-educated tribal member who is bilingual and bicultural is an emblematic figure, poised between two worlds, bringing the best messages of both.

A second experience from the field trip provides an important example about the nature of legitimacy in the framework of the hearing of an actual case. In this instance, Chief Judge Marshall was hearing a small claims matter between a grandmother and her daughter concerning the alleged failure of the daughter to pay the grandmother for taking care of her children.[58] Both parties were tribal members and were unrepresented, as is the norm in both tribal and state small claims proceedings.

Chief Judge Marshall requested the plaintiff to tell her story. She began and went on for some time in a seemingly long and circular narrative. Chief Judge Marshall spoke to her several times briefly in Lakota, the tribal language of the Rosebud Sioux. She answered in Lakota and went on mixing English and Lakota. When she finally finished, he asked several direct questions necessary to making appropriate findings of fact. He then proceeded to address and listen to the defendant in exactly the same manner. He concluded by informing the parties that he needed additional documentation; after he received it, he would make a prompt decision.

It was readily apparent that an unusual rapport was established between the judge and the parties. They could speak without interruption (a cultural prerogative of elders) and in their first language. Contextual legitimacy was palpable; yet the entire case and its hearing raised ongoing questions about the nature of legitimacy in tribal settings.

The process of striving for legitimacy is far from over and must continue as a dynamic force in Indian country. Many questions remain, including the development of traditional and customary law, the separation of powers, authentic appeal, and the enforcement of individual civil rights within the tribal context. In particular, the example cited above illustrates the need to discover the best possible means for resolving disputes that are primarily cultural rather than strictly legal. Yet, as always, the core of legitimacy rests with the people themselves. Without their support and understanding, there can be little hope for continued advancement and growth.

A review of the elements of legitimacy of the dominant legal system as a whole also provides a fruitful comparison. The legal system merits the support of the people if it serves three functions related to stable features of the social, historical, and cultural context: (1) providing a professional community to run and watch the system on a case-by-case basis; (2) offering institutions that operate at some distance from majoritarian politics; and (3) using a legal language and reasoning in the search for a more orderly and just society to augment lawmaking processes that reflect majoritarian and other political preferences.[59]

A PROFESSIONAL COMMUNITY

What is the nature of the "professional" community that runs and watches the legal system on a case-by-case basis? Most tribal codes admit two quite different groups to the community of recognized practitioners, namely, law-trained individuals (i.e., Indians and non-Indians who are law school graduates and admitted to practice in some state or federal jurisdiction) and tribal advocates (i.e., tribal members admitted to tribal practice generally without any education or examination requirement).

The issue here is how these groups come together, or can come together, to form a community helping to carry out an important legitimating function. Some suggestions for strengthening the tribal court legal community include the development of a tribal bar examination,[60] the provision of tribally sponsored CLE (continuing legal education) programs, and the adoption and enforcement of a tribal ethics code. The development and implementation of a tribal bar examination would aid in securing a professional community that shares a common legal and cultural understanding of the procedural and substantive legal matrix (including tradition and custom) that governs in tribal court. A tribal bar examination, in addition to furthering basic tribal legal community competence in accordance with tribally developed standards, serves to advance legitimacy by assisting in the fulfillment of the expectation of responsible self-government. It reflects an exercise of autonomous power that is credible and necessary to maintain and to increase parity with other sovereigns within (and even beyond) the federal system. The implementation of a tribal bar exam requirement illustrates institution building that does not simply mimic or rely on state-developed credentials or requirements.

Second, tribal bar–sponsored CLE programs would augment professional community competence and understanding of new legal developments, especially within the context of federal Indian law and local tribal law changes. In the latter category, programs involving such topics as the development of tribal tradition and customary law, the enforcement of judgments, and client counseling would seem particularly appropriate.[61] CLE programs would also provide one of the few opportunities for tribal bar members to come together informally and to socialize in order to form a face-to-face community with a better understanding of each other as *individuals* participating in a community of common endeavor.

A third important area is the development of an effective ethics code and enforcement program to deal with those few individuals who do not comport with tribal standards. The ethics code must not only establish appropriate standards of representation but also provide the necessary administrative machinery to hear complaints and, if necessary, apply sanctions.[62] Any professional community worthy of the name must be able to maintain standards of integrity and safeguard the interests of litigants from the gross improprieties of their legal representatives. In recent years the legal community in general has been subject to growing criticism from the public because of its seeming inability or unwillingness to adequately police its own members. Tribal bars should not let themselves get caught in that web of criticism and distrust.

These three elements, if instituted in a vigorous and timely manner, can do much to develop a well-trained, up-to-date, and self-policing organization to which the entire community can entrust the day-to-day monitoring of the legal system. Such efforts would further augment the message that Chief Judge Marshall and other tribal judges would be able to take to the community.

Such efforts, of course, take time, money, and commitment. Yet time is plentiful, the cost is not prohibitive, and the commitment to improvement certainly exists on most reservations. It is more a matter of placing these efforts in the necessary pipeline of tribal priorities in order to ensure the necessary tribal legislative, executive, and judicial commitment. In fact, in recent years many of these developments have become increasingly apparent in tribal courts throughout Indian country.

INSTITUTIONS OUTSIDE MAJORITARIAN POLITICS

The second component of legitimacy concerns the existence of legal institutions that operate at some distance from majoritarian politics and seek to resolve the dilemma that majoritarian views alone cannot achieve legitimacy for all segments of a society or tribe. For example, during large parts of American history, majorities have been able to enslave or oppress substantial minority communities, including African Americans, women, and Native Americans. The legal system and the professional community operating within it—however imperfectly—have often been able to establish the rights of individuals and groups to be treated equally and fairly under the law.

The legitimacy of the system is particularly enhanced if it protects the rights of and advances justice for individuals or groups who are unable to protect their basic rights and interests through majoritarian politics. Litigation and adjudication thus provide a meaningful alternative to disobedience, which is a manifest rejection of the dominant system's claims to legitimacy.[63]

Such a view raises poignant questions in the context of tribal court systems. This dilemma is particularly acute when considering the nature of the rights sought to be recognized within tribal systems. The controversy over the Indian Civil Rights Act (ICRA) of 1968[64] is particularly instructive. In that controversy, the notion of strong individual rights that could be enforced against the majority government was alien to the traditions and customs of many tribes, where the group, not the individual, is primary.[65] The Act was further criticized as another example of the unilateral imposition of federal standards[66] that abridged tribal sovereignty.

These elements of controversy were at least partially addressed by the U.S. Supreme Court in *Santa Clara Pueblo v. Martinez.*[67] *Martinez* made it clear that tribal courts were the appropriate forums for adjudication of individual claims concerning such ICRA individual guarantees as due process and equal protection. Other federal court decisions held that tribal courts would be accorded some leeway in determining the exact substantive content of these provisions.[68]

Tribal councils and other decision makers are increasingly faced with this dilemma of individual rights. There is a need to fashion remedies in tribal court that allow for some resolution of individual claims against the tribe, but there is also a need to balance bona fide tribal concern that such relief might grind tribal activity to a halt or impoverish a tribal treasury. The prospect of unlimited or paralyzing injunctive relief justifiably concerns many tribes, particularly when there may be limited access to other tribal or federal appellate review. Accommodation and the fashioning of limited relief in the form of declaratory judgments, limited monetary recovery, and modest injunctive relief would constitute a viable starting point. Many tribes have successfully moved in this direction, which is clearly the line of current momentum.

Inaction on this issue might aggravate the perception of illegitimacy by tribal members and many non-Indians and could result in further federal standards encroaching on tribal sovereignty. Tribes need to continue, and in some cases to begin, moving cautiously forward to avoid these inimical results. Increasingly, tribal courts have demonstrated the ability to craft thoughtful and enforceable decisions in this delicate area.[69]

Such skill is particularly necessary in light of concerns over the separation of powers. Most tribal constitutions do not provide for separation of powers,[70] and the tribal courts are direct legislative creatures subject to defeasance and even complete control (including the removal of personnel) by tribal councils. Such situations are not structurally conducive to dependable neutral adjudication on the merits. Many tribes are sensitive to this problem and have moved to a policy of de facto, if not de jure, separation of powers.[71] The separation of powers issue can be, at least in the short run, resolved by such a de facto approach. Nevertheless, more detailed and thoughtful approaches are needed to meet the persistent, long-term need for legitimacy that rests, in part, on the institutional integrity of the tribal judiciary. In fact, a number of tribes, including the Cheyenne River Sioux Tribe in South Dakota, have recently amended their constitutions to provide for a formal separation of powers.[72]

LEGAL REASONING

The third element contributing to contextual legitimacy involves a commitment to legal reasoning as a potent device for securing a more orderly and just society and developing a body of law to complement the lawmaking of majoritarian elected officials.[73] The force of legal reasoning in daily adjudication is important, for it raises the question of the appropriate kind of legal reasoning to be advanced in tribal courts.

The recognized standard and style of legal reasoning that is appropriate for tribal court adjudication remains to be developed. Such a standard and style is necessary to establish a sufficient *common ground* for advocates and judges that permits intelligent consideration of the issues before the court in any particular case. Without such common ground, reasoned adjudication and adequate representation of litigants' claims are unlikely. This is not to suggest that the legal reasoning (and attendant values) must be like those of the dominant legal system. Instead, there must be an adequate agreement and understanding of the kind of legal reasoning that is appropriate in a tribal court context.

It is therefore critical that the parameters of proper reasoning and argument before tribal courts be better demarcated. It is essential to describe, for example, the style of argument to be practiced before the courts and to determine the applicable authority deriving from such sources as tribal oral tradition or state and federal law. This notion of how best to articulate the manner in which to develop argument and to create the resulting judge-made law is critical in creating legitimacy within the tribal legal community itself. Tribal practitioners, law trained or not, must act and argue in concordance with an understanding of and belief in the legitimacy of their advocacy. In contrast to the other aspects of contextual legitimacy, legal reasoning does not lend itself to any particular commitment to reform or change but only to developing growing sensitivity and refinement as to what is actually permitted and what ought to be encouraged in tribal court argument. In other words, what is needed is a commitment to developing an interpretive community.

THE TRIBAL BAR AS AN INTERPRETIVE COMMUNITY

The legal community as a whole plays a significant role in guiding the adjudication of cases as they come before all courts, including tribal courts. In this respect, the legal community serves as an interpretive community:[74] that is, a community of practitioners who largely determine what is permitted and what is normative in the context of arguing and developing the law in the process of adjudication. This interpretive community plays several important roles in guiding the adjudication of cases in the established state and federal systems. At least two of these roles raise important questions about the nature of adjudication in tribal courts.

One role is that of establishing the nature and style of permissible argument in actual cases. The second role, which is more intangible but no less critical, is that of identifying, if not actually defining, the central values of the legal system. As to these concerns, it has been suggested that

> [w]hat distinguishes the legal community from other interpretive communities is the presence of order and justice at the center of our webs of beliefs about law, the principles of legitimacy, stare decisis, and legislative supremacy near the center, and the commitment to legal reasoning in bringing these values and principles to bear in particular cases.[75]

The function of the legal community as an interpretive community is therefore, in part, to define the acceptable parameters of the legal reasoning brought to bear in deciding cases. These recognized conventions include (1) the language of legal discourse, (2) the practice of developing argument through legal research, and (3) the commitment to the rule of law.[76] These conventions also constrain judges to rule and decide cases within this generalized framework. The importance of these precepts is that they establish sufficient common ground to allow members of the legal community to present claims in a manner that may be intelligently understood, debated, and decided.

Such rules are necessary to assure litigants that their claims will be clearly understood and that they stand on equal footing with all other participants in the system. It is in this regard that tribal court adjudication is often uncertain as to the appropriate legal conventions of discourse, argument, and authority. The question is, How does one argue (and then decide) cases in tribal court? Without this framework, unnecessary uncertainty may become apparent. Attorneys, tribal advocates, and tribal judges must all recognize the nature of proper argument within a tribal court. Without it, justice and fair representation are not possible.

The easy answer is to say, of course, that argument before a tribal court should not differ from that which is expected in state or federal court. Yet I do not think that this is by any means the consensus. If tribal courts are different (e.g., by cultural choice or by their relative youth), how is the nature of legal argument different? Tribal courts, for example, are often described as less formal than state or federal courts.[77] But what does that mean? Obviously, many cases handled by any court, particularly local state and tribal courts, are quotidian, routine. In the routine cases, the less formal style has no great significance, but in contested cases it is different. In such circumstances, does less formal mean less rigorous, requiring less procedural precision in terms of the admissibility of evidence? Does less formal mean there is a lower expectation or standard for the marshaling of coherent substantive argument? Or does less formal mean less rigid constraints in seeking fairness and justice, or less concern with the artificial and often extrinsic rule of law?

More broadly, is conventional legal reasoning too narrow and restrictive in that it rules out important tribal knowledge and wisdom, such as in the realm of spiritual metaphysics and community insight? This is not, of course, as extreme as it seems when thinking about native societies that do not necessarily recognize or accept the secular/sectarian, rational/spiritual dichotomies taken for granted in the dominant society. This is particularly true, for example, in the context of tribal oral tradition and customary law as sources of normative and substantive rules.

The point of all this is not which of these approaches (including many possibilities not mentioned) is better, but rather the necessity of developing agreement of what is required within the interpretive community. In other words, the need is to ensure litigants, whether Indian or non-Indian, that they will have an opportunity to be heard and to have a meaningful day in court. "Meaningful" should be defined in terms of both the form *and* content of their claims and argument.

Legal argument in actual cases depends on what members of the legal community let pass without objection as acceptable legal reasoning.[78] Newly created tribal bars must therefore strive to identify and to articulate these canons. This will not necessarily be easily achieved, but such articulation is more likely to occur if attention is directed toward the problem. It is also more likely to emerge or become apparent if tribal bars come together more frequently and more directly to address these and other related matters. This is particularly true when tribal advocates who are not law trained, but are members of the tribal bar, play a significant role in providing representation before tribal courts including tribal appeals courts.

One of the functions of legal education, apart from substantive training, is socialization into the profession, a process involving explicit and implicit training in what cases to argue and how to argue them. Tribal advocates, in this respect, need exposure to these realities. Or if the nature of advocacy in tribal forums is contrary to this training, law-trained individuals need to be disabused of that part of their tradition.

Part of this notion of the role played by an interpretive community is especially important in the context of building and developing tribal institutions. By any measure, formal tribal courts—most of which were established after passage of the IRA—are young, developing institutions. Part of the benefit of such relative youth is that they have the ability to chart the future on their own terms. Tribal courts are in the process of becoming; they are not calcified into any particular form.

An interpretive community aids in this ongoing process of forging and clarifying the values that underlie the process of adjudication and the legal system as a whole. For example, the values of order and justice are most often mentioned in descriptions of the dominant legal system.[79] Are tribal legal systems committed to the same web of values in the same proportion, or are there equal concerns for such competing values as cooperation, community, and conciliation? The point is that tribal courts do not have to blindly imitate the interpretive strategies and canons displayed in federal and state settings. If tribal interpretive strategies and goals are to be different, it is necessary for all concerned to be conscious of why and how this should be so. If tribes and tribal members and practitioners are interested in actively directing this process, tribal bars provide an ample opportunity to provide guidance in the direction of desired growth. Again, this ongoing process is subtle and not always visible in the tribal courts' daily work of deciding cases and creating a recognizable body of reported decisions and tribal common law. It is therefore not easily subject to legislative direction. Yet it bears thinking about what practitioners in tribal courts ought to be doing and saying and why.

The former Intertribal Court of Appeals in South Dakota,[80] for example, explicitly recognized and addressed this phenomenon in at least one respect. Rule 17 of the court stated that "in recognition of the oral tradition in tribal history and culture, and to speed the hearing and just disposition of cases on appeal, the Court may waive the requirement of legal briefs in selected cases."[81] Yet this rule was applied only when *both* parties proceed pro se.[82] The waiver of written briefs was not available to represented parties. This approach, of course, treated all members of the tribal bar, law trained or not, as members of the same professional, interpretive community responsible to the same standard of competence and performance. Was this a good rule properly situated and defined? Should it be used or extended in the future? What values are advanced or submerged by the rule?

Tribal courts perform important adjudicatory functions within the tribal system, but more important, they are the primary tribal institutions charged with carrying the flame of sovereignty and self-government. In their difficult and challenging position, they face important questions related to contextual legitimacy and the role of nascent tribal bars as interpretive communities identifying core values and techniques that promote tribal court maturity, competence, and fulfillment.

The need for both the respect and allegiance of the communities which these courts serve, as well as the comity and deference of state and federal judicial systems, also places great weight on the shoulders of tribal courts and tribal bars. The future of tribal justice and integrity hangs in the balance.

JURISDICTION IN INDIAN COUNTRY

As tribal courts engage the more internal question of legitimacy, they must simultaneously confront the more palpable and public

issue of the permissible scope of their jurisdiction. This encounter
with the force field of jurisdiction requires the development of an
appropriate analytical framework to apply to these issues. The
allocation of jurisdiction in Indian country[83] and the often competing interests of federal, state, and tribal governments create a
unique jurisdictional collage. Issues of tribal jurisdiction often
emerge from this web of interests and rules. Therefore, an explanation of the genesis of tribal jurisdiction provides the necessary
background for a proper understanding of its parameters and its
future.

CRIMINAL JURISDICTION

Two major federal statutes govern the primary apportionment of
criminal jurisdiction in Indian Country: the Indian Country
Crimes Act[84] and the Major Crimes Act.[85] The Indian Country
Crimes Act provides for federal, not state, jurisdiction over interracial crimes occurring in Indian country.[86] The reference to "the
local law of the tribe" permits concurrent tribal jurisdiction,[87]
and although the statute, on its face, makes no exception for
crimes committed by one non-Indian against another non-Indian,
such an exception was carved out in *United States v. McBratney*.[88] As a result, the statute essentially governs interracial criminal activity in Indian country.

The Assimilative Crimes Act[89] is a general law of the United
States, made applicable to Indian country through the Indian
Country Crimes Act. It permits federal prosecutions by "assimi-
lating" state criminal law as a "gap-filling" device, when there is
no applicable federal substantive criminal law. These prosecutions seem unwarranted in light of the ability of the tribal court
to punish minor crimes involving Indian defendants. Nevertheless, the application of the Act is undisputed.[90]

In 1883, in the case of *Ex Parte Crow Dog*,[91] the Supreme
Court ruled that tribes had exclusive jurisdiction over crimes
among Indians: that is, in any offense involving Indians as both
perpetrators and victims. Congress abrogated this rule two years
later by enacting the Major Crimes Act. The Act mandated federal jurisdiction over seven major crimes and made no provision

for state jurisdiction. Congress has since amended the Act several times, so that it now includes a total of sixteen major crimes.[92] The Major Crimes Act applies only when the perpetrator of the enumerated crime is Indian.[93] Despite the occasional applicability of state law,[94] all prosecutions are federal proceedings in federal court. It is unsettled whether the Major Crimes Act divests the tribal courts of concurrent jurisdiction.[95]

Tribal courts have exclusive criminal jurisdiction over Indian defendants for all crimes not covered by the Indian Country Crimes Act or the Major Crimes Act and concurrent jurisdiction over matters involving the former, and possibly the latter, of these statutes.[96] Tribal courts do not have any criminal jurisdiction over non-Indians.[97] These rules govern most criminal jurisdictional issues, but occasional questions remain concerning "victimless" crimes,[98] the applicability of the Assimilative Crimes Act,[99] and criminal jurisdiction over nonmember Indians.[100]

CIVIL JURISDICTION

Civil jurisdiction in Indian country, in contrast to criminal jurisdiction, is *not* largely governed by federal statutes, and its contours are therefore less clear.[101] The Supreme Court's recent decisions render the scope of tribal court jurisdiction ever more uncertain. For example, in *National Farmers Union,* the Court refused to extend into the civil arena *Oliphant*'s bright line rule rejecting tribal (criminal) jurisdiction over non-Indians.[102] While undoubtedly a correct result, the Court, by so holding, increased rather than decreased the complexity in determining tribal courts' civil jurisdiction. The Court's ruling in *National Farmers Union,* which requires plaintiffs to exhaust tribal court remedies, bolsters the authority of tribal courts and correspondingly increases the volume of the litigation in those courts, but it fails to establish clear guidelines for deciding in what circumstances tribal court jurisdiction is appropriate. This complexity is extended even further with the corollary recognition articulated in *Iowa Mutual* that "tribal authority over the activities of non-Indians on reservation land is an important part of tribal sovereignty."[103]

This unresolved issue[104] usually manifests itself in one or both of the following questions:

1. What is the extent of tribal court judicial jurisdiction over non-Indians and their property?

2. What is the extent of tribal legislative and regulatory authority over non-Indians and their property?

LEGISLATIVE VERSUS JUDICIAL JURISDICTION

Tribal legislative jurisdiction and tribal judicial jurisdiction are *not* the same thing. They may often intersect and overlap, but they are not necessarily coterminous. Each of these strands requires independent treatment to describe the unique rules and treatment the federal courts have provided in each area. Tribal legislative jurisdiction concerns the issues of whether a tribal legislative body, such as a tribal council, has the authority as a matter of tribal law to make laws governing the conduct of non-Indians and whether such authority is proscribed by federal law. Tribal judicial jurisdiction refers to the questions of whether a tribal court is empowered by tribal law to hear a particular kind of case and whether such tribal court authority is not limited by federal law.

For example, if a tribal court decides that it does not have judicial jurisdiction, it cannot reach the issue of legislative jurisdiction and must dismiss the case for want of jurisdiction. If a tribal court decides it has proper judicial jurisdiction over the lawsuit, it must then decide whether the tribe has proper legislative jurisdiction to establish the particular laws governing non-Indian conduct. If there is no legislative jurisdiction, the action must also be dismissed for failure to state a cause of action on which relief may be granted. Only after a tribal court decides first that it has judicial jurisdiction and second that the tribe itself has legislative jurisdiction can it then proceed to decide the case on the merits. This distinction between legislative and judicial jurisdiction was particularly emphasized in the *Iowa Mutual* case.

In *Iowa Mutual,* the Supreme Court emphasized that the tribal court must decide two separate issues. First, the tribal court must determine whether it possesses judicial jurisdiction over the suit. Second, the court must resolve whether the tribe has the legislative authority to regulate the conduct of non-Indians engaged in the activities at issue.[105] The *Iowa Mutual* court did not rule on the tribal court's findings that it had judicial jurisdiction over the controversy and that the tribe had legislative jurisdiction over the non-Indian tortious conduct in issue, but remanded for further proceedings consistent with its opinion.[106] The failure of the Court to demonstrate or spell out the kind of analysis it expects in this area unnecessarily reinforces the lack of clarity that often permeates questions of Indian law jurisdiction. In the wake of *Iowa Mutual,* lower federal courts have taken different, largely inconsistent approaches to the appropriate standard of review of tribal court findings of fact and tribal court interpretations of tribal and federal law.[107]

TRIBAL JURISDICTION OVER NON-INDIANS

The extent of tribal authority over non-Indians and their property depends largely on an analysis of the extent of tribal sovereignty in the particular circumstances at issue. The classic statement on tribal sovereignty comes from Felix Cohen:

> The whole course of judicial decision on the nature of Indian tribal powers is marked by adherence to three fundamental principles: (1) An Indian tribe possesses, in the first instance, all the power of any sovereign state. (2) Conquest renders the tribe subject to the legislative power of the United States and, in substance, terminates the external powers of the sovereignty of the tribe, e.g., its power to enter into treaties with foreign nations, but does not by itself affect the internal sovereignty of the tribe, i.e., its powers of local self-government. (3) These powers are subject to qualification by treaties and by express legislation of Congress, but save as thus expressly qualified, full powers of internal sovereignty are vested in the Indian tribes and in their duly constituted organs of government.[108]

The federal courts, however, have not consistently adhered to Cohen's formulation. In fact, some scholars[109] suggest that at the beginning of the modern era two parallel but contradictory lines of authority developed. Decisions such as *Ex Parte Crow Dog*[110] and *Talton v. Mayes*[111] were prototypical affirmations of the tribal sovereignty doctrine, while such cases as *United States v. Kagama*,[112] *Lone Wolf v. Hitchcock*,[113] and *United States v. McBratney*[114] all evinced a view that the authority of Indian tribes had been severely eroded by the increased presence and dominance of non-Indian society and that tribal sovereignty must therefore be appropriately reduced.[115] None of these cases specifically concerned or addressed the ambit of tribal jurisdiction over non-Indians and their property, but they do provide a striking overview of the conceptual contrast that the courts continue to grapple with. This contrast often focuses on the issue of how much weight should be accorded to the change of circumstances on any particular reservation. This approach frequently examines such questions as whether, and under what circumstances, the tribe has historically exerted the authority at issue or whether it has previously deferred or accommodated itself to the state exercise of that authority. Of course, historical particulars alone do not always provide definitive answers, and it is therefore necessary to review as well the nature of a tribe's sovereignty in terms of treaties, the current status of the tribe's own laws and judicial system, the nature of the landholding patterns on the reservation, and the federal government activity in the particular area. As a result, there has been no ease or real predictability in determining the extent of tribal jurisdiction over non-Indians.

TRIBAL JUDICIAL JURISDICTION

A proper analysis of whether a tribal court has judicial jurisdiction over any particular lawsuit involves an examination of at least three issues: whether the tribal court has proper subject matter, personal, and territorial jurisdiction over the controversy. Additional collateral and ancillary issues may arise from questions concerning the local execution of judgments and comity and recognition of tribal judgments in sister jurisdictions. These latter concerns do not directly affect whether a tribal court has jurisdiction over a particular matter but more often raise questions of litigation strategy and choice of forum.

The most concise and effective analysis of these issues flows from a two-stage approach. The first stage requires an inspection of federal Indian law to determine whether there are any controlling federal statutes, decisional law, or treaties. If the tribal court's jurisdiction is thus limited, the pertinent statutes, judicial decisions, or treaties must be given decisive effect. For example, under the Supreme Court's decision in *Oliphant v. Suquamish Indian Tribe*,[116] a tribal court does not have criminal jurisdiction over non-Indians,[117] and any assertion of such jurisdiction must necessarily fail, preferably as a result of the tribal court's own decision and analysis. Interestingly enough, no federal statutes or decisions categorically bar tribal court jurisdiction over certain civil matters. Because of the general absence of federal statutes that deal with the allocation of civil jurisdiction, few civil cases will be disposed of at this stage of analysis.

SUBJECT MATTER JURISDICTION

After an issue of tribal court jurisdiction has been refracted through the pertinent body of federal Indian law without adverse result, the second stage of analysis begins. This analysis involves an examination of whether the tribal court has jurisdiction as a matter of tribal law. In the absence of controlling federal law, tribal courts presumably have jurisdiction over disputes involving Indians and non-Indians on the reservation.[118] Nevertheless, this range of judicial jurisdiction may be limited by express restrictions found within tribal law itself or even, occasionally, by the absence of positive tribal law on point.

This line of analysis requires a threshold examination to identify the sources of tribal law available for scrutiny. The primary sources of tribal law include treaties, the tribal constitution, the tribal code, and tribal decisional law. Two potential additional sources of tribal law should be mentioned. The first is tribal customary and traditional law, which is seldom codified and must often be identified as part of the oral tradition and culture. The second is a directive—mandatory or directory in nature—within a tribal code to consider and/or apply pertinent federal or state law. For example, the Tribal Code of the Sisseton-Wahpeton Tribe of South Dakota provides that civil matters shall be governed by the laws, customs, and usage of the tribe. The tribal code also provides that the laws of the State of South Dakota may be employed as a guide.[119]

This tribal statutory provision neatly illustrates the range of analysis. In any situation, federal Indian law is primary and pre-empts any tribal law to the contrary.[120] In the absence of conflicting federal Indian law, tribal law controls. In the example of the Sisseton-Wahpeton tribal code, tribal law includes noncodified tribal custom and usage. If there is doubt about a particular custom and usage, advice and testimony of tribal elders familiar with tribal traditions should be sought. If after such an analysis there is still a gap of applicable law, it is permissible to use pertinent South Dakota state law. Even in the absence of such a graceful statutory scheme, this form and order of analysis is richly suggestive of a helpful conceptual approach to the necessary jurisdictional scrutiny.

To determine whether a tribal court has subject matter jurisdiction over a particular controversy, it will be necessary to determine whether tribal law authorizes, and federal law does not prohibit, such a cause of action. If none of the above sources, such as the tribal constitution, the tribal code, tribal decisional law, or tribal custom, specifically recognizes (or prohibits) the contemplated cause of action, it may be urged on the tribal court that, as a court of general jurisdiction, it may entertain jurisdiction in the contemplated cause of action as part of its inherent judicial sovereignty. In this regard, the most fruitful analogy is to the general jurisdiction of state courts. Despite the fact that general subject matter jurisdiction may exist in a tribal court, there may be self-imposed tribal limitations regarding available remedies. For example, a tribal code may place a ceiling on monetary damages[121] or explicitly bar certain kinds of relief.[122]

PERSONAL JURISDICTION

Even though there may be subject matter jurisdiction over the cause of action, tribal court judicial jurisdiction may still fail because of the inability to obtain personal jurisdiction over the individual or corporate defendant(s). Constraints involving personal jurisdiction may arise, again, through self-imposed limitations and through perceived gaps in tribal law. Tribally imposed limitations in the area of personal jurisdiction are exemplified in such matters as race and residence. For example, the Rosebud Sioux Tribal Code,[123] prior to its recent amendment, provided that in civil actions jurisdiction obtained only in those situations where the defendant was a resident of the reservation. Therefore, any plaintiff (whether a reservation resident or not) in a reservation-based cause of action with a nonresident would be foreclosed from establishing tribal court jurisdiction.[124] The shortcomings of such a provision led to the recent amendment.

More curious, perhaps, are the instances where tribal constitutions or codes limit or condition jurisdiction based on "race" or tribal enrollment. For example, the Cheyenne River Sioux Tribe of South Dakota, until its recent amendment, conditioned civil jurisdiction in a suit between Indians and non-Indians by requiring a stipulation of the parties.[125] This is not the prototypical situation where the parties attempt to circumvent or to invoke a court's jurisdiction by private agreement but rather the converse, where the jurisdiction's organic law itself requires a stipulation of the parties. The Oglala Sioux Tribal Constitution contains a similar limitation by providing that its judicial powers shall extend to all cases involving members of the Oglala Sioux Tribe arising under the constitution, bylaws, or ordinances of the tribe and to other cases in which all parties consent to jurisdiction.[126]

These provisions, which were part of the original tribal constitutions and bylaws enacted respectively in 1934 and 1935, seem to reflect the handiwork of the Bureau of Indian Affairs and its commitment to act cautiously with regard to jurisdiction involving non-Indians. Whatever the philosophy at the time, this policy is clearly at odds with the current trend toward meaningful self-determination[127] and the support for tribal court authority evinced in the *National Farmers Union* and *Iowa Mutual* cases. Such limitations can also create jurisdictional voids and the potentially volatile "no forum" situations in which no court—tribal, state, or federal—has jurisdiction and may develop a situation in which the federally recognized allocation of jurisdictional authority is subject to change in a way that is likely to be adverse to tribes. Such jurisdictional limitations that exist in a tribe's organic law are subject to melioration through tribally initiated amendments in the necessary organic law.[128]

These limitations also raise potential due process and equal protection claims under the Indian Civil Rights Act of 1968[129] and similar tribally adopted protections.[130] This is particularly likely if the tribe is asserting legislative jurisdiction over non-Indians. Such concerns raise the question of whether a tribe may regulate non-Indian conduct legislatively but condition access (by requiring a stipulation by the parties) to its courts to litigate claims centering on the same subject matter. For example, suppose that a tribe passes an ordinance requiring all retail sellers of used cars to provide a thirty-day written warranty to purchasers and that failure to provide such a warranty subjects the retailer to a fine of $500 and revocation of its tribal business license. The statute is enforced by the tribe's Department of Consumer Affairs. May a tribe regulate commercial activities in this manner and yet, at the same time, condition non-Indians' access to tribal courts to collect on a defaulting Indian consumer by requiring the defaulting consumer's consent?[131]

The incongruities created by these limitations do not appear to reflect any coherent policy considerations that would justify their continued use. Not only are these anomalies[132] without public policy justification, but they suggest serious due process, equal protection, and potential "no forum" problems that are inimical to tribal sovereignty in general and tribal court development and integrity in particular. Such problems, which are often permeated with unique historical and policy considerations,[133] illustrate the complex issues that tribal courts often confront.

These difficulties exist independently of service of process issues posed by a defendant who is not present on the reservation. Again, proper analysis, federal authority to one side, begins with the tribal constitution and code. In the absence of an applicable code provision, at least one tribal court has applied traditional federal "long arm" jurisdictional analysis.

In *Rosebud Housing Authority v. LaCreek Electric Cooperative*,[134] the issue before the tribal court was whether there was personal jurisdiction over the LaCreek Electric Cooperative, which provided and performed services on the reservation but maintained no specific office or "residence" on the reservation. After reviewing the holding of the U.S. Supreme Court in the seminal personal jurisdiction case of *International Shoe v. Washington*,[135] the tribal court held that it had personal jurisdiction over the defendant because there were sufficient "minimum contacts" to establish the necessary "presence" to avoid a due process challenge.[136]

By adopting the rationale of *International Shoe*, the tribal court demonstrated a commitment to recognize extensive personal jurisdiction as long as it comported with tribal law and the basic concepts of due process. It is interesting to note in this regard that the notion of due process in *Rosebud Housing*, which is so central in such an analysis, does not emanate, despite the ambiguous language in the opinion, from the U.S. Constitution but rather from the Indian Civil Rights Act of 1968 and the dictates of *tribal* constitutional provisions.[137] The tribal court's thoughtful rationale seems firmly grounded in its commitment to tribal sovereignty.

Service of process[138] and full faith and credit[139] deserve brief note because they can occasionally lead to unique problems that do not arise in a state or federal context. In the state or federal context, nonresident defendants seldom ignore service of process on them because the likely result will be a default judgment, which is subject to execution in any state or federal court pursuant to the Full Faith and Credit provisions of the U.S. Constitution.[140] However, the Full Faith and Credit clause, by its terms,[141] does not apply to tribes, and therefore the enforcement of tribal court judgments in other jurisdictions is more problematic and wholly dependent on the local law of the enforcing jurisdiction. A few states,[142] as a matter of state statutory or decisional law, require that full faith and credit be given to tribal court judgments, while most other states apply some form of the principle of comity.[143]

The South Dakota statute requires reciprocity in most instances as a necessary condition for the application of its comity doctrine, but even if all the statutory conditions are met, comity apparently remains discretionary. These same problems arise with respect to the enforcement of state court orders or judgments as well as other tribal court orders or judgments in a particular tribal court. For example, only two of the eight largest tribes in South Dakota specifically provide for the enforcement of foreign judgments.[144] The lone federal statute which deals with this issue is the Indian Child Welfare Act,[145] which requires as a matter of federal law that states give full faith and credit to *all* tribal court orders and judgments rendered pursuant to the Act.[146]

TERRITORIAL JURISDICTION

A number of reservations in Indian country have been diminished.[147] This means that their original boundaries as established by treaty or agreement were reduced by subsequent treaties or agreements or by unilateral acts of Congress. One of the results of diminishment is that there often continues to be both tribal and individual Indian trust land located outside the boundaries of the diminished reservation.[148] This trust land, as well as any "dependent Indian community,"[149] nevertheless remains part of Indian country[150] and therefore constitutes a potential basis for tribal court jurisdiction. Despite the fact that the definition of "Indian country" is part of a criminal statute, the Supreme Court has found that it "generally applies as well to questions of civil jurisdiction."[151]

The fact of diminishment can thus become a complicating factor in considering issues of tribal court jurisdiction. Does a tribal court have civil jurisdiction over a civil transaction that took place outside the boundaries of the diminished reservation but on trust land within the original borders of the reservation? The apparent answer is yes.[152] Without federal statutory law or case law to the contrary, the focus of analysis must be on tribal law. Accordingly, the proper inquiry is whether the tribal constitution, pertinent tribal statute, or case law specifically limits tribal court jurisdiction to the territorial boundaries of the diminished reservation. The analysis should also consider whether there is an affirmative claim of territorial jurisdiction within the original boundaries of the reservation or, alternatively, whether the situation is ambiguously silent.

In the absence of dispositive tribal law, a credible argument might emphasize that because tribal and trust land, as well as individual Indians and non-Indians, are involved, the tribe, and not the state or federal government, has an enduring responsibility to provide a local forum for adjudication of cases. The holding of *Williams v. Lee*[153] supports this view that state jurisdiction ought not to infringe the right of reservation Indians to make their own laws and be governed by them.[154] Such a result is particularly compelling if there are recognized Indian communities and individuals in these areas who participate in the social, cultural, and political life of the particular tribe. Regardless of outcome, the fact of diminishment makes geography a pertinent factor in ascertaining tribal court jurisdiction and is a salutary reminder that jurisdictional concerns do not automatically end at a diminished reservation's boundaries. Jurisdictional analyses must therefore be flexible and responsive to the unique history of any particular reservation.

TRIBAL LEGISLATIVE AUTHORITY

As discussed above,[155] after a tribal court determines that it has judicial jurisdiction over a controversy, it must then decide whether the tribe has the necessary legislative authority to enact the laws governing the non-Indian conduct at issue. The leading contemporary case involving the extent of tribal legislative authority over non-Indians and their property is *Montana v. United States*.[156] In that case, the central issue was whether the Crow Tribe of Montana could regulate duck hunting and trout fishing by non-Indians within the reservation. The Ninth Circuit Court of Appeals ruled the tribe could regulate such hunting and fishing of non-Indians on both tribal and other trust land and on non-Indian fee patented land.[157] The Supreme Court readily agreed that the tribe had the authority to regulate non-Indian hunting and fishing on tribal and other trust lands[158] but reversed the Ninth Circuit's conclusion that the tribe could regulate hunting and fishing on fee patented land within the reservation.[159]

In reaching that decision, the Court reviewed the doctrine of tribal sovereignty and found that incorporation of the tribe into the United States along with treaties, statutes, and other actions resulted in the loss of many attributes of sovereignty.[160] The Court specifically stated that the "exercise of tribal power beyond what is necessary to protect tribal self-government or to control internal relations is inconsistent with the dependent status of tribes, and so cannot survive without express congressional delegation."[161] From the *Oliphant* case, which held that tribes do not have criminal jurisdiction over non-Indians,[162] the Court extrapolated the general proposition that the inherent powers of an Indian tribe do not extend to the activities of nonmembers of the tribe.[163] Nevertheless, this sweeping statement was immediately and substantially qualified by Justice Stewart's caveat that tribes retained authority over non-Indians who enter consensual relationships with the tribe or its members or whose activities otherwise directly affect the political integrity, economic security, or health or welfare of the tribe.[164]

The Court's extensive caveat might well permit tribal regulations of hunting and fishing on fee patented lands on another reservation *if* other facts were present. The Court specified two unique sets of facts on the Crow Reservation that precluded tribal regulation. First, despite treaty recognition of hunting and fishing rights, the Crows were a nomadic tribe dependent chiefly on buffalo, and fishing and hunting were not important to their diet or way of life at the time these treaty rights were established.[165] Second, and perhaps even more important, was the Court's finding that the state of Montana had exercised "near exclusive" jurisdiction over hunting and fishing on fee lands within the reservation and that the parties had accommodated themselves to state regulation.[166] Given this history, the Court held that tribal regulation was not necessary to Crow self-government.[167]

Montana v. United States does not establish a bright line test for tribal regulatory and legislative jurisdiction over non-Indian activity on fee land, but it does identify the crucial variables in such determinations. They include the history of such regulation on the particular reservation, treaty provisions and tribal practices, consensual arrangements involving Indians and non-Indians, and activity that affects the political integrity, economic security, or health and welfare of the tribe. The primary effect of *Montana* is to create a threshold presumption that tribes do not have legislative and regulatory jurisdiction over non-Indians on fee lands within the reservation. This view contrasts sharply with the Court's own analysis of tribal court *judicial* jurisdiction as articulated in the *National Farmers Union* and *Iowa Mutual* cases. There the Court evinced a unique commitment to tribal courts as the primary forums for adjudicating civil disputes on the reservation.[168]

It is interesting to note that in each decision the Court took a different view about the importance of the *Oliphant* case in the civil arena. In *Montana,* the Court found that, despite the fact that *Oliphant* involved a question of criminal jurisdiction over non-Indians, "the principles on which it relied support the general proposition that the inherent sovereign powers of an Indian tribe do not extend to the activities of nonmembers of the tribe."[169] In contrast, the same Supreme Court in *National Farmers Union* explicitly rejected an analogous extension of *Oliphant* into the area of tribal judicial jurisdiction. The Court said, "Thus, we conclude that the answer to the question of whether a tribal court has the power to exercise civil subject matter jurisdiction over non-Indians in a case of this kind is not automatically foreclosed, as an extension of *Oliphant* would require."[170] This inconsistent analysis by the Supreme Court continues to vitiate any hope for conceptual coherence and analytical unity within Indian law. This troubling inconsistency appears rooted in the Court's continuing inability to identify, much less apply, appropriate doctrinal formulations with which to analyze issues of tribal jurisdiction.

The narrow presumption against tribal legislative and regulatory authority over non-Indians on fee land that is articulated in the *Montana* case is often successfully rebutted. Subsequent cases, including both federal and tribal court decisions, uphold tribal legislative and regulatory authority over non-Indians on fee land within the reservation. The cases affirm tribal legislative and regulatory authority in such diverse matters as zoning,[171] health regulation,[172] riparian rights,[173] and seismic activity of mineral lessees.[174] Tribal courts have also upheld tribal legislative and regulatory authority in other areas such as contracts,[175] corporate business activities,[176] and the tortious conduct of a non-Indian school district.[177] The *Brendale* case discussed in chapter 5 has added yet more difficult wrinkles to such analysis. It is also important to remember that there is a presumption *in favor* of tribal jurisdiction over non-Indians for activities that take place on trust land within the reservation or, more broadly, within Indian country.

Tribal legislative and regulatory authority over non-Indians can also be affected by the existence of any pertinent federal statute. For example, in *United States v. Mazurie*[178] the Supreme Court upheld a congressional delegation of authority to tribes, conditioned on approval of individual tribal ordinances by the Secretary of the Interior, to regulate the introduction of liquor into Indian country by both Indians and non-Indians, so long as state law was not violated. Tribal regulatory authority does not, however, automatically require federal approval of the Secretary of the Interior unless it is specified by statute.[179] Such requirements may, however, be part of tribal constitutions[180] and create self-imposed provisos to the exercise of authority over non-Indians.

Tribal taxation of non-Indians and their property, often the crux of true self-determination and economic development, raises special questions. The tribal power to tax non-Indians and non-Indian corporate entities involved in transactions on reservation lands involving a tribe or its members is a fundamental attribute of sovereignty, which the tribes retain unless divested of it by federal law or the necessary implication of their dependent status.[181] In analyzing specific tribal taxes, the Court often closely examines a tribe's specific history, its provision of services to the individuals and entities taxed, the question of whether the economic value of the resource is generated on the reservation, and the existence of any legitimate state interests to the contrary.[182] The two most potentially explosive tribal taxes involving non-Indians would likely be property and income taxes, but neither of these has been asserted and consequently there is no decisional law on point.[183] Such taxes, if and when they come, will certainly extend tribal legislative and regulatory authority to its broadest, most significant limits.

TRIBAL COURTS AND THE FEDERAL SYSTEM

Beneath the geologic holdings of the *National Farmers Union* and the *Iowa Mutual* cases, the tectonics of the Supreme Court seem to be slowly bringing together the separate continents of federal and tribal courts. The Court, without articulating and perhaps without even realizing it, appears to be gradually identifying the contours of the relationship of tribal courts to the federal system.[184] This process contains several paradoxical lines of development. For example, on the one hand there is increasing recognition of the stature of tribal courts, but on the other hand there is the companion development which seems to bring tribal courts more directly into the orbit of federal review. Or to say it another way, the more important tribal courts become, particularly in their authority over non-Indians, the more need there seems to be for increasing federal scrutiny.

Before *Santa Clara Pueblo*,[185] *National Farmers Union*,[186] and *Iowa Mutual*,[187] it was relatively easy to circumvent tribal courts. The notions of a direct federal cause of action under the ICRA of 1968, federal question jurisdiction, and diversity jurisdiction permitted a significant bulk of civil causes of action occurring on the reservation to be brought directly in federal courts, without any concern for the tribal forum. As a result, there was little federal concern for what occurred in tribal courts. There was also scant interest in the question of federal review and in the overall relationship of tribal courts to the federal system. But when direct access to federal courts was sharply curtailed, there was a concomitant growth of tribal court litigation and a renewed litigant and federal interest in prescribing the boundaries of tribal authority.

National Farmers Union and *Iowa Mutual* have staked out some of the territory.[188] Federal review, on the exhaustion of tribal remedies, is available under the federal question doctrine to determine whether tribal courts have exceeded their jurisdiction. This much is clear. Federal review of tribal court decision making on the merits is decidedly less lucid. The limited review afforded by the habeas provision[189] of the ICRA of 1968 is the only specific federal enactment in this area. Even under this provision, however, it remains unclear whether federal review will require tribal courts to meet the substantive standards of the analogous provisions in the Bill of Rights or whether there will be a greater degree of flexibility in determining these standards.[190]

The amount of review provided by federal habeas relief seems ample. Tribal courts ought to be able to interpret and declare what tribal law is, for if tribal sovereignty and self-determination mean anything, they mean the authority to declare and interpret the law that will govern in tribal forums. Federal courts should therefore stay their hands unless tribal decision making offends some specific federal law that applies to the tribes. Of course, under the plenary power doctrine, tribes remain subject to the supreme legislative authority of the United States.[191]

Yet another paradox is at work here. Increased federal respect and deference to tribal courts are premised on a national policy that supports the growth and development of tribal courts. The paradox centers on what constitutes the growth, development, and competence of tribal courts. Is it simply the adequate mimicry of non-Indian state and federal courts? Or is it a commitment to a reasonable autonomy for tribes and tribal courts to develop to meet the needs of local people, which in turn permits or recognizes the possibility of some divergence from the dominant canon?

The mandate for continuing tribal activity in these areas is as pressing as ever. Yet it is important to note that tribal actions in these matters must not lose sight of the interest and concerns of the tribe's primary constituents. That is, what is the best law to be used in such situations as seen from the perspective of tribal members? For ultimately the law is designed to serve the people, not the dictates of attorneys and the federal courts standing alone. As there is federal scrutiny from "above," there is also the more important scrutiny from "below." This is the scrutiny of culture and the people themselves. While federal courts, rightly or wrongly, loom large in this process, they ought not to be made more ascendant than they lawfully are. In this regard, it is the wisdom and integrity of tribal law and tribal courts, properly and consistently informed by tradition and evolving contemporary tribal standards, that will stand as the best bulwark against federal encroachment. Without this continuing development, there can be little expectation for stability and equilibrium.

Tribal courts function at the very edge of tribal sovereignty, and as a result they face steep challenges. This discussion has attempted to set out a reliable conceptual framework with which tribal courts may properly analyze the parameters of their authority. In responding to the federal issues imposed from above, tribal courts must not lose touch with the people and traditions that nourish them from below. However, this intense pressure may fuel creative and progressive tension that will help tribal courts to continue to evolve to meet the yoked objectives of federal deference and tribal legitimacy.

The perspective that animates this discussion is that of the tribal courts. From their viewpoint, how might these pressing issues of sovereignty and analytic rigor appear? That is, what is the vantage point of an important tribal institution which must enact a discourse on sovereignty within the context of a case-by-case adjudication of disputes that come before it? Robert Williams describes this challenge and opportunity as follows:

> The decision in *National Farmers Union* places a tremendous responsibility upon, and presents a tremendous opportunity for, tribal courts and those who litigate disputes before these vital institutions of Indian self-government. Through the tools of the adversary process, relevant statutes, treaties, Executive Branch policy, and judicial decisions must be presented to tribal court as they decide in the first instance what tribal sovereignty means for their particular tribe's self-governing vision. The adequacy and thoroughness of the relevant record and judicial reasoning upon that record at the tribal court level will likely have a determinative impact on a non-Indian federal court's review of the initial tribal decision. Thus, Indian tribal courts have been presented with a unique wedge to drive home an Indian vision of tribal sovereignty in United States society. If affirmed by federal courts, the vision and discourse of sovereignty articulated in the tribal court opinion will have the force of law in United States society. Of course, there is no guarantee that this vision articulated by tribal courts will always be affirmed.[192]

The Supreme Court decisions in the *National Farmers Union* and *Iowa Mutual Insurance* cases vigorously reaffirm the federal policy of encouraging tribal self-determination and tribal self-government. Tribal courts are properly seen as vital institutions for implementing this important national policy. As a result, tribal courts are the very visible explorers charting much of the future of tribal self-determination. As part of this mission, they need greater understanding, growing support, and continued recognition as the enduring forums for rendering justice and fair play throughout Indian country.[193]

CHAPTER FOUR

Liberation, Dreams, and Hard Work

A *View of Tribal Court Jurisprudence*

THE DILEMMA OF DIFFERENCE

Tribal courts do not exist solely to reproduce or replicate the dominant canon appearing in state and federal courts.[1] If they did, the process of colonization would be complete and the unique legal cultures of the tribes fully extirpated. Nevertheless, tribal legal cultures—given even the most benign view of Indian–non-Indian history—also do not reflect pre-Columbian tribal standards and norms.[2] This is so because there has always been a unique legal reality created by tribal resistance to the process of colonization and assimilation.[3] The process of decolonization can *never* lead back to a precolonized society. The dynamics of history and the attendant psychological and sociological changes make such a return impossible. This does *not* mean, however, that liberating forces cannot synthesize the best of the indigenous past and present. Confidence, balance, and respect for roots are key elements in this process. The exercise of wise choice among competing possibilities offers the best likelihood for an optimal future. The riprap created by these forces provides an opportunity for tribal courts to forge a unique jurisprudence from the varied materials created by the ravages of colonialism and the persistence of a tribal commitment to traditional cultural values.

Along this line of tension one can see, and feel, the additional pressures facing tribal courts. A concern about the role "differences" might play in tribal court jurisprudence generates these forces. The resulting fault line, in turn, traces the shifting tectonic plates of tribal sovereignty. The concept of sovereignty consists of two main components: the recognition of a government's proper zones of authority free from intrusion by other sovereigns within the society, and the understanding that within these zones the sovereign may enact substantive rules that are potentially divergent or "different" from that of other—even dominant—sovereigns within the system. Although the notion of separate sovereigns is primarily concerned with formal constraints on power (i.e., circumscribing the powers of limited sovereigns), it is also related to the recognition of different legal approaches to human problems. This may be thought of, in part, as the function of the "other" in the legal domain.[4]

From the federal perspective, when the "other" is the state, the differences are likely to be relatively slender because of the similarity of origin and experience. When the "other" is the tribe, the potential for difference is rather large, for there are great differences in origin and experience. The federal record, however, evinces a tolerance of similarity rather than dissimilarity. The history of the pressures to "civilize" and assimilate Indians provides more than ample support for this description of federal-tribal relations.[5] Despite these enormous pressures, tribal courts continue their struggles to maintain their identities and to resist the ongoing forces of assimilation.[6] This is particularly important given the current federal policy commitment to tribal self-government and self-determination, which seems to recognize, at least rhetorically, the possibility of difference in theory, if not in practice.

For the federalist, the immediate task lies in identifying the best legal norms by which to measure the appropriate level of "tolerance." While this discussion has historically taken place under the rubric of sovereignty, it is perhaps more accurately tracked within the context of the exploration of difference. As suggested by Professor Judith Resnik:

> From the perspective of the dominant society, the question is how much "subversion" and "invention" should be tolerated and encouraged. At the core of federal courts' jurisprudence is a question that

has often gone under the name of "sovereignty" but may more fruitfully be explored in the context of difference. If the word "sovereign" has any meaning in contemporary federal courts' jurisprudence, its meaning comes from a state's or a tribe's ability to maintain different modes from those of the federal government. The United States has often made claims about the richness of its pluralist society—made claims that the loss of state or tribal identity would not only be a loss to states and tribes, but would also harm all citizens because of the benefit of living in a country in which not all are required to follow the same norms. Some deep-seated emotional respect for group governance may be at work here, some sense that these self-contained communities are "jurisgenerative" (again, to borrow from Robert Cover) and that their traditions and customs must sometimes be respected and preserved. In the tribes, cities, states, and regions of the country, one can find not only individuals, but also the individual as part of a community—a community that has had continuity over time. In these communities there are social ties, there is a shared history, there is a network of relatedness. In contrast, the federal system appears to some as individualistic and atomistic. We are attracted by these smaller institutions, these subsets, these multiple sovereignties; we like the scale, the sense of history, the intimacy.[7]

An exploration of the dilemma of difference, while very helpful in understanding the quandary of tribal courts, contains its own paradoxes. These include considerations of the definition of difference, the meaning of difference, and the treatment of difference. Differences, for example, are not inherent but rather are social creations based on some kind of comparison to an often unstated norm. For example, notions about the qualities of women, minorities, and the handicapped are often based on the unstated comparison to white, able-bodied males. Societies inevitably assign people to categories in order to organize reality and to provide a framework for economics, politics and government.[8] The important question, of course, becomes how the differences are assigned and how they are treated in terms of power and opportunity. The categories themselves are human constructs subject to change and reorganization.

Differences also offer a way of addressing issues of connections and boundaries. The constant stream of social, economic, and political experience in the life of a society needs to be sorted and given meaning. Connections and boundaries help us to do this. Because connections and boundaries are interdependent terms, society need not choose between them but must instead identify the kinds of boundaries and connections it chooses to recognize and enforce.[9] This issue is especially keen, even poignant, in the field of Indian law, where the federal government has often done much to eradicate physical boundaries in Indian country and to obliterate the Native American landscape which is often the very basis for making connections in the first instance.[10]

To construct differences, however, merely begs the question: Are the differences positive or negative? In the context of colonialism or other oppressive forces, the majoritarian society often defines differences as negative. For example, the history of Indian–non-Indian relations is replete with negative labels such as "primitive," "uncivilized," and "inferior" being assigned to Indians. Categorization of this type creates the stigma of difference.[11] Such a label of difference is often the product of the unilateral exercise of dominant power.

The legal treatment of the stigma of difference highlights the overall "dilemma of difference." After we have decided to eradicate the stigma of difference, the question becomes how best to achieve this goal. The stigma of difference may be recreated both by ignoring it and by focusing on it. For example, in the context of bilingual or special education, the question may be how to deal with those defined as different, such as students who do not speak English or who have mental disabilities. As Professor Martha Minow suggests, the problem often becomes "When does treating people differently emphasize their difference and stigmatize and hinder them on that basis, and when does treating people the same become insensitive to their difference and likely to stigmatize or hinder them on *that* basis?"[12] Solutions to the dilemma of difference cluster around choices between integration and separation, between similar treatment and special treatment, and between government neutrality and government accommodation.[13]

In the context of Indian law, federal Indian policy has inexorably pressed toward assimilation and has tolerated only minor or "quaint" differences. Some might call this an admirable but incomplete commitment to eradicate the stigma of difference. Yoked to the stigma of difference, however, is the pride that Indian tribal communities take in pre-Columbian sources of cultural continuity and spiritual richness. This pride of difference is at the heart of claims of tribal sovereignty. Neither the legal community nor the dominant community at large fully understands this pride of difference, which tests the vitality of "old promises" in a diverse society that professes a commitment to both equality and pluralism.

Tribal courts are often confronted with the dilemma of resolving this apparent contradiction between "stigma" and "pride," not in the context of airy academic discussion about sovereignty but in forums involving vigorously litigated and hotly contested claims. For example, how should tribal courts deal with issues such as child custody, nonperformance of contracts, and trespass to property? Each of these questions suggests the potential for rules or results at odds with those of the dominant legal system. The ability to understand and to articulate the basis of difference therefore becomes critical. This is true not only within the language of sovereignty itself but also within the daily effort of respecting cultural differences.

Tribal courts have their work cut out. This work is essentially twofold: to transcend the ravages of colonialism while simultaneously animating traditional values in contemporary circumstances. Some of the tools for this work include language, narrative, and the pursuit of justice.

LANGUAGE

Law consists of two main components: language and power. Language is the means of expressing the power of law, and therefore it is often slavish to the dictates of power. Language is also a force in its own right capable of expressing aspirations, even transcendence, within legal discourse. The language of tribal court jurisprudence needs to be sensitive to these disparate possibilities, especially when the language of discourse is almost always English, which may itself be an inadequate vessel to express certain traditional values and concepts embedded in tribal culture. In addition, the language and law of the colonizer should always be inherently suspect.

These diverse possibilities of language have been forcefully expressed in many contexts. As noted by Vaclav Havel, the playwright and leader of the Czech Republic: "Words that electrify society with their freedom and truthfulness are matched by words that mesmerize, deceive, enflame, madden, beguile, words that are harmful—lethal, even. The word as arrow." [14] Words or phrases from the field of Indian law, such as "assimilation" and "plenary power," have triggered lethal effects, aiding in the expropriation of Indian land and the denial of tribal culture.

Tribal courts must unpack and subvert these and other lethal albeit legal doctrines rather than simply defer to their power. Tribal courts may accomplish this task in part by reading these texts from a new, indigenous perspective. Because all law must be "read" to glean its meaning, this almost pristine activity may be reasonably governed by an appropriate set of protocols.

Such a set of protocols might include the following elements. Reading has two faces. One is the text or source of law anchored in some time past. The second is the current situation of the reader presently seeking to understand the text and to apply it to the situation at hand. The resulting "reading," whatever it is, meshes two times, two places, and two interpretations. [15] This process is essentially dialectic in nature and entertains (at least theoretically) the possibility of the emergence of a new synthesis that is less lethal or even nonlethal. As the legal reader must respect the text, however oppressive it might be, so too the text must respect the reader's aspiration and otherness. [16] In a sense, there must be a protocol of mutual respect. This is especially appropriate in the context of Indian law given its potential for reconciliation and meaningful self-determination. Such protocols do not guarantee anything except possibility; nevertheless, it is a possibility and an initiative that tribal courts must understand and pursue. "Obviously this is not just a linguistic task. Responsibility for and towards words is a task which is intrinsically ethical." [17] It is a task which must also be encountered by an equally ethical and respectful federal legal culture in the courts and in the halls of Congress.

Language also has the potential to mislead us. Instead of honoring the sacredness of people and cultures, it can reify abstractions and deflect attention from their particularity and irrepressible reality. Vine Deloria, Jr., a leading Sioux intellectual and Indian law scholar, is most attentive to this phenomenon within Indian law and has accurately dubbed it "the Fallacy of Misplaced Concreteness."[18] It is instructive to note that his warning is directed neither to Congress nor to the federal courts (though it might well be) but rather to the arguably "friendly" community of practitioners and Indian law scholars. Tribal courts and the entire field of Indian law need to guard against this fallacy, but they also need to extend their perceptual net outside the field of Indian law for relevant insights from other disciplines, such as politics, history, economics, philosophy, and linguistics.[19] These insights need to be gathered not in the pursuit of further abstraction but in the pursuit of a better understanding of the reality and dilemma of tribal cultures and Indian law. The object is not to multiply the loaves and fishes of abstraction but to heed the prophetic observation that "what is missing in federal Indian law are the Indians."[20]

Language can further obscure the reality of power and the necessity for action. This message, for example, is central to liberation theology,[21] which plays a prominent role in the political struggles in much of Central and South America. Liberation theology focuses on the inadequacy of most of the Catholic response to the world in which we live. In a world that teems with injustice and the violent marginalization of the poor, liberation theology teaches that it is simply not enough to attend mass, to say a few prayers, and then to go on one's prosperous way. That is not the message of the Gospels and the life of Christ. Jesus spoke, suffered, and acted *in* history—not outside it—in order to redeem His promise of liberation. Liberation theory holds that any belief in redemption outside the travail of human history is a denial of the Word and essentially sinful in its repudiation of the necessity to act *in* history on behalf of ourselves and the most marginalized in our society.

This might seem a curious if not wholly misplaced analogy for tribal courts to consider. Yet it is peculiarly resonant in that it is a potent reminder that tribal courts (as well as their federal counterparts) do act in history, and sometimes they do have to take the measure of that oppressive reality. In the legal domain of Indian law, the words and actions of tribal courts do have their own unique "redemptive" potential, but only if they stay their course and keep their cultural and analytical balance.

In addition, words both assemble and disassemble. Words are often all we have to reach out to one another across communities, traditions, and cultures. But they are also tools which we can use to avoid the actions and commitments that give words meaning in the first instance. It is necessary to stand by words and to understand the sacred covenants that hold their utterances in place, unless they are to be lost in the prairie winds. These are the covenants of justice, friendship, and compassion and their application to the predicament and place of each other in the struggle to resolve the paradoxes embedded in Indian law and tribal court jurisprudence. Tribal courts must hold themselves to words of assembly and union and *not* fall prey to a language of disconnection and distance.[22]

Words are also a means of intensifying consciousness.[23] It is here on the powerful borders of words that poets speak most forcefully not only to lovers of poetry but to anyone committed to truth and justice. For example, the poet Adrienne Rich has explored the "tension between the possibilities in language for mere containment and the possibilities for expansion, for liberation."[24] In the commitment to liberation is the need to be painfully sensitive to "the oppressor's language, a language that is no longer useful, and the need to find a new language, a common language, if you will. It's the question of associations with words and of the history of words, and how they come down to us and how we go on with them."[25] This is particularly evident in the law—especially Indian law—where words in the form of doctrine and precedent certainly "come down to us," often in the most oppressive way in such formulations as the doctrines of discovery, plenary power, and a sovereignty subject "to complete defeasance." The enduring challenge for tribal courts is to discover how they can "go on with them" in seeking a new and common language to help define a permanent tribal sovereignty and a supportive legal reality.

There is, finally, the spiritual dimension of words. This concept itself is particularly significant within tribal cultures but is viewed as almost anathema in the dominant legal culture. Understanding the spiritual capacity and impact of language is a crucial source of strength and wisdom within a tribal judiciary. This dilemma of spiritual language and law is artfully described by the Native American writer Linda Hogan:

> As one of our Indian elders has said, there are laws beyond our human laws, and ways that are above ours.
> We have no words for this in our language [i.e., English], or even for our experience of being there. Ours is a language of commerce and trade, of laws that can be bent in order that treaties might be broken, land wounded beyond healing. . . . The ears of this language do not often hear the songs of the white egrets, the rain falling into stone bowls. So we make our own songs to contain these things, make ceremonies and poems, searching for a new way to speak, to say we want a new way to live in the world.[26]

Tribal courts, in their pursuit of truth and justice, must also look for a "new way to speak, to say we want a new way to live in the world." This is the burden, and the bounty, of cultivating a future that is rooted in a vital continuity with the past.

Language in the Native American tradition contains other timely insights. Although there is no shortage to the barrage of words that permeate the dominant culture's advertising, its news reporting, and even its legal system, one result of this verbal inflation is a deterioration of our sensitivity to language.[27] But within the oral tradition, as suggested by the noted Native American writer N. Scott Momaday,

> one stands in a different relation to language. Words are rare and therefore clear. They are zealously preserved in the ear and in the mind. Words are spoken with great care, and they are heard. They matter greatly, and they must not be taken for granted, they must be taken seriously, and they must be remembered.[28]

The words that are chosen to define and to express a tribal court jurisprudence must also, therefore, strive to achieve an equivalent respect for, and belief in, the efficacy and power of language.

NARRATIVE AND STORY

In Indian law—and especially in the tribal court setting—federal statutes and case law tend to swagger with some odd combination of alleged wisdom and routine dominance. Part of this swagger is the pure (legal) arrogance of federal hegemony, but part of it is also related to the inability and perhaps even the unwillingness of federal courts and Congress to understand the cultural and narrative, much less the legal, drive propelling tribal courts and their jurisprudence in the first instance. The use of narrative and story by tribal courts, therefore, is potentially a valuable strategy to deal with this arrogance. It may also be an important means to clarify and elucidate the vision of tribal sovereignty to tribal courts themselves.[29]

Tribal court narrative and legal storytelling provide perhaps the most trenchant means of confronting federal hegemony in Indian law. This hegemony, which has legal roots in such pernicious concepts as the plenary power doctrine[30] and a dependent tribal sovereignty,[31] contains its own "story." As Professor Richard Delgado has noted: "The dominant group creates its own stories, as well. The stories or narratives told by the ingroup reminds it of its identity in relation to outgroups, and provides it with a form of shared reality in which its own superior position is seen as natural."[32] Federal Indian law doctrines are grounded in "stories" of conquest, (cultural) superiority, and a guardianward relationship.[33] Tribal court narratives may seek to unravel such stories that manifest a "mind-set" justifying the world as it is,[34] with tribal existence beholden to federal benevolence.

Stories and narratives "are powerful means for destroying mindset—the bundle of presuppositions, received wisdom, and shared understanding against a background in which legal and political discourse takes place."[35] For example, in a recent decision[36] of the Cheyenne River Sioux Tribal Court of Appeals, the court spent a considerable part of its opinion discussing the intrusive role of the Bureau of Indian Affairs in the original drafting and preparation of the tribal constitution—particularly in regard to a provision that might be claimed to limit tribal court jurisdiction over lawsuits involving Indians and non-Indians.[37] Specifically, the court noted:

It is well established that these IRA constitutions were prepared in advance by the Bureau of Indian Affairs—almost in boilerplate fashion without any meaningful input or discussion at the local tribal level. Therefore, it is clear that this "oddity" in Cheyenne River Sioux Tribal law—which has no comparable analogue in the United States or any state constitution—does *not* have its roots in any considered decision of the Cheyenne River Sioux people, but rather in some gross B.I.A. oversight or self-imposed legal concern to tread cautiously when potential non-Indian interests are involved. Neither of these concerns were authorized by federal statute and ought not be given the force or respect of law.[38]

The court's language suggests a counternarrative, one that exposes colonial interference in tribal courts and its need to be properly identified and corrected. In this new light, the courts of the dominant society[39] might properly reject such colonial interference as inimical to the democratic values of pluralism and the current federal policy of meaningful self-determination. Without this opposing light, federal courts are all too free to see such issues as problems of the tribes' own making rather than a legacy of colonial dominance. This is not, however, to suggest that all the problem or responsibility lies with the federal government, but only that there is need for a new dialogue on the issues facing tribal courts.

The force of narrative and story within the oral tradition of most Native American cultures is especially compelling. In the oral tradition and especially under conditions of oppression, the tradition may end in one generation. Under these conditions, "to be careless in the presence of words or the inside of language, is to violate a fundamental morality."[40] Narrative and story are not extrinsic niceties but are basic life forces needed to establish and to preserve communities and "to develop a common culture of shared understandings, and deeper, more vital ethics."[41]

In the Native American context, much of the narrative intensifies a particular light of intelligence and experience.

This light, like that of long ago, is the light of thought about the past and present, about the lives Native people live as hostages in our own land, and about the overreaching power and living presence of the land over which, finally, no one can tyrannize. . . . We Indian women who write have articulated and rendered the experience of being in a state of war for five hundred years. While non-Indians are largely unconscious of this struggle, we cannot afford that luxury.[42]

Narrative and stories in tribal court jurisprudence are valuable not only as an omega of resistance set against the dominant narrative but also as an alpha of aspiration to connect the past with the future. This is one feature of stories as the connective tissue of memory:

> That's what stories are for. Stories are for joining the past to the future. Stories are for those late hours in the night when you can't remember how you got from where you were to where you are. Stories are for eternity, when memory is erased, when there is nothing to remember except the story.[43]

Indeed, without stories the collective memory of culture will be severely impoverished, if not eradicated. In turn, the culture will become increasingly susceptible to being swallowed whole by the great American maw of assimilation and uniformity. Similar pressures of assimilation and cultural forgetfulness are powerfully illustrated by the quandary of the Palestinians living in Israel. The Israelis hoped that the Palestinians, in their pursuit of economic survival, "would prosper as individuals but remain impoverished as a community."[44] The dominant society, even when providing some modest economic access, prefers to do so on individual terms that do not encourage a land-based cultural pluralism.

These individual and cultural pressures to survive are thus sometimes pitted against each other as alternative rather than mutually reinforcing commitments. These pressures are painful and potentially divisive. Again the Palestinians' situation is instructive. According to Sari Nusseibeh, a young Palestinian philosopher, "Although as individuals we talked about Palestinian independence and uniqueness, as a community we believed just the opposite."[45] This is a valuable insight in the tribal court context. Individuals may say anything, but it is ultimately the words and actions of the tribe and its institutions that will determine survival and continuity with a cultural past. When communities fail to maintain such historical links, a great deal may be lost:

[T]he Israeli world enveloping them [the Palestinians] only left them feeling like strangers in their own land. . . . For the Israeli shadow that followed Palestinians wherever they went was a shadow with a voice, and the voice kept whispering in every Palestinian's ear, "It's not yours. Palestine is not yours. It's ours." [46]

Yet the recent Israeli-Palestinian accord may redress this historical split involving claims over land, political participation, and mutual respect.

In such struggles, stories sometimes provide nurture and sustenance more important than food itself. As the character Badger notes in the instructive fable *Crow and Weasel:*

"I would want you to remember only this one thing," said Badger. "The stories people tell have a way of taking care of them. If stories come to you, care for them. And learn to give them where they are needed. Sometimes a person needs a story more than food to stay alive. That is why we put these stories in each other's memories. This is how people care for themselves." [47]

And with such "care," stories "help us all remember to remember":

As long as we refuse to remember to know that our whole life is a ceremony and that the only temptation is really a temptation to forget God, then we will continue to hate and continue to be lost. Medicine and food and religion are one thing. In the old days, when a man got up he prayed toward the rising sun, and then remembered God all day. [48]

The challenge of this spirit and wisdom is not at the edge but rather at the heart of tribal court jurisprudence. This has been most eloquently articulated as a general jurisprudential rule by the late Robert Cover:

I have argued not only that the nature of law is a bridge to the future, but also that each community builds its bridges [w]ith the materials of sacred narrative. . . . The commitments that are the materials of our bridge to the future are recorded and expressed through sacred stories. [49]

There is, of course, no telling what a federal reviewing court might make of such stories embedded in tribal court jurisprudence. And perhaps in these conservative times, expectations should accordingly be minimized. Yet behind the courts there is "the people." As trenchantly noted by a leading commentator in the context of recent liberal U.S. Supreme Court dissents:

> Surely "the People" will be far more likely to pick up the slack if they can somehow come to have a stake in—to feel responsible for— these threatened causes, views, creeds, and lives. Thus, if the practices of the Native American Church are rendered *familiar*—if we can somehow come to sympathize with the religious impulse they represent, whether or not we agree with the content of the creed— we will be far more likely to "have a stake" in their maintenance.[50]

In addition, tribal court opinions more generally can serve as educational tools to instruct the dominant society at large, insisting on the responsibilities of a liberal society to nurture and protect alternative cultures.[51] Yet such stories and opinions must be properly anchored in the analytic processes of the law in order to be both compelling and persuasive and to promote understanding and respect.

Last, tribal court jurisprudence needs to clarify and to integrate all the interdependent narrative and analytical strands. Again the quandary of the Palestinians is highly revealing: "The Palestinians . . . didn't just want to tell the Israelis, 'We are not you.' They also wanted to tell the Israelis and themselves who *they* were."[52] That is the challenge and promise of a tribal court body of law grounded in story, narrative, reason, and justice. Such an undertaking, though fraught with the obvious perils posed by federal hegemony and limited resources, remains a work of local autonomy and culture. As suggested by the poet and essayist Wendell Berry in a similar setting, this task must "be done not from the outside by the instruction of visiting experts, but from the inside by the ancient rule of neighborliness, by the love of precious things, and by the wish to be at home."[53]

JUSTICE

In law, narrative and analytical rigor need to serve the ends of justice. Without this convergence, the processes of law—including tribal law—serve only top-down order, hierarchy, and special interests. The meaning and definition of justice are not always perfectly clear; nonetheless, the pursuit of justice within tribal court jurisprudence must be a central concern if the claim of sovereignty is to have any true meaning beyond the mere arrogation of power.

To think more precisely about what justice means, or might mean, in the tribal court context, we must first consider broader questions about the nature and function of law generally. Two visions of law presently dominate most legal thinking and scholarship. Formalists see the law as a set of rules issuing from a political sovereign—passed by the legislature or articulated in judicial opinions. The goal of such a set of rules or principles is to act as a means of social control that affects human behavior in desired ways.[54] By contrast, legal realists claim to pierce this formalism and examine what "really happens" as the result of law. This view reveals not high-minded concerns for neutral rules but rather the manipulation of law with the "aim of inducing those most injured by the political process to acquiesce in it."[55]

Law may be thought about in yet a third way—a way that is particularly resonant in Native American communities, where law has played and continues to play a dominant, if not dominating, role in tribal life. This third view sees law as a "culture which constitutes a world of meaning and action. It is a culture that establishes and maintains community through its practice of language. In this sense the law is an ethical and political activity and should be understood and judged as such."[56]

In this vision of legal culture, the law is not merely an obvious set of rules governing current reality; more significantly, it may also inspire the attainment of a more enlightened reality. If our legal texts reflect the political and economic context of our lives, the law (particularly foundational texts such as constitutions and treaties) may also be imbued with a commitment to change contexts in line with a more idealized version of ourselves and our communities.[57]

This legal potential is especially significant within the context of tribal court jurisprudence. First, it prescribes a method for approaching federal law and precedent not so much as unavoidable literal proscriptions but as potential statements of an overarching federal commitment to respect tribal sovereignty and meaningful self-determination. Second, it offers tribes a way of thinking about their own law and judicial decision making as a means of transforming their colonized context.[58]

This legal vision can sound rather "soft" in the hardball reality of actually making law and deciding contested cases, but that is no reason to disregard it. In fact, it is all the more reason to embrace it. If the law and the pursuit of justice are subsumed completely under the rubric of applying the appropriate legal rules to a single fact pattern, the law readily collapses into a mechanical and ideological means for maintaining the status quo. All of this does *not* negate the important idea that precedent and law play in helping to realize other significant values, such as order and predictability within the legal system. Rather, it helps to achieve a better balance between stasis and movement, between the real and the ideal, between injustice and justice. In a developing tribal court jurisprudence, attention to such issues is especially critical, lest tribal courts inadvertently reproduce the distortions that permeate majoritarian courts and their jurisprudence.

It remains necessary to suggest what the meaning or pursuit of justice consists of in this legal conception. Professor James Boyd White's exegesis is particularly informative in this regard. He suggests that justice is not any fixed quantity or even consequence but who we are to each other:

> This is the radical question of justice, too: not, "How much do I get?" but "Who are we to each other?" What place is there for me in your universe, or for you in mine? Upon what understandings, giving rise to what expectations, do we talk? What world, what relations do we make together? These are the questions we ask our law to answer.[59]

The notion of justice as essentially relational resonates well within Native American communities. For example, throughout the Lakota tribal world, all prayers and many public addresses conclude with the speaker uttering the phrase "*mitakuye oyasin*," which literally means "all my relations." This utterance seeks to recognize and to create a connection between the speaker and her listeners. For in the Lakota worldview, without relationships there is no way to connect or have meaningful exchanges with one another.[60]

The pursuit of justice described by Professor White is captured by the word and process of "translation." Again, the very word "translation" occupies a central place in many Native American traditions because of its connections with bilingualism and with the spiritual domain of traditional healers who "translate" the messages from the spirit world. Translation in the legal realm involves taking the law or text of the past and removing it from the associations of its origin and relocating it in a new set of associations and circumstances. "The text remains the same, but its translation—its being carried over—to our own time locates it in a new context of particularities which will, and should, give it a transformed meaning."[61] Such an approach to law and justice may ultimately hold sway within tribal courts because it holds the promise of transformation and reconsideration of a legal past largely dominated by the forces of colonization and assimilation.

Finally, this notion of translation is also an ethical and political dictate—a protocol of reciprocity, as it were:

> In this sense translation forces us to respect the other—the other language, the other text—yet it nonetheless requires us to assert ourselves, and our own languages, in relation to it. It requires us to create a frame that includes both self and other, both familiar and strange; in this I believe it serves as a model for all ethical and political thought.[62]

Considerations of "justice as translation" provide an innovative perspective for thinking about the thrust of law and the attainment of justice. Yet it remains unclear how this perspective functions in solving concrete legal problems. In this arena, the work of Professor Martha Minow is illuminating, refreshing, and cautionary. An important aspect of her work is its focus on relationships rather than rights. It is also true that her work "discovers" much of what already inheres in Native American legal and cultural thought but which the distortions of colonialism obscure from view.

Some preliminary discussion of the more traditional solution of "rights" is needed. This solution holds that the universal recognition and enforcement of rights—especially for marginalized women, minorities, the poor, and the disabled—would go far to achieve justice. However, this stated solution is only partly valid. One problem lies in identifying what rights (and values) initially exist or ought to exist.[63] A second problem, which is especially acute in the Native American community, is the notion of a right being held by an abstract individual "independent of social context, relationship with others, or historical setting."[64]

No one doubts that rights are significant in one's relationship to government, be it federal, state, or tribal. Rights are, for example, the whole premise of the Federal Bill of Rights[65] and the Indian Civil Rights Act of 1968,[66] as well as bill of rights provisions in tribal constitutions.[67] However, in addition to having a "rights standing" with their government, individuals also have significant interaction with others outside the governmental sphere. These situations have traditionally been defined more as ones of "relationship" rather than rights and have been mediated (rather than litigated) by institutions outside the court, such as the family, church, and community. Yet with the weakening of these institutions in the dominant society, "relationship" is threatened to be subsumed by the growing assertion of rights to be litigated by atomized individuals in the private sphere. Many Native American societies find this development threatening, because it is potentially invasive of that fundamental web of relationships defined by family, community, and culture that holds individuals and the tribe together.

Tribal court jurisprudence needs to heed this distinction. Perhaps it is possible, or even necessary, for tribes to see their citizens as located on one side of a triangle with a rights-mediated standing to their government on another side of the triangle and a relationship model of interaction with other individuals and people on the third side of the triangle. The model of dominant jurisprudence seems at times to imagine society as consisting of thousands of particles defined only by quasi-physical laws. This view of society as an entropic system is clearly at odds with the view of most indigenous communities that define their existence in terms of *relatedness* among individuals and groups, not in terms of the rights of isolated, contingent individuals.

Since law both reflects and constructs reality, such views are not without effect on the social and cultural fabric of tribal life. For example, the legal decision whether or not to grant "standing" in a custody dispute to a member of the extended family or *tiyospaye*[68] who is neither the mother nor the father of the child has readily identifiable implications for the family and the cultural values. Similarly, in a contract dispute there are deep cultural implications in the potential tribal court decision to render a judgment involving not only money damages or specific performance but a remedial performance of some kind—such as caring for a neighbor's cattle or garden—in order to heal the relationship between the parties and to maintain the well-being of the community. As Professor Minow observes: "Beyond our talk of rights we have each other and the steady burden of learning to live together and apart."[69]

Another limitation of the "rights" approach to certain legal issues is its tendency to locate the problem in the person with the "difference" rather than in the community itself (even when the system may ameliorate the "difference" based on the asserted "right").[70] For example, what is the appropriate approach to dealing with a hearing-impaired child in a public school? What are her "rights" to "special" treatment? What must the school do to meet her "special" needs? These formulations of the problem lead to answers that focus on this "different" child. Yet another way of defining the problem involves not only the hearing-impaired student but also the whole class and the relationships among *all* the students and the teacher.

This approach relocates the problem of difference in the community as a whole rather than in the individual. In the example given, one solution would suggest classwide instruction in sign language so that all students (and the teacher) would be better able to communicate with one another. As a result, "all students could learn to struggle with problems of translation and learn to empathize by experiencing first hand discomfort with an unfamiliar mode of expression."[71] Of course, there would be the expected objections that the solution is impractical and too costly.

These objections may be relevant, but that does not take away from the insight of how distributing the problem *within* the community can potentially help to alleviate the stigma associated with locating the problem *within the person.*

This example is particularly resonant within the bilingual, bicultural context present on many reservations. In this view, the importance of bilingual, bicultural education is not only to "help" the "different" Native American students academically or even to preserve and to advance Native American language and culture; rather, the purpose is also to expose non-Indian students to a linguistic, cultural, and legal reality that will in turn narrow the "differences" between Indians and non-Indians that prevent or obstruct the communication that is absolutely essential to mutual respect and understanding. The object here is not to eradicate difference through assimilative education but to preserve differences through increased awareness of their necessity and importance to the well-being of *all.* This understanding can be advanced effectively through creative use of a relational model.

I do not mean to disparage the importance of rights discourse within tribal court jurisprudence; rather, I want to suggest that attention to rights is only *part* of the solution. That "rights" are paramount for the well-being of tribal citizens vis-à-vis their government (and in particular the state and federal governments) is almost axiomatic. These rights need not, however, simply replicate the content of rights in the federal and state setting. Instead, rights in the tribal court setting may require their own unique parameters.[72]

Yet in the private and communal relationships of the tribal context, which often holds "relatedness" to be a central value, a complementary jurisprudence needs to assert itself.[73] A jurisprudence that conceives of justice as essentially relational in nature must also take root in tribal juridical soil. For example, the Native American writer Ella Deloria has observed that the ultimate goal of Dakota (Sioux) life is to "be a good relative"[74] and that "every other consideration [is] secondary—property, personal ambition, glory, good times, life itself."[75] If this traditional value remains vital today, tribal court jurisprudence needs to reflect its contours. This is no easy matter given the weight of the dominant jurisprudence to the contrary and the ongoing historic pressures of assimilation. Nevertheless, this is the essence of the struggle to achieve a cultural fidelity to the past and a communal integrity in the present.

Tribal court jurisprudence also finds unique challenges in its legal strategies for dealing with nature and the environment. Simply put, the poverty on many reservations places intense pressure on tribes to pursue economic development in an attempt to alleviate material deprivation.[76] This in turn creates a growing burden on the tribes to develop their natural resources.[77] The model of the dominant society is just this: the value of natural resources lies in developing and exploiting them for the "benefit" of the human community. This simplistic notion necessarily elides the distortions and ravages of much of modern capitalism and industrial socialism.

At first glance, most of the decision making in this area actually seems more political and economic rather than legal and cultural. But on closer inspection this is not really so. Eventually tribal courts will have to confront the legal facet of natural resources: whether rivers, trees, and salmon have legal rights of their own independent of the human community or whether they are simply commodities awaiting development.[78] For the Native American reverence for the life and spiritual nature of all of creation to be truly meaningful, it must receive legal recognition within tribal court jurisprudence. If it does not, the observation embodies nothing more than a romantic cliché.

The cultural expressions of such principles are often quite evocative and demanding:

> According to Koyukon teachers, the tree I lean against *feels* me, hears what I say about it, and engages me in moral reciprocity based on responsible use. In their tradition, the forest is both a provider and a community of spiritually empowered beings. There is no emptiness in the forest, no unwatched solitude, no wilderness where a person moves outside moral judgments and law.[79]

The legal demand of such teachings presses toward the development of a true tribal jurisprudence of place: a jurisprudence committed not only to justice for the members of the human community but to justice and honor for the community of nature that helps to sustain the human community. The contours of such a jurisprudence of place remain to be fashioned, but the necessity of engaging its challenge already calls to us.

HORIZONS

Tribal court jurisprudence must also consider federal constitutional law and international law in order to connect itself to the national and world contexts. Because tribal sovereignty is so precariously situated within much of federal constitutional law,[80] tribal court adjudication presents an opportunity to present views of federal constitutional law and theory seeking to restore the constitutional integrity of the relationship between the federal government and Indian tribes. As noted in chapter 2,[81] concepts of plenary authority and a sovereignty subject to complete defeasance are insufficient for ensuring any kind of a meaningful constitutional relationship. Reference to international law provides an opportunity to draw on the emerging law of the rights of indigenous people as a progressive global doctrine, which may in turn affect the actions and theory of Western European settler states such as the United States in dealing with their own indigenous populations.

CONSTITUTIONAL LAW

In the arena of federal constitutional law, several tribal court approaches are apparent. These include describing the essential constitutional incoherence that currently manifests itself in federal Indian law, identifying the appropriate federal constitutional benchmarks for engaging in dialogue about tribal sovereignty, and reemphasizing the moral and ethical commitments that ought to animate federal-tribal interaction.

In a constitutional republic premised on the authority of limited sovereigns and the consent of the governed, federal doctrines of plenary power and unilateral abrogation of tribal authority are clearly extraconstitutional and ought to be considered beyond the scope of national authority. Unfortunately they are not,

and tribal courts need to fashion their own constitutional arguments to confront this disturbing reality. One such argument includes delineating the constitutionally insupportable rationale for
these doctrines: namely, that no adequate constitutional justification exists for such doctrines that by definition eschew the constitutional permanence of tribal sovereignty and place unlimited
authority in the hands of the federal sovereign when dealing with
tribes.

Another argument involves the Indian Commerce Clause[82] in
the U.S. Constitution, which recognizes the right of Congress to
regulate trade with Indian tribes. The Indian Commerce Clause
by its own terms acknowledges Indian tribes as sovereigns, sovereigns other than states for which the federal government needs
delegated authority to regulate. Broad as the authority conferred
in the Indian Commerce Clause might be, it cannot include the
right to annul or otherwise unfairly limit the right of tribes to
exist[83] and to exercise reasonable authority within their borders.
Tribal courts are ideally situated as the judicial arms of these
enumerated sovereigns to make these arguments in their most
compelling manner.

Tribal courts are also well positioned to delineate the appropriate constitutional benchmark for tribal-federal dialogue concerning the parameters of tribal sovereignty. This would likely
include the dynamic recognition of tribal sovereignty in treaties
as well as the sovereignty acknowledged in the Indian Commerce
Clause. From the tribal perspective, treaties are critical because
they represent the true interaction of mutual sovereigns. Treaties
in many instances embody a standing of equals, a parity of authority and recognition. Treaties are paramount in discussions
of tribal sovereignty not only because they recognize tribes as
sovereigns but also because they reveal the contours of the pivotal exchanges that undergird the federal-tribal relationship.[84]

As noted in chapter 1, the quality of these exchanges has varied significantly. Many tribes were forced to agree to small reservations in regions removed from their traditional territories because the federal government had the strong military upper hand.
Yet in other cases—particularly involving the Lakota of the Great
Sioux Nation in South Dakota—there was a virtual military

standoff, and the reservations were established in the heart of the traditional Sioux homeland in the Dakota Territory.

The recognition of tribal sovereignty does not in itself solve complex contemporary problems of jurisdiction, but it does provide the necessary common ground from which problems of the allocation of tribal-federal and tribal-state authority can be better understood. Furthermore, it relieves tribes of the constant destabilizing threat to their very existence and right to self-determination that the full potential of the plenary power doctrine represents.[85] President William Clinton himself recently reaffirmed this historic government-to-government relationship. The President's words need to find their way into tribal court jurisprudence:

> So much of who we are comes from who you are. Long before others came to these shores, there were powerful and sophisticated cultures and societies here, and they were yours. Because of your ancestors, democracy existed here long before the Constitution. . . .
>
> In every relationship between our people, our first principle must be to respect your right to remain who you are and to live the way you want to live. And I believe the best way to do that is to acknowledge the unique government-to-government relationship we have enjoyed over time.
>
> Today, I re-affirm our commitment to self-determination for tribal governments. Today I pledge to fulfill the trust obligations of the federal government. Today I vow to honor and respect tribal sovereignty based upon our unique historical relationship.[86]

Treaties remain the "supreme law" of the land under the U.S. Constitution.[87] Tribal courts need to call on federal courts to heed this solemn dictate with a fidelity that is often and inexcusably missing from our national jurisprudence.

Last, tribal courts need to remind federal courts of the ethical imperative that "[g]reat nations, like great men, should keep their word."[88] This imperative is in the service not of abstraction and rhetoric but of real people and communities seeking to realize a future that is both continuous with a cultural past and responsive to the demands of the historical present. Moreover, this obligation is in keeping with our national commitment to justice, pluralism, and a guarantee of a "measured separatism"[89] to Indian tribes.

INTERNATIONAL LAW

International law provides another valuable source with which to enrich tribal court jurisprudence. Many new legal insights leading to increased recognition of collective group rights have been developed on the frontier of international law development. Tribal court adjudication is a crucible for the local application of these emerging international norms and covenants. Such applications may serve to give unique meaning to the axiom "Think globally and act locally" and thus help to complete the jurisprudential loop from the reservation to the world.

International law not only provides legal insight about the struggle of indigenous people for voice and recognition but also helps to illuminate the constraints on that development which find their roots in certain *foundational* Indian law principles. Until quite recently, for example, international law norms, as applied to the situation of indigenous peoples, have focused on individual rights that derive from principles associated with the European doctrine of discovery.[90] This doctrine finds its central elaboration in the seminal case of *Johnson v. McIntosh*,[91] in which the U.S. Supreme Court held that European explorers' "discovery" of land occupied by Indian tribes gave the discovering European nation "an exclusive right to extinguish the Indian titles of occupancy, either by purchase or conquest."[92]

The doctrine of discovery was extended in early international law scholarship to mean that the only territorial titles recognized by international law were those held by the "civilized" members of the family of European nations.[93] The pervasive termination and assimilation policies in domestic Indian law complemented this doctrine. For example, "'Civilized' states pursued a sacred duty of trust by dismantling 'tribal organization' and treating indigenous peoples 'as individuals under guardianship.'"[94] The yoke of these mutually reinforcing objectives was to effectively dismiss indigenous people as proper subjects of international law and scholarship.[95]

These colonial doctrines have been the subject both of renewed criticism in the stories and narratives of indigenous people themselves and of scholarly examinations of the rights of indigenous people. Consequently, a movement begun in the 1970s led ultimately to the formation of the United Nations Working Group on Indigenous Populations in 1981.[96]

The United Nations Working Group is charged with the task of developing international legal standards for the protection of indigenous peoples' human rights. The Working Group's activities are intended to culminate in a Universal Declaration on Rights of Indigenous People to be forwarded to the U.N. General Assembly for ratification.[97] On ratification, the Universal Declaration will become an authoritative international human rights instrument in the world legal order. It will declare the international community's minimum legal standards for the protection of indigenous peoples' rights to survival.[98]

Professor Robert A. Williams separates this bundle of emerging rights into four categories most prominent in the international testimony of indigenous people: (1) the distinctive nature of indigenous peoples' collective rights; (2) the centrality of territorial rights to indigenous survival; (3) the recognition of indigenous peoples' right to self-determining autonomy; and (4) international legal protection of indigenous rights.[99] All of these principles speak directly to the current struggles that dominate Indian law; they need application and elucidation in the tribal court context.

These themes are significant for tribal courts in a number of important ways. So much of tribal history and culture—including its thought and philosophy—is collective and communal in nature that it has often been difficult to frame such an indigenous legal discourse within and at the margin of a dominant jurisprudence based on *individuals*. European legal thought is premised on individuals who precede the state, while much of Native American thought is premised on the centrality and primacy of groups such as families, communities, and tribes themselves.[100] This dichotomy is well captured by the contrast between the European aphorism "I think therefore I am" and its indigenous counterpart "I belong therefore I am."

This concept of collective rights is also a central tenet that may be used to resist ongoing cultural and legal pressures to assimilate and fall prey to "ethnocide."[101] Because Indian people are federal and state citizens, assimilation often seems benevolent, merely a means of escaping poverty and discrimination. Yet these pressures are ultimately lethal for people whose primary identity is with a group and culture that the forces of assimilation seek to dismantle. As a good friend, Elizabeth Little Elk, once said to me: "I cannot live without the reservation. It is like oxygen to me."[102]

The right of territorial integrity, one element in emerging international human rights law, has long been a staple of domestic Native American struggles within the United States. The historical ravages of the allotment,[103] termination,[104] and diminishment[105] processes have been extensive. All have contributed substantially to the erosion of tribal lands within the United States. For people intimately connected with the land as a source of identity and spiritual strength, the loss has been much more than economic and political; it has been culturally devastating. International human rights law is beginning to recognize and to address this reality. For example, the current Working Group's Draft Declaration of Indigenous Peoples' Rights specifically recognizes the right of indigenous peoples to "ownership, possession and uses of lands which they have traditionally occupied or used."[106] This growing international legal recognition of the centrality of land to the survival and well-being of indigenous people directly validates the ongoing commitment of tribes to maintain and to enhance their reservation-based way of life—a way of life that draws on the land's economic potential and numinous bounty.

The global human rights theme of self-determination employs almost identical language, which compares very favorably to that used in the context of much contemporary Indian law discourse. The label "meaningful self-determination" purports to describe current federal policy.[107] An international thrust in the same direction ought to help reinforce this sometimes wavering federal commitment. "Self-determination" is sometimes difficult to define at its outer edges. However, from the tribal perspective the doctrine clearly includes the authority to govern all individuals and property found within the reservation's borders. This important international development recognizes a tribe's right to govern its own affairs, as well as the right of its citizens to fully participate in the society at large.[108]

Finally, there is the broad development of the growing recognition of the legitimate international legal status of indigenous people. Consistent with the doctrine of discovery and most colonial policy, indigenous people have not been generally recognized as having "standing" in international law.[109] For example, indigenous people have almost always been foreclosed from access to international tribunals, where standing is reserved to states.

Indigenous people have consistently argued that because they have negotiated treaties with European settler states since initial contact more than four hundred years ago, such treaties by their very nature recognize tribal sovereignty and statehood as a matter of domestic and international law. The Working Group's Draft Universal Declaration incorporates much of this argument with its recognition of indigenous peoples' right "to claim that states honor treaties and other agreements concluded with indigenous people" [110] as well as the right to seek domestic and international redress for treaty violations.[111] This increased international visibility and standing ought, in turn, to increase the credence and durability of a tribal court jurisprudence that explores and elucidates the same themes in the local context. In fact, given the absence of clarity about the relationship of tribal courts to federal courts,[112] there may even be the innovative possibility of building a relationship between tribal courts and international forums, including such features as concurrent jurisdiction or a trial-appellate court system.

These powerful international law developments provide much new doctrinal footing and support with which to enhance the depth and breadth of tribal court jurisprudence. They cannot help but boost tribal courts' morale about the importance and significance of what they are doing, and they also provide valuable legal support for work in the area of treaties, self-determination, and territorial integrity.[113]

DREAMS AND HARD WORK

Inevitably, the theory and reality of law and legal development place substantial burdens on judges and practitioners committed to undoing a legacy of discrimination and oppression as well as forging a jurisprudence of justice and hope. These burdens include the issues of resources, competence, and the continuing encroachment of the majoritarian legal system and its tradition.

The effort required to establish a new tribal jurisprudence is both personal and institutional and involves attorneys and judges who work and practice in tribal courts, as well as the support staff of secretaries, clerks, and lay counselors. The overwhelming number of people who work in tribal courts, at least those in South Dakota, are tribal members who take great pride in their work.[114] In part, this pride is engendered by the recognition that tribal courts are rapidly developing into significant tribal institutions embodying the struggle to realize sovereignty and to achieve justice.

Hallmarks of this development include the growing number of law-trained Indian attorneys and judges who constitute the tribal court bar, the increasing importance and volume of civil legislation in tribal courts, and the development of active and flourishing tribal appellate courts. For example, in 1973 there was not a single law-trained Indian tribal judge in South Dakota. Now more than half of the chief tribal judges are law-trained Indians. In addition, fully functioning appellate courts exist on all the reservations. The opinions of these courts are regularly reported in the national *Indian Law Reporter* and rival the complexity and sophistication of many state and federal courts. Also of note is the fact that *eight* out of eighteen tribal trial judges in South Dakota are Native American women (both law and non-law trained), while only *one* out of thirty-five circuit (i.e., trial) judges in the South Dakota state system is a woman.[115]

Many courts and tribes are also actively contemplating constitutional and other legal reforms to enhance their institutional strength and competence. These reforms most often include considerations of the separation of powers, judicial improvements such as increased training, and expansion of the body of law available for tribal court application and review.[116] For example, a recent amendment to the Rosebud Sioux Tribal Constitution creates a mechanism to convene a tribal constitutional convention.[117] Other tribal initiatives range from legislative consideration of commercial codes governing commercial activities on the reservation to setting up culturally appropriate methods of civil dispute resolution, such as mediation by respected elders.[118] Although the success of these efforts is still unknown, they nonetheless demonstrate that tribal courts and their jurisprudence are in a period of exciting and innovative change—a change commensurate with their growing local and national status and responsibility. Attendant challenges, however, may thwart this growth and development.[119]

Much of the hard work necessary to overcome these pressures falls on judges and practitioners in tribal courts. Few tribal courts have the advantage of law clerks and sumptuous law libraries to supplement the research that practitioners develop in their written briefs.[120] Therefore, the burden on practitioners and tribal judges is extensive. Practitioners and judges need to cast their jurisprudential nets widely in order to better encompass the possibilities for rich and diverse legal thought. The practitioners often have a much narrower focus: they desire to win cases. Nevertheless, winning cases and enriching legal thought are not mutually exclusive acts, particularly in the tribal court context.

For example, many practitioners—particularly non-Indian attorneys—who appear before tribal trial and appellate courts in South Dakota regularly cite South Dakota cases as dispositive precedent. This approach is unduly narrow if not actually counterproductive. Because the questions before tribal courts are often ones of first impression,[121] there may not be any dispositive local tribal precedent on point. Tribal precedents from other reservations, however, may be relevant. Such precedent will most often be found in the national *Indian Law Reporter* that reports all tribal court opinions that it receives.[122] Nevertheless, this reporter service is a research tool to which few South Dakota practitioners subscribe. In a close case the court might well follow tribal rather than state precedent because of its greater similarity of history and circumstance.

Standing alone, state law precedent is merely persuasive, not binding. Just because the state and reservation are physically contiguous is not enough to justify the routine application of state court precedent, especially in light of the history of animosity and colonialism. In these situations, precedent from another tribal court might be more pertinent. At a minimum, practitioners need to articulate why the principle of law, rather than the simple fact that it is embedded in South Dakota precedent (or other tribal precedent for that matter), is good and just and should be followed on its *merits*.

In light of many tribal courts' relative youth,[123] much tribal court litigation involves cases in which there is no controlling authority. This alone suggests the possibility for innovative and creative lawyering, which, as a necessary by-product, can help to forge a meaningful and enduring tribal jurisprudence. Conversely, treating tribal court litigation as so much "business as usual" risks creating a colonial jurisprudence of imitation, a jurisprudence guided by the expedience and propinquity of available state court decisional law rather than a jurisprudence grounded in cultural integrity with global horizons. The depth and quality of tribal court jurisprudence is largely the product of the engagement and critical intelligence of the practicing and judging bar—a bar which must now rise to the challenges of both culture and history *and* individual client representation.

It is also true, as noted above, that tribal courts often lack up-to-date and efficient legal resources and record management systems. Tribal law libraries tend to be bare-bones. They often include no more than the tribal code, a smattering of volumes of the *United States Code,* the *Code of Federal Regulations,* and some state, federal, and Indian law reporters. Law clerks and computerized research component facilities are virtually unknown luxuries. The research resources of many tribal courts are therefore seriously limited. This basic deficiency, however, can be readily overcome, primarily through an infusion of money. If the federal government desires to advance meaningful tribal self-determination, funds for tribal court development would seem a most felicitous investment.

A statute that goes far in attempting to meet this need recently passed Congress. The Indian Tribal Judicial Act[124] specifically addresses needs relative to improved access to law libraries, improved court records management systems, continuing legal education, and technical assistance.[125] The Act calls for more than $50 million to be spent over five years. Funds would be provided through agreements or contracts to award financial assistance to any Indian tribe for developing, enhancing, or continuing a tribal judicial system pursuant to the Indian Self-Determination Act.[126] In addition to stating important policy objectives and providing reasonable levels of funding, the statute explicitly recognizes that "tribal justice systems are an essential part of tribal governments and serve as important forums for ensuring public health and safety and the political integrity of tribal governments."[127]

Regardless of its ultimate success, the statute clearly addresses important tribal court needs and endorses their premier role in achieving self-determination and rendering justice in Indian country. Such an ongoing federal commitment can go a long way to complement the hard work of tribal court personnel and to aid in the realization of their dreams of justice, sovereignty, and durability. In fact, the Indian Tribal Judicial Act helps to avoid hegemonic paternalism, creating instead a model of federal-tribal partnership.

COMMUNITY AND INSTITUTION BUILDING

The law is partly about power—the jurisdictional power to render justice and to achieve other socially important goals. However, the ability to realize worthy objectives requires more than jurisdiction and power; it also requires expertise, resources, and community support. Practitioners and scholars of Indian law are often not sensitive enough to this political and social reality. Theory and practice in Indian law are too often unhinged from the political commitment to institution building which is necessary to make the possibilities of the law meaningful. Any tribal jurisdictional authority confirmed by Congress or the U.S. Supreme Court must in turn be complemented by tribal resources and institutions capable of implementing that authority in such a way that the ideals and principles of the law are realized in practice. Without this understanding, much Indian law scholarship is in danger of becoming a misleading abstraction cut off from the frontiers of significant tribal development. A supportive body of federal Indian law is a necessary but not sufficient condition for building a flourishing cultural and institutional future in Indian country. The field of Indian law needs to extend its range, to ground itself in tribal reality, and to avoid the temptation of becoming a thing unto itself—a useless reification.[128]

An important and related caution to heed is the fact that the law in general, and Indian law in particular, cannot be an end in itself. The law does not make things happen; rather, it creates a normative space[129] in which to realize individual and cultural values. The normative space created by tribal sovereignty validated by federal Indian law stands in need of creative and viable tribal institutions in order to achieve the social and cultural objectives embodied in the law. This latter effort is often a long, unheralded struggle, but it is arguably the most important foundation for the future. It is important not to lose sight of the fact that all significant public values are realized through institutions. Better institutions are essential to better lives.[130]

Unfortunately, many in the field of Indian law, including scholarly commentators, often pay insufficient attention to this issue.[131] The result is to create a grossly distorted picture of the relationship of law to sovereignty. It further obscures the relationship of politics and institution building to law and the realization of significant tribal values. For example, the fact that tribal sovereignty and federal Indian law currently endorse the significance of tribal courts[132] cannot deflect concern from the concomitant necessity for tribal courts to continue to develop their resources, competence, and insights. For it is, after all, both theory and practice, both authority and its implementation, that determine the quality of justice.

This foundational predicate includes the necessity of developing increasing political support and understanding of tribal courts. Institutional support needs to come from all quarters, but particularly from both the Indian and non-Indian communities subject to the authority of tribal courts, including those members of the legal profession who practice before them. For example, on the Rosebud Sioux Reservation, Chief Trial Judge Sherman Marshall[133] holds an annual weeklong Tribal Court Open House in which members of the tribal and general public are invited to visit the courthouse and listen to a series of presentations on the policies and procedures of the tribal court. The topics of these presentations range from the filling out of forms to the structure and function of the tribal court appellate system. Chief Judge Marshall also makes it a point to visit all the tribal communities to explain the nature and duties of the tribal court. This is particularly important, because as Chief Judge Marshall notes,[134] many tribal people do not understand, and have a negative view of, their tribal courts. Such institution building is closely related to the matters of legitimacy discussed in chapter 3.

In addition, Chief Judge Marshall has organized a group of Indian and non-Indian attorneys who appear regularly before the Rosebud Sioux Tribal Court to serve as an advisory group concerning legal practice issues before the court. This group is clearly a precursor to a functioning tribal bar association.[135] Without this kind of understanding and action, tribal sovereignty and federal Indian law are in danger of becoming abstractions disconnected from the reality and challenge of community and institutional life on the reservation. Even worse, tribal sovereignty itself may be threatened by the very failure to establish an adequate base of financial resources and institutional development. For example, at recent hearings of the U.S. House of Representatives Committee on Interior and Insular Affairs in South Dakota, most of the testimony provided about tribal courts focused on how well they are working or not working in their day-to-day operation rather than on their theoretical or jurisdictional underpinnings. This is the kind of "reality" that is likely to affect Congress, for good or ill, rather than any general analysis of federal Indian law.

A MISSING WEB OF BELIEFS

Much of the problem concerning tribal sovereignty within the national, state, and even many tribal legal communities is the absence of any foundational web of beliefs about tribal sovereignty. Without this foundational agreement or understanding that tribal sovereignty exists and what its roots and branches are, the entire field is in jeopardy. Tribal sovereignty often seems to be extraordinarily precarious. For example, virtually none of the members of the state and federal practicing bar and judiciary have any training in Indian law. Furthermore, since the Indian law presence is only nominal in other parts of the curriculum,[136] most members of the practicing bar and judiciary have no sense of what tribal sovereignty and the principles of self-determination mean. As a result, the legal and constitutional context of tribal sovereignty is not readily apparent. Therefore, almost every instance of discourse on Indian law requires substantial "education" in order to achieve any threshold understanding of the most important concepts within the field. This incredibly burdensome but necessary task reflects the pervasive ignorance and distortion that permeate the understanding of sovereignty and Indian law doctrine within the national and state legal communities.

This problem is exacerbated because the thrust of tribal sovereignty is often counter to the thrust of that of other minority groups within this country. The object of almost all litigation of other minorities in this society is increased access to rights and institutions within the dominant society. This goal is well understood, even if resisted, within the dominant legal and judicial community. However, the object of most, if not all, tribally initiated or defended Indian law litigation is to establish and vindicate a historical, nonassimilated right to an autonomy that seeks to preserve a "measured separatism."[137] This emphasis is not recognized within the national and state legal communities' web of beliefs. To expand this web of beliefs, we must labor to create mutuality and dialogue in the context of federal and state awareness and understanding of tribal court decision making.

Belief in tribal sovereignty does not, at least to me, mean that tribes always "win." Rather, it means that their basic sovereignty is recognized as permanent, enduring, and located in, and vouchsafed by, the federal constitution. Only when this status is widely accepted will it be truly possible to determine the specifics of tribal sovereignty in the thick detail and practice of adjudicating individual cases, just as it occurs in the context of state and federal sovereignty.

The absence of any truly constitutionalized understanding of tribal sovereignty is, of course, problematic at the level of political and legal rhetoric; more important, it is a serious destabilizing force in the day-to-day political, cultural, and institutional life of tribes. Any project, particularly one concerning law and jurisdiction, is subject to unilateral defeasance by Congress or the federal courts.[138] A sovereignty of sufferance, oxymoronic on its face, does not provide an environment conducive to meaningful self-determination or realization.

The process of tribal court decision making and constitutional adjudication promises to articulate an emerging vision of tribal sovereignty. It will also, in parallel fashion, advance the process which recognizes, from the tribal perspective, the authenticity of tribal courts as legitimate and significant tribal institutions. Tribal authenticity is, of course, not a given because tribal courts, like most other tribal institutions, do not have their structural foundations in precontact, precolonial times.[139] This "inside-out" authenticity, in turn, must meet the potential constraints of judicial and congressional review that is necessary to achieve a complementary "top-down" authenticity. It is the delicate synthesis of these often competing sources of validation that holds the key to a meaningful and flourishing future.

This chapter speaks ultimately of love[140] and its ability to define an indigenous jurisprudence that is committed to "a new and sweeping utopia of life, where no one will be able to decide for others how they die, where love will prove true and happiness be possible, and where the races condemned to one hundred years of solitude will have, at last and forever, a second opportunity on earth."[141] Such an understanding clearly endeavors to transcend the ravages of history and to avoid the canon of despair. As noted by the poet Adrienne Rich, "[T]he search for justice and compassion is the great wellspring for poetry in our time"; she herself "draw[s] strength from the traditions of all those who, with every reason to despair, have refused to do so."[142] These claims for the potential of tribal jurisprudence are not meant to be extreme; rather, they are elemental in their call to the roots of tradition to guide contemporary struggle and to shape modern tribal competence with wisdom and grace.

In light of this evolving pattern, the encroachment of the dominant legal tradition must abate. It too has something to offer to this progression, namely the foundational insight of a constitutional faith that sees law not only as a field of force but as a ground of aspiration for individual and group self-realization. With this understanding, the separate strands in the braid of a pluralistic legal tradition may converge ever closer. For example, as recently noted by the Supreme Court of the Oglala Sioux Tribe:

> It should not have to be for the Congress of the United States or the Federal Court of Appeals to tell us when to give due process. Due process is a concept that has always been with us. Although it is a legal phrase and has legal meaning, due process means nothing more than being fair and honest in our dealings with each other. We are allowed to disagree. . . . What must be remembered is that we must allow the other side the opportunity to be heard.[143]

Inevitably, there will also be differences between the dominant and indigenous jurisprudential views that cannot be resolved so easily, but these differences too must be reconciled without force and with due deference and respect—a deference and respect that seeks to honor the fundamental guarantee of treaties of a measured separatism for Indian tribes. This achievement contains the potential to complete the circle and to confirm and to give renewed meaning to the struggle for justice and liberation that animates the *ideals* of both the majoritarian and tribal legal traditions. For it is true, finally, that without the torment of the ideal,[144] there is little hope for significant and enduring change.

PART THREE

Issues in the Western Landscape

A Regional Perspective

Federal hegemony in Indian law and affairs not only obscures the importance of developments at the tribal level but also deflects attention from significant issues at the regional level. These issues include the economic, political, and cultural role of tribes in the life of the West as well as the texture and parameters of tribal-state relations. The West—which may be defined as the region beyond the hundredth meridian—is physically characterized chiefly by its relative aridity and its wide-open spaces. These ecological determinants impose certain limitations and exact a premium for successful living and development.

These constraints, in turn, create a unique set of challenges—challenges that come from the harsh environment and a history of federal dominance (of both tribes and states) and outside exploitation. Despite these common challenges and the need for creative solutions to them, tribes are often ignored within the western context. And when not ignored, their interests and concerns are often perceived as inimical to those of the rest of the region. The old myths of cowboys and Indians die hard. Yet that is the very point that needs to be made. These old myths are pernicious and harmful to all concerned. What is needed in the West is a *new* ethic and story to create a greater sense of solidarity and common interest between Indians and non-Indians, between the tribes and the states. As noted by the novelist Wallace Stegner, the American West is a living space of real and mythical promise.

The nature and texture of tribal-state relations are central elements in the field of Indian law as well as powerful coordinates in assaying the future of the West, particularly in the critical matters of water and natural resources that are vital to the well-being of the region. In addition, these relationships often serve as the first point of localized face-to-face contact between Indian and non-Indians and the racial animosity that often permeates this interaction. Despite these facts, not much scholarly effort focuses on these important contours. Despite the widely acknowledged agreement that the key questions in Indian law involve questions of tribal regulatory and jurisdictional authority over resources and non-Indians in Indian country, the major attention centers on federal decision making. This, of course, makes a good deal of sense given that federal forums have been the principal arenas of decision making. Yet this approach has primarily yielded a legacy of substantial tribal-state friction and continuing uncertainty, while also being extremely costly to all.

There are better, though perhaps less explored, relationships that might serve as a hallmark for the future of tribal-state and regional relations, and it is time to explore them. However, the pressing issues of contemporary Indian–non-Indian relationships within the West cannot be properly understood without examining the roots of early federal, tribal, and state interaction from which many current paradoxes and problems have grown.

A core challenge within this cluster of regional concerns is the issue of economic development in Indian country. Many now claim that economic development can provide a pathway to economic sovereignty and constitutes a necessary complement to an agenda of political and legal sovereignty. The specific causes of the widespread poverty in Indian country remain somewhat elusive, yet the call for economic development is almost unanimous. Unfortunately, however, the content of the "answer" to the question of economic development is not self-evident. Too often in the past, the question of what economic development is needed in Indian country has yielded very specific "answers," such as the massive leasing of tribal natural resources, capital-intensive manufacturing, large-scale agribusiness ventures—and, most recently, Indian gaming. These "answers," as a rule, were developed with little understanding of the difficult and subtle issues involved. As a result, there has been neither sustained economic growth nor increased cultural meaning.

The issues of tribal-state relations and economic development in Indian country are central to the regional destiny of the West. The vitality of both the states and the tribes are inextricably bound together. The tribes and the states need to parse their differences and parley their similarities into a creative synthesis that will enable each side individually, and the region collectively, to flourish.

CHAPTER FIVE

Tribal-State Relations

Hope for the Future?

The legal relationship of tribes to the states has been unclear from the very beginning of the republic. It finds, for example, no elucidation in the U.S. Constitution, which is the primary national document to allocate authority between sovereigns.[1] There is no constitutional analogy to the Tenth Amendment,[2] which establishes a constitutional benchmark for dialogue about the relationship of federal and state sovereignty. Nor can there be found a true description of the state-tribal relationship within any state[3] or tribal constitution.[4]

The tribes and states stand as mutual sovereigns which share contiguous physical areas and some common citizens—tribal members who reside on the reservation are both tribal and state citizens, while non-Indian residents of the reservation are state citizens but not tribal citizens. Nevertheless, tribes often see the states as relentlessly expansionary in seeking to extend their authority over the reservations and, in the process, to limit the tribes' authority and demean their very existence.[5]

The doctrines that attempt to describe the early contours of tribal-state relations are even more disparate and evanescent than those that undergird the federal-tribal relationship. In addition, they represent several missed doctrinal opportunities. There have been at least two watershed attempts to define the nature of tribal-state relations, but they have only been temporarily and minimally successful before being severely limited by subsequent historical events and legal interpretations.

The first and earliest attempt to address the nature of tribal-state relations can be found in *Worcester v. Georgia.*[6] Although the case is central to identifying some of the early contours of federal-tribal relations, perhaps inextricably it also attempts to limn the nature of tribal-state interaction. The Court—particularly Chief Justice Marshall's opinion—proceeds in a straightforward manner. The relationship between the federal government and the tribes is special and unique—one sovereign to another—and *exclusive.* Justice Marshall's opinion proclaims that "[t]he treaties and laws of the United States contemplate the Indian territory as completely separated from that of the states; and provide that all intercourse with them shall be carried on exclusively by the government of the Union."[7] This *exclusive* federal-tribal relationship bars the intrusion of any state authority in Indian country.

In addition, there is the apparent strength of independent tribal sovereignty as its own barrier to state authority:

> The Cherokee Nation, then, is a distinct community, occupying its own territory, with boundaries accurately described, in which the laws of Georgia can have no force, and which the citizens of Georgia have no right to enter, but with assent of the Cherokee themselves, or in conformity with treaties and with acts of congress.[8]

The late-nineteenth-century case *United States v. Kagama*[9] probably represents the apotheosis of this line of legal thinking which is premised on the centrality of federalism in Indian affairs. In that case, which challenged Congress's authority to enact the Major Crimes Act,[10] the court upheld Congress's power, particularly noting its necessity to protect tribes from states:

> These Indian tribes *are* the wards of the nation. They are communities *dependent* on the United States,—dependent largely for their daily food; dependent for their political rights. They owe no allegiance to the states, and receive from them no protection. Because of the local ill feeling, the people of the states where they are found are often their deadliest enemies. From their very weakness and helplessness, so largely due to the course of dealing of the Federal Government with them, and the treaties in which it has been promised,

there arises the duty of protection, and with it the power. This has always been recognized by the executive, and by congress, and by this court, whenever the question has arisen.[11]

It is, however, unsettling to note that this "duty of protection" is apparently unfettered, clearly presaging the full-blown plenary power doctrine and its erosion of tribal sovereignty.

Yet this original federal and tribal certainty rebuking state authority in Indian country has become vastly diluted and uncertain. Federal-tribal relations are no longer exclusive but have narrowed into the notion of federal preemption,[12] declaring that the federal government must *affirmatively* assert its authority in order to foreclose any potential state claims of authority. This doctrine has become a thin reed in many areas—particularly in the critical civil regulatory area, where federal preemption activity is mostly nonexistent. Even when it is nominally applied, federal preemption analysis serves as little more than a balancing test, where tribal sovereignty is relegated to a "backdrop"[13] from which the Court examines

the language of the relevant federal treaties and statutes in terms of both the broad policies that underlie them and the notions of sovereignty that have developed from historical traditions of tribal independence. This inquiry is not dependent on mechanical or absolute conceptions of state or tribal sovereignty, but has called for a particularized inquiry into the nature of the state, federal, and tribal interests at stake, an inquiry designed to determine whether, in the specific context, the exercise of state authority would violate federal law.[14]

The second and arguably the most propitious historical moment in which to examine the contours of tribal-state relations is probably the latter part of the nineteenth century, when many states—particularly in the West—joined the Union. The enabling acts admitting most states to the Union, including South Dakota in 1889, provided Congress with ample opportunity to consider the relationship of these new states to Indian people and reservations within their borders. Yet the results proved inadequate and short-lived. Most enabling acts contained only vague "disclaimer clauses" in which the new states generally agreed that "said Indian land shall remain under the absolute jurisdiction and control of the United States."[15] At the time, such a statement undoubt-edly seemed sufficient to address the issue since most reservations were comprised almost entirely of Indian land and Indians. States basically had no jurisdiction in Indian country.

However, historical forces and subsequent judicial interpreta-tions have rendered this injunction almost useless. Courts have *not* found these "disclaimer clauses"[16] particularly significant in dealing with the ravages of the allotment policy, which brought significant numbers of non-Indians to Indian country and permit-ted the passage of vast amounts of tribal land into non-Indian hands.[17] The key contemporary issue of whether the tribe or state has jurisdiction over non-Indians and non-Indian lands slipped away, and tribal-state relations were once again uncoupled from any conceptual unity.

Despite the absence of any readily applicable doctrine for un-derstanding or describing tribal-state relations, there potentially exists a vital zone for creative free play and mutual governmental respect and advancement. Unfortunately, such an approach has been the exception to the rule of enmity between the tribes and the state.

CURRENT CONTOURS IN TRIBAL-STATE RELATIONS

There can be little doubt that tribal-state relations questions are the most significant issues in Indian law today. In the last decade the bulk of U.S. Supreme Court litigation in Indian law has fo-cused on these issues. A survey of that litigation provides a valu-able thermometer with which to access the health of present-day tribal-state relations.

Supreme Court litigation in the area of tribal-state relations has drifted further and further away from the foundational mooring of *Worcester v. Georgia*,[18] out past the abandoned buoys of the infringement and preemption tests[19] and into the uncharted seas of doctrinal incoherence in such recent cases as *Montana v. United States*,[20] *Cotton Petroleum v. New Mexico*,[21] *Brendale v. Confederated Tribes and Bands of Yakima Indian Nation*,[22] and *South Dakota v. Bourland*.[23] In *Worcester* the Su-preme Court made it clear that tribal reservations were extraterritorial to states whose borders nominally contained Indian reservations. The decision in *Worcester,* which resulted in a total exclusion of state authority in Indian country, was based on the twin tenets of tribal sovereignty and federal exclusivity and hegemony in tribal affairs.[24]

The modern watershed case in tribal-state jurisprudence is often thought to be *Williams v. Lee.*[25] In *Williams,* a non-Indian store owner on the Navajo Reservation attempted to sue a Navajo defendant in state court for an unsatisfied debt that arose on the reservation.[26] On one level, it might have appeared that this case would be disposed of with dispatch by reference to the holding of *Worcester.* The Court did pay homage to the "courageous and eloquent"[27] opinion of Chief Justice Marshall but went on to enumerate the "infringement" test, which holds that "[e]ssentially, absent governing acts of Congress, the question has always been whether the state action infringed on the right of reservation Indians to make their own laws and be ruled by them."[28] The Court dismissed the case, readily finding the necessary infringement.[29]

Six years later, in 1965, in the case of *Warren Trading Post v. Arizona Tax Commission*[30] the Court faced the quandary of whether the state of Arizona might assert a gross proceeds or sales tax on a non-Indian business engaged in retail trading with Indians on the Navajo Reservation.[31] The Court held in the negative but did not apply either the *Worcester* or *Williams* analyses. Instead, the Court fashioned the preemption test, which holds that Congress possesses the necessary legislative authority to affirmatively control any subject matter area in Indian country, effectively ousting any claim of potential state authority on the reservation over Indians and/or non-Indians.[32] The Court, for example, specifically noted that the pertinent federal trading statutes and regulations "seem in themselves sufficient to show that Congress has taken the business of Indian trading on reservations so fully in hand that no room remains for state laws imposing additional burdens upon traders."[33]

In each of these cases, the Court noted that the Navajo Reservation was set apart as a "permanent home"[34] for the Navajo Tribe in the Treaty of 1868. The Court acknowledged Navajo powers of self-government, but the concept of tribal sovereignty was clearly not dispositive.

In *McClanahan v. Arizona Tax Commission*[35] the Court struck down an attempt by the state of Arizona to collect state income tax on income earned by Navajo Indians within the Navajo Reservation.[36] In so doing, the Court "clarified" the role that tribal sovereignty plays in its jurisdictional analysis. The tribal sovereignty recognized in *Worcester v. Georgia* "has undergone considerable evolution in response to changed circumstances."[37] Specifically,

> [t]he trend has been away from the idea of inherent Indian sovereignty as a bar to state jurisdiction and toward reliance on federal pre-emption. . . . The modern cases thus tend to avoid reliance on platonic notions of Indian sovereignty and to look instead to the applicable treaties and statutes which define the limits of state power.
> . . .
> The Indian sovereignty doctrine is relevant, then, not because it provides a definitive resolution of the issue in this suit, but because it provides a backdrop against which the applicable treaties and federal statutes must be read.[38]

The Court's most comprehensive synthesis of these diverse strands is found in *White Mountain Apache Tribe v. Bracker*.[39] In the context of striking down an attempt by the state of Arizona to assert vehicle license and fuel use taxes on a non-Indian corporation doing business with a tribal entity on the White Mountain Apache Reservation,[40] the Court summarized its view of the applicable jurisdictional analysis:

> Congress has broad power to regulate tribal affairs under the Indian Commerce Clause, Art. 1, § 8, cl. 3. . . . This Congressional authority and the "semi-independent position" of Indian tribes have given rise to two independent but related barriers to the assertion of state regulatory authority over tribal reservations and members. First, the exercise of such authority may be preempted by federal law. Second, it may unlawfully infringe "on the right of reservation Indians to make their own laws and be ruled by them." The two barriers are independent because either, standing alone, can be a sufficient basis for holding state law inapplicable to activity undertaken on the reservation or by tribal members. They are related, however, in two important ways. The right of tribal self-government is ultimately dependent on and subject to the broad power of Congress. Even so,

traditional notions of Indian self-government are so deeply ingrained in our jurisprudence that they have provided an important "backdrop" against which vague or ambiguous federal enactments must always be measured. . . .

. . . This inquiry is not dependent on mechanical or absolute conceptions of state or tribal sovereignty, but has called for a particularized inquiry into the nature of the state, federal, and tribal interests at stake, an inquiry designed to determine whether, in the specific context, the exercise of state authority would violate federal law.[41]

This comprehensive view has fallen on hard times recently. The Court has apparently discarded this analytic framework in the context of cases involving tribal regulatory authority over non-Indians on non-Indian land within the reservation, as will be seen in the discussion of the *Montana*,[42] *Brendale*,[43] and *Bourland*[44] cases. In addition, the *Bracker* test has become so "flexible"[45] that it has lost its essential character and utility, as a review of the *Cotton Petroleum*[46] case will amply demonstrate.

In the *Cotton Petroleum* case, a sequel to *Merrion v. Jicarilla Apache Tribe*,[47] the Supreme Court confronted the issue of whether the State of New Mexico could continue to impose its severance taxes on (non-Indian) Cotton Petroleum's production of oil and gas, which was already taxed by the Jicarilla Apache Tribe.[48] The Court held that it could.[49] The Court noted that questions such as this "are not controlled by 'mechanical or absolute conceptions of state or tribal sovereignty.' " Instead,

we have applied a flexible pre-emption analysis sensitive to the particular facts and legislation involved. Each case "requires a particularized examination by the relevant state, federal, and tribal interests." . . . It bears emphasis that although congressional silence no longer entails a broad-based immunity from taxation for private parties doing business with Indian tribes, federal pre-emption is not limited to cases in which Congress has expressly—as impliedly—preempted the state activity.[50]

In a two-tier analysis, the Court found no federal preemption and no undue burden on the tribe. The Court arrived at this conclusion despite a contrary finding in *Montana v. Blackfeet Tribe of Indians*[51] and even though the 1938 Indian Mineral Leasing Act no longer expressly permitted state taxation.[52] The Court supported its finding by stating that "this is not a case in which a state has nothing to do with a reservation activity, save tax it. Nor is this a case in which an unusually large state tax has imposed a substantial burden on the tribe."[53] The Court was also broadly unsympathetic to any notion that the state's right to tax would impair the ability of the tribe to carry out its legal and economic functions free from burdensome state interference.[54]

The dissent, written by Justice Blackmun, takes the majority sharply to task, arguing that "[the majority] distorts the legal standard it purports to apply."[55] The dissent vigorously criticizes the majority analysis under the preemption test:

> Instead of engaging in a careful examination of state, tribal, and federal interests required by our precedents, ... the majority has adopted the principle of "inexorable zero." ... Under the majority's approach, there is no preemption unless the States are *entirely* excluded from a sphere of activity and provide *no* services to the Indians or to the lessees they seek to tax. That extreme approach is hardly consistent with the "flexible" standard the majority purports to apply.[56]

All of this is, of course, a long way from *Worcester v. Georgia* and seems to make that seminal case's parsimonious reading of state authority in Indian country rather evanescent after all.

In *Montana v. United States* and *Brendale v. Confederated Tribes of the Yakima Nation,* the Supreme Court appears to wholly dispense with the preemption/infringement synthesis articulated in *Bracker.* The Court does not bother to explain why it is appropriate to ignore that synthesis; rather, it simply proceeds in a different fashion. In *Montana* the Court faced the issue of whether the Crow Tribe could regulate the hunting and fishing[57] of non-Indians on fee lands within the Crow Reservation.[58] The Court ruled that it could not.[59] The Court's analysis is hurried and, for the most part, heedless of its own past. For example, *Worcester* is not even cited, much less discussed. The Court notes that allotment of the Crow Reservation pursuant to the General Allotment Act and Crow Allotment Act effectively reduced the tribe's authority over alienated reservation lands, despite the guarantee in the Fort Laramie Treaty of 1868 that recognized the Crow Reservation as "set apart for the absolute and undisturbed use and occupation of the Indians herein named."[60] The

Court bluntly states that "treaty rights with respect to reservation lands must be read in light of the subsequent alienation of those lands. Accordingly, the language of the 1868 treaty provides no support for tribal authority to regulate hunting and fishing on land owned by non-Indians." [61]

The Court blended this finding, which strips the Fort Laramie Treaty of 1868 as a source of tribal authority over non-Indians, with the notion that the "exercise of tribal power beyond what is necessary to protect tribal self-government or to control internal relations is inconsistent with the dependent status of the tribes, and so cannot survive without express congressional delegation." [62] This sweeping generalization was nevertheless limited by a substantial proviso:

> To be sure, Indian tribes retain inherent sovereign power to exercise some forms of civil jurisdiction over non-Indians on their reservations, even on non-Indian fee lands. A tribe may regulate, through taxation, licensing, or other means, the activities of nonmembers who enter consensual relationships with the tribe or its members, through commercial dealing, contracts, leases, or other arrangements. A tribe may also retain inherent power to exercise civil authority over the conduct of non-Indians on fee lands within its reservation when that conduct threatens or has some direct effect on the political integrity, the economic security, or the health or welfare of the tribe. [63]

The exact meaning of this analysis by the Court became the subject of intensive debate within the Court in the *Brendale* case. In *Brendale* the Court confronted the issue of whether the Yakima Indian Nation or the County of Yakima (a governmental unit of the State of Washington) has the authority to zone fee lands owned by nonmembers of the tribe located within the boundaries of the Yakima Reservation. [64] The Court reached no firm conclusion on the issue but rather issued three separate plurality opinions that seemingly obscured rather than clarified the issue at hand. [65]

Justice White's opinion, which was joined by Chief Justice Rehnquist and Justices Scalia and Kennedy, essentially relied on its reading of *Montana* that tribes, in the aftermath of the allotment process, presumptively do *not* have authority over fee lands within the reservation unless there is an express congressional delegation to the contrary.[66] This opinion disposes of the *Montana* exception or proviso with dispatch. The facts at issue demonstrated no consensual agreement between the parties, and somewhat amazingly, the second part of the proviso ("threatens or has some direct effect on the political integrity, the economic security, or the health or welfare of the tribe") merely creates a potentially "protectable interest" that may be vindicated in federal court and would be binding on the states via the supremacy clause.[67]

The second opinion, authored by Justice Stevens and joined by Justice O'Connor, ultimately opted for a factual examination of the demographics and land tenure patterns within the reservation as a whole or the portion of the reservation at issue. In a graphic metaphor, Justice Stevens identifies the question as "whether the owners of a small amount of fee land may bring a pig into the parlor."[68] He answers that question in the negative,[69] but he also finds that if the area in question has lost its "essential character" as Indian land as a result of the allotment process and adverse demographic patterns, the tribe's legitimate interest in land use regulation is consequently diminished.[70]

Justice Stevens concludes that "[a]ny difficulty courts may encounter in drawing the line between 'closed' and 'open' portions of reservations simply reflects that the factual predicate to these cases is itself complicated."[71] Justice Stevens did not find *Montana* to be an apposite precedent because it involved an alleged discriminatory land use regulation, the state stocked much of the fish and game on the reservation, and the state owned the riverbed of the Big Horn River.[72]

Justice Blackmun, joined by Justices Brennan and Marshall, authored an opinion concurring in Justice Stevens's decision and dissenting from the decision announced by Justice White. This opinion makes a significant attempt to clarify the meaning of *Montana* within the framework of 150 years of Indian law jurisprudence.[73] Justice Blackmun's effort is laudable if not completely successful. The opinion honestly and correctly notes that although *Montana* is an anomaly, it is nevertheless a serviceable precedent:

[Having] strangely reversed the otherwise consistent presumption in favor of inherent tribal sovereignty over reservation lands is not [necessarily] to excise the decision from our jurisprudence. Despite the reversed presumption, the plain language of *Montana* itself expressly preserves substantial tribal authority over non-Indian activity on reservations, including fee lands, and, more particularly, may sensibly be read as recognizing inherent tribal authority to zone fee lands.[74]

This authority to zone, the opinion states, is clearly located within the *Montana* proviso concerning a "significant tribal interest"[75] in that zoning is a "critical aspect of self-government and the ultimate instrument of 'territorial management.' "[76]

Justice Blackmun's opinion excoriates the views of both Justice White and Justice Stevens. Justice White is accused of "legal tokenism"[77] and misreading "the Court's decisions defining the limits of inherent tribal sovereignty,"[78] while Justice Stevens is charged with "disregarding those decisions altogether."[79] Stay tuned for round two.

The *Brendale* decision, I think, places the Court at a crossroads in Indian law jurisprudence. Whither the issue of tribal sovereignty and tribal jurisdiction over non-Indians on fee lands within the reservation? The doctrinal center no longer seems to hold.[80]

One way of thinking about these recent cases that does provide more conceptional coherence is in terms of individual property rights. Although the Court itself has *not* articulated this line of thinking, it appears to be embedded in its analysis. The allotment process does not have to be seen strictly in terms of how it alters the jurisdictional spheres of the tribes and the states. It can also be viewed in terms of the individual property rights originally granted by the federal government to non-Indian homesteaders on the reservation. One view of that bundle of rights is that it included the "right" to be free from tribal regulation in certain activities that have a "private" character (such as hunting and fishing or basic land use) unless such activities go too far, butting up against the concerns set out in the *Montana* proviso.[81]

Such analysis is not only more coherent but more historically logical in regard to the nature of the allotment process, which was designed not to transfer significant portions of reservations from tribal to state jurisdiction but simply to allow non-Indians to settle on most reservations and to grant them certain (limited) property rights. Of course, the practical result is the same: the tribes do lose jurisdictional ground to the states. Yet such a view may well serve to limit further losses of jurisdiction by noting that the property rights of non-Indians are limited. Further wholesale erosion of tribal authority over non-Indians and their property could then be seen as contrary to both the purpose and historical logic of the allotment policy, as well as to the foundational analysis in *Worcester* on the nature of tribal-state relations.

Most recently, in *South Dakota v. Bourland*,[82] the Supreme Court not only avoided such analysis but seemed to jettison the remnants of whatever doctrinal center remained. *Bourland* raised the question of the extent of tribal authority over non-Indian fishing and hunting activities on *federal* land within the reservation. Specifically, the case focused on 104,420 acres of trust land "taken" by the federal government on the Cheyenne River Sioux Reservation as part of the Oahe Dam hydroelectric and flood control project on the upper Missouri River.[83]

Neither the Flood Control Act of 1944[84] which took the land nor the Cheyenne River Sioux Act of 1954[85] which set compensation for the "taking" *specifically* extinguished tribal jurisdictional authority. Yet the Court, with Justice Thomas writing his first Indian law opinion, presumed no tribal sovereignty, paid no apparent heed to treaty rights, seemed untroubled by the fact that *no* individual non-Indian property rights were involved, and scarcely mentioned the canon of construction that requires treaty ambiguities to be construed in favor of Indians. The whole history of Indian law doctrine disappeared down a rabbit hole like something out of *Alice in Wonderland*.

Congress, exercising its plenary authority, may certainly "take" (and provide compensation for) Indian land and even transfer jurisdiction to itself or the state. Yet such action, especially when it is in derogation of a treaty (such as, in this case, the Fort Laramie Treaty of 1868), must be express and explicit on Congress's part. The Court was apparently untroubled by these doctrinal constraints and found that the less than precise language of section 4 of the Flood Control Act, opening to "public use" recreational facilities established on land taken for the Oahe Reservoir, and the language of section 2 of the Cheyenne River Sioux Act, setting out compensation to be paid to the tribe for the land taken, sufficient to strip the tribe of its authority.

As Justice Blackmun's dissent notes, Congress's intent was clear. It wanted to build a dam, not alter the tribe's jurisdictional authority.[86] The accuracy and simplicity of this observation and its attempt to hold fast to basic Indian law doctrine stand in stark contrast to the doctrinal amnesia of the majority.

The infection eating way at tribal authority over non-Indians on *fee land* has now spread to federal land within the reservation. It remains to be seen whether the infection will spread further or whether the Court will remember and apply the (doctrinal) antidote with which to treat this spreading but wholly curable problem.

TOWARD A MORE MEANINGFUL FUTURE

Despite the problems that beset tribal-state relations, the discussions and options relative to this critical area of Indian law can be advanced and reinvigorated in a number of ways. These include exploration of such ideas as sovereignty accords, the development of thoughtful and comprehensive state and tribal policies relative to state-tribal relations, significant educational reform, and an increase of state and regional forums to pursue meaningful dialogue.

SOVEREIGNTY ACCORDS

Particularly in states such as South Dakota, tribal-state relations are often caught in a history of actions that are perceived (rightly or wrongly) by many tribes as having as their main objective the undermining of the tribe's very existence.[87] The playing field has never been level. This unfair slope could be corrected if certain principles could be embedded in a set of negotiated sovereignty accords.[88] These accords would involve no waiver or abridgment of any rights on either side but would simply take the word "respect"—the Governor of South Dakota's own litmus test in the

1990 Year of Reconciliation[89] (since expanded into the Decade of Reconciliation)—and apply it to the legal realm. The quality and texture of tribal-state relations are such that states must demonstrate publicly and in writing that they recognize tribal sovereignty—that is, the right of tribal governments to exist, to endure, and to flourish. A set of accords might establish innovative new political and diplomatic protocols leading to a more fulfilling and successful future.

Accords of this nature were entered into in 1989 by the State of Washington and the sovereign tribes of that area. For example, the Washington Centennial Accord provides that

> [e]ach party to this Accord respects the sovereignty of the other. The respective sovereignty of the state and each federally recognized tribe provide paramount authority for that party to exist and to govern. The parties share in their relationship particular respect for the values and cultures represented by tribal governments. Further, the parties share a desire for a complete accord between the State of Washington and federally recognized tribes in Washington respecting a full government to government relationship and will work with all state and tribal governments to achieve such an Accord.[90]

Such accords alone, of course, do not solve difficult problems, but they do offer a significant opportunity to advance vigorous, fair-minded, and mutual problem solving. This is a process, it might be added, that is not nearly as expensive as traditional tribal-state litigation. Such accords can do much to put the state and the tribes on the same emotional and political footing.

STATE PUBLIC POLICY CONCERNING INDIANS

In state-tribal relations, there is an acute paucity of state *public* (not litigious) policy; therefore, a more responsive and creative public policy needs to be developed. One way to establish such a process would be for the governor of every western state to appoint a commission of Indian and non-Indian experts from within the state and the reservations to prepare a public report to review the status of tribal-state relations within the particular state. The report would review the history of tribal-state relations, discuss current problems, and suggest policy options for the future.[91]

Such a report needs also to address important questions about the allocation of authority within state governments in the area of tribal-state relations. The making of such public policy, at least in its broadest sense, is a *legislative* function. This is so because it is the legislative duty to make law (embodying the attendant values and public policy concerns) which is to be carried out by the executive branch and, when contested, interpreted by the judicial branch. However, in a state like South Dakota where there has been little if any meaningful legislative activity in tribal-state relations, much of this authority is exercised de facto, if not de jure, in the executive branch, particularly in the attorney general's office.[92] The attorney general's office has no written policy and, perhaps because of its "prosecutorial" mentality, tends to litigate matters on an ad hoc basis without apparent thought for the overall implications for tribal-state relations. Such a course of action is unlikely to ameliorate the situation.

Again, the Washington Centennial Accord is instructive. The accord seems particularly sensitive to this pattern of authority and explicitly directs actions within the executive branch:

> The chief of staff of the governor of the State of Washington is accountable to the governor for implementation of the Accord. . . . Each director will initiate a procedure within his/her agency by which the government to government policy will be implemented. Among other things, these procedures will require persons responsible for dealing with issues of mutual concern to respect the government to government relationship within which the issue must be addressed. Each agency will establish a documented plan of accountability and may establish more detailed implementation procedures in subsequent agreements between tribes and the particular agency.[93]

Similar accountability is required of tribal officials: "the parties will review and evaluate at the annual meeting the implementation of the government to government relationship. A management report will be issued summarizing this evaluation and will include joint strategies and specific agreements to outline tasks, overcome obstacles, and achieve specific goals."[94] All of this points to the necessity, from both legislative and executive perspectives, to specify the framework for the government-to-government relationship between tribes and the state; it also necessitates ongoing review and accountability within that framework. Without these elements, there is too much opportunity for the unbalancing forces of "prosecutorial" zeal, ineffective communication, and continued racism and misunderstanding.

Tribal communities must also realize that dialogue and negotiation with the state on legitimate issues is not a "sell-out" of tribal sovereignty but simply part of the contemporary political and legal struggle to achieve a tribal sovereignty that advances the flourishing of tribal life. It is here that there needs to be continuing political discussion within tribal communities and tribal councils to forge a wide-ranging and thoughtful tribal public policy on tribal-state relations, complete with specific goals, objectives, and attendant strategies.

EDUCATIONAL REFORM

Any effort to advance tribal-state relations in South Dakota and throughout the West needs the underpinning of substantial educational reform if it is to have any longevity and permanence. This is so because of the incredible ignorance that has taken root in the arid historical and political soil that permeates much of the region.[95]

This destructive ignorance finds emblematic articulation in the statement by the recent South Dakota Attorney General that "Indian reservations are a 'divisive system' of government that have outlived their usefulness."[96] This statement shows an astonishing failure on the part of the Attorney General to comprehend the treaty-based guarantees of a "measured separatism" to Indian tribes on reservations. The South Dakota Attorney General ought to know something about tribal sovereignty and its parity with state authority. Yet this reaction is typical. During the ten years I lived and worked on the Rosebud Sioux Reservation as a teacher and a lawyer, non-Indian people were genuinely surprised, if not astounded, that anyone, whether Indian or non-

Indian, would choose to live on the reservation. This reaction always puzzled me. Part of it is racism, but ultimately, I think, racism is only a small part of the response. The larger part of the reaction reflects the institutional and governmental victimization of citizens throughout most of the West.

This victimization has not been seriously questioned because most ordinary citizens do not even perceive that they have been victimized. As a result, governmental inertia or, even worse, governmental design in this area goes unchecked. This governmental silence also contributes to the continuing refusal throughout much of the region to confront the dismal history of tribal-state and Indian–non-Indian relations.

It *is* hard even for well-meaning people to understand life on the reservation when they do not know anything about it. Why don't people in South Dakota and throughout the West know anything about reservation life? The answer lies in the fact that state and local governments simply do not educate their citizens about reservations, treaties, and tribal governments. For example, it is still possible to be educated in South Dakota from kindergarten through college and *not* learn anything about tribes and reservations, including their permanent and enduring reality. It is not surprising that when many South Dakotans become adult citizens they do not have even the *baseline* concepts and understandings to bring to real tribal-state problems involving such issues as water, land, jurisdiction, and the environment. And without an informed citizenry, the political leadership of most states in the West is free to be equally uninformed and misdirected in its responses to these issues.

Beyond the absence of this foundational knowledge about treaties and the permanency of reservations and tribal governments lies something even more nefarious. Education determines what is authentic, meaningful, and legitimate; it is the touchstone for civic discourse and problem solving. Thus, the educational void that obscures tribes and reservations also sends the implicit message that tribal governments and reservations are not meaningful and legitimate, and therefore they cannot have problems and claims that merit the serious attention of fellow citizens.

This failing in regard to education about treaties and reservations is instructive in other ways. It reflects the inability in South Dakota and much of the West to identify the features that are unique to the region and that need to be preserved in order to mold a meaningful future. For example, if South Dakota values local and rural life as much as it claims, why are the young leaving in such terrific numbers? One reason may be that very little in their education, particularly at the university level, teaches students the value and challenge of rural life.

South Dakota and other states throughout the region can no longer blithely exploit their citizens by depriving them of the opportunity to learn about the enduring and important contributions of the tribes and the reservations to the state and region. Without such efforts, there can be little hope for the improvement of tribal-state relations in the West. There will only be a continued and inexcusable ignorance and an ugly educational apartheid.

DEVELOPMENT OF FORUMS

One of the principal problems of tribal-state relations is the absence of forums—both formal and informal—in which Indians and non-Indians and tribal and state officials come together to discuss important issues. Given this lack, the resulting gulf in communication is all too easily filled with pernicious gossip and relentless stereotypes.

This state of affairs needs to be eradicated, and various means are available to begin the process. Some of these means are implicit in what has been discussed above. The development of sovereignty accords, the adoption of thoughtful and explicit public policy, and the implementation of educational reforms will all go a long way to bridging the communications gap between the two sides. Yet other means are available and ought to be pursued. These include joint training for state and tribal employees who work in the same substantive areas, such as law enforcement, tax collection, and game management. In addition, state and tribal department heads and policymakers need to come together regularly to share their issues and concerns. Such changes would, of course, lead to improved communication on substantive matters;

perhaps more important, the people involved would learn to appreciate one another *as* people who share similar job challenges, rewards, and frustrations.

At the state level, specific and precise state legislation will probably be required to ensure this kind of cross-communication. In addition, such legislation might mandate the preparation of an annual report for legislative, executive, and public review that would evaluate, in some detail, the nature and quality of tribal-state relations for the year. Such reports, in turn, would provide an ongoing record with which to measure the accomplishments and direction of tribal-state relations.

Perhaps most startling in this area, at least in South Dakota, is that tribal-state relations and Indian issues in general play absolutely no role in the life of the Republican and Democratic parties within the state. Therefore, there is no discourse within the statewide political process about tribal-state relations, and this lack greatly aggravates and undermines the likelihood for tribal-state issues to be meaningfully addressed within the political and electoral context.

This absence of discussion also permits and even encourages political (and ethical) ignorance of issues that are pivotal to state and regional well-being. The major political parties need to develop thoughtful and meaningful "planks" within their respective parties, to make special efforts to reach out to Native Americans within the party system, and to increase their recruitment of Native Americans. And, in the spirit of interrelatedness, this process can be advanced, in part, by making the parties *responsive* to the very issues of tribal-state relations and Indian affairs they currently ignore. For example, for all the discussion in 1990 about reconciliation in South Dakota, neither the Democratic nor the Republican parties made tribal-state relations an issue in the statewide elections in 1990 or 1992. This process of change will not be easy, but it is absolutely necessary if there is to be any claim for a truly inclusive politics within South Dakota and much of the region. In fact, most recently, the state Democratic Party, in preparation for the 1994 elections, did adopt a platform supportive of tribes in matters of gaming and welfare reform.[97]

The notion of an inclusive politics and political discourse throughout the West on Indian affairs also raises the issue of regional (and mutual) discourse on these issues. Many of these questions, particularly in matters of water and natural resources, concern natural phenomena and ecological boundaries that transcend state and reservation boundaries. And while there is some regional state discourse (through, for example, the Western Conference of State Governors)[98] and some regional tribal discourse (through, for example, the Council of Energy and Resource Tribes [CERT]),[99] no concerted effort has been made to bring both sides together. Such an effort would seem to be an ideal project in the regional context—particularly, perhaps, with an emphasis on developing nonlitigative approaches to regional problem solving.

Nonlitigative strategies—particularly those that fall under the conceptual rubric of alternative dispute resolution (ADR)[100]— are playing a growing role in tribal-state relations. For example, the Western Network, an organization that facilitates environmental and tribal-state negotiations, recently helped form the National Association of Counties Task Force on Indian Affairs as a part of the National Association of Counties, the representative organization for all county governments throughout the United States.[101] One of the task force's key recommendations was the creation of a County/Tribal Mediation Model.[102]

Other instances of nonlitigative approaches include the individual state-tribal water compacts that have been negotiated between individual tribes and the states of Wyoming and Montana. In addition, tribal and state courts have undertaken new and noteworthy cooperative efforts:

> In response to growing concern over the lack of effective resolution of disputes between state and tribal courts over civil jurisdiction matters, the Conference of Chief Justices (CCJ) established a Committee on Civil Jurisdiction in Indian Country. The significance and complexity of these issues led the committee to recommend that the state judiciaries encourage tribal and state governments to cooperate in resolving jurisdictional problems at tribal, state, and local levels. Subsequently, CCJ endorsed a project, designed by the National Center for State Courts and later funded by the State Justice Institute, that would provide a research basis and model approaches to dispute resolution that tribal and state courts could use cooperatively to resolve disputes in constructive, nonlitigative ways. A 13-member coordinating council composed of state appellate justices, tribal court

judges, state trial court judges, federal judges, an Indian and non-Indian attorney, a state court administrator, and legal scholars and consultants guides the project.[103]

A national conference sponsored by both state and tribal court organizations, entitled "Civil Jurisdiction of Tribal and State Courts: From Conflict to Common Ground," was held in the summer of 1991; a follow-up conference, entitled "Building on Common Ground: A Leadership Conference to Develop a National Agenda to Reduce Jurisdictional Disputes Between Tribal, State, and Federal Courts," was held in the fall of 1993. It is also significant to note that in 1991 Chief Justice Robert Miller of the South Dakota Supreme Court organized a successful Tribal-State Judicial Conference. This landmark tribal-state cooperative judicial effort may develop the most promising model for mutual tribal-state problem solving.

Tribal-state relations have floundered conceptually, politically, and economically from the earliest days of this republic. Racism, competition for resources, and ignorance have all exacted tribute from any potential alliance against the real raptors from beyond the region who plunder the tribes and the states alike. Both the tribes and the states need to know that their greatest "enemies" come from commercial and exploitative interests outside the region.[104] Each side has to see, or at least explore, the potential for identifying *local* common ground on which to make a stand.

It is, of course, also true that manifold problems exist between tribes and states, but they are not intractable. In fact, these problems often grow and fester in the recesses of inattention and cultural and political ignorance. There are exciting and creative ways to move tribal-state relations forward. Yet there is also the concomitant need for mutual goodwill, the timely deployment of resources, and a leadership and citizenry who possess a vision committed to an ethical and flourishing future for all.

This process has already started;[105] let us continue it in a spirit of respect—with forthright, provocative, and civil exchange. Without talk and conversation, there is no hope for the future of tribal-state relations. Yet hope must encourage the energetic dialogue that animates and gives meaning to hope in the first instance.

CHAPTER SIX

Economic Development in Indian Country

Poverty in Indian country, particularly in South Dakota and throughout much of the West, continues to be substantial. Several reservation counties, such as Shannon County on the Pine Ridge Reservation, Buffalo County on the Crow Creek Reservation, Ziebach County on the Cheyenne River Reservation, and Todd County on the Rosebud Reservation, are among the poorest in the United States.[1] The per capita income for the eight largest tribes in South Dakota ranges from $2,166 to $2,801; all are well below the national poverty standard.[2] From 28.6 to 54.9 percent of these tribal populations are below the poverty line.[3] The number of individuals in these populations receiving some form of welfare assistance is exceptionally high.[4] Staggering unemployment is the norm, averaging 71 percent on Indian reservations within the state.[5]

The dilemma of economic development requires that the underlying questions be rigorously framed and analyzed. The issue of economic development must be approached through an incremental process of devising approximate answers to the "right" questions. There are no specific answers; rather, individuals and groups must make the best possible choices under circumstances involving some constraint and indeterminacy. This chapter seeks to elucidate some of the contours of the "right" questions by examining the context, goals, and strategies of development and the deeper concerns of culture and meaning.

In most scholarly writing on economic development in Indian country, broad generalizations are made with little sensitivity or attention to tribes' past experiences, except in noting their general lack of success. Most tribes are clearly underdeveloped by almost any definition,[6] and the usual ways suggested to overcome underdevelopment are agricultural development,[7] community economic development,[8] and escape from the shackles of the "colonizer-oppressor."[9] Such standard approaches place the issue of economic development in a tidy framework that misrepresents the reality the authors seek to address. This initial misunderstanding of the economic situation fatally distorts any future development project, often in a manner that directly leads to failure. These standard approaches are beneficial only when they are employed with a proper understanding of the particular tribal and reservation context in which they are to apply.

The emphasis on tribal context is rooted in an "inside-out" policy analysis framework. The development problem is too often treated as a material entity, part of "a well structured world of unambiguous objectives, mutually exclusive choice, authoritative decision making and willing decision endurers."[10] Actually, a more intractable reality "involves a staggering variety of people and organizations, all pulling, pushing and otherwise interacting with each other in pursuit of their various interests."[11] The first task, then, is to turn this "mess" into a problem about which something constructive can be done. This is not easy, but it is fundamental.

It may be possible to untangle such "messes" by focusing on the tribal context of the people, their interactions, and the institutional settings in which these interactions take place. Considerable emphasis must be placed on the various entities, including political groups, families, and community organizations, that mediate these interactions. Development efforts do not proceed with a clean slate. The ongoing social reality permeates the design of any development effort because development policies "are not designed but redesigned as modifications of existing policies which in turn provide foundations for policies that will follow."[12]

Past experience is therefore one element that must be closely examined. We cannot learn from past experiences, both successes and failures, until they are diagnosed and understood. This diagnosis is not always readily apparent. What went wrong with past development efforts? On the Rosebud Sioux Reservation, for example, what actually caused the demise of Rosebud Electronics, Lakota Products, and the Sicangu Arts and Crafts Cooperative? What caused the persistent failures of the Rosebud Sioux Tribal Ranch? Were there failures of program design, capital resources, management expertise, marketing, or employee motivation? What about the forces of political divisiveness, social upheaval, and unfavorable macroeconomic trends? Successes need the same scrutiny. Why did something go right? In much of Indian country, data from the past are extremely limited, but retrospective efforts will nevertheless be quite useful. These initial forays may be primitive methodologically, but close examination of the evidence may yield valuable insights.

The past not only informs the social reality that influences the making of development policy but also affects individuals. Past experience with development projects often shapes personal commitment. For example, any reservation-based employment training project in South Dakota must consider that during the past decade many eligible individuals will have been through three or four similar programs, such as the federal Comprehensive Employment and Training Act (CETA),[13] BIA Employment Assistance,[14] Community Action Program (CAP) Employment Training,[15] and South Dakota State Vocational and Technical Training.[16] As the ever-increasing unemployment rates on reservations confirm, these projects all failed because they provided good skills training but no permanent employment or, in the case of CETA, temporary jobs with no training. The end result is the same: when the program is over, the individual is still unemployed. Such experience often withers both personal enthusiasm and the work ethic. These problems must be taken into account. They are not insurmountable, but if ignored they invite the likelihood of future project failures.

Raking the coals of the past is central to any competent problem analysis. "The goal is to extract from past experience some enlightening perspectives from which to redesign [rural] development. By better understanding past experience, we hope better to profit from its successes and better to avoid its mistakes." [17] Retrospection alone, however, is perilous; it does not carry us forward with sufficient vision. It needs the complement of a conceptual framework for evaluating the long-term consequences of present actions, often referred to by business managers as "assessing the futurity." Of the small number of initially successful development projects, too many fail because this conceptual analysis is missing. Many good projects end because they cannot be sustained. Their resources, including human and financial capital, are not properly integrated into the development equation and are often exhausted without possibility of replacement or renewal. "The assessment of futurities is an exercise in identifying option generating and option foreclosing actions, in articulating major tradeoffs and complementarities, and generally, in appreciating some of the long term implications inherent in policy choice." [18] It is a process which seeks to thrust the lessons of the past into the future.

A strategic analysis for development also requires a method of weighing the nature and quality of present conditions for economic development in the tribal context. Such investigation and evaluation need not entail cumbersome longitudinal research. There are very real limits on the usefulness of any analysis; beyond those limits lie impotence and needless abstraction. The analysis must be, in economic parlance, "optimal," arraying time and resources in their most productive fashion given the existing constraints. The goal is fruitful action, not analytic nicety. Therefore, the most erudite or precise approach is not necessarily the best.

A reliable guideline here is simplicity. "In place of spurious pretense of comprehensive authority, we have found that analysis benefits from being 'as ruthlessly parsimonious and economical as possible while still retaining responsiveness to the management objectives and actions appropriate to the problem.' " [19] The experts serve the analysis and not vice versa. The product is a set of reliable questions whose answers form an agenda for action.

We focus first on the most intensely felt needs of the policy endurers: What is wrong with the present situation? What specific evils are most in need of mitigation? What aspects of past policies require correction? We next turn to the specific actions or interventions which policy makers and implementors believe to be potentially feasible and desirable: What actually might be done? What resources are available? What political coalitions are needed and possible? Finally, we proceed to mobilize the small subset of expert knowledge or experience which is necessary to establish relationships between the implementors' action and the endurers' needs. To be sure, things are left out of such an analysis. Optimal prescriptions are not even aspired to; the modest hope is to find something merely better; with luck and cunning, the exercise has been known to produce insights and progress.[20]

The goal is not to eliminate uncertainty but to contain and accommodate it more successfully. "In practical terms, this means using the best analysis and knowledge that we can muster to help policy makers to see a little further ahead, to comprehend a few more interactions, and to avoid some of the truly disastrous and irreversible mistakes to which development is prone."[21] The goal is to minimize error and to maximize successful adaptation: to move forward to reduce the ravages of poverty and stasis.

WHAT ARE THE GOALS OF DEVELOPMENT?

The goals of development often appear self-evident, even facile. Development means economic growth, more jobs, a better standard of living. Yet the empirical results, particularly from the developing nations, are dismaying. Economic growth in certain segments of a society may actually increase income disparities and further depress the income of the poorest class: ironically, economic growth may eliminate jobs for the poor.[22] Significant economic growth, particularly in rural areas, often simply does not occur.[23] Many developing countries have had painful experiences with development. As a result, there has been a substantial revision of development policy.

The most consistent articulation of this rethinking emphasizes four objectives: (1) creating self-sustaining, cumulative economic growth; (2) expanding employment; (3) reducing poverty; and (4) slowing population growth. These objectives are often dislodged in practice by competing interests with more political clout or by macroeconomic forces that are too pervasive and too powerful for localized projects to overcome. Therefore, in many cases these four goals are unrealized. Nevertheless, they suggest a clear standard by which to measure comparable efforts in Indian country.

The development literature about Indian country is not extensive. The most comprehensive economic development manual flatly asserts that "tribes have found it difficult deciding where to start and how to proceed in developing their economies. They have no appropriate economic development theories or practical guides that tribal leaders have found helpful."[24] The authors conclude that

> tribes can wait no longer for private initiative to play the pivotal role in reservation economic development. Tribal leadership must take the initiative. It must institute central economic planning at the tribal level which spells out a logical sequence of direct interventions designed to stimulate and support income and job generating activities on the reservation. Tribes must manage and nurture growth on their own reservations, by combining public sector and private sector involvement.[25]

A central issue, then, is who is to be the prime beneficiary of economic activity on reservations—the tribes or the individual tribal members? This question has important implications. In most instances, especially in South Dakota, tribal governments themselves are greatly impoverished. They have no independent revenues except from minor tribal ventures and, in the case of the Rosebud Sioux Tribe, the Oglala Sioux Tribe, and the Cheyenne River Sioux Tribe, a joint sales tax administered and shared with the state.[26] These revenues are only a small part of the tribes' budget funds, which are almost totally derived from federal grants and BIA allocations.[27] These funds are "soft" because they rest on largely discretionary decisions made by Congress and the federal bureaucracy and are therefore almost totally unreviewable. The tribes are also greatly restricted in how they may spend this money.[28] As a result, the tribes possess little disposable income and an even smaller say over how it is disbursed. Therefore, many argue that development must focus on the tribes. They further argue that as the tribes develop new revenue, they will be able to invest this income in other employment and income-generating ventures on the reservations. Given that no South Dakota tribe has any broad taxing schemes in place, increased employment alone will not do much to increase tribal revenues.

Supporters of this approach often add that economic development must focus on the tribes because the tribes, despite their penurious state, are the primary and perhaps the sole entities capable of generating substantial income-producing activity on the reservations.[29] The tribes control so many of the development variables that they must be the principal agents or catalysts in the development process. They also greatly shape the institutional settings and structural prerequisites of development. This is especially true in the burgeoning activity involving tribal gaming operations.

Others contend that the tribes themselves hinder any meaningful advance, and therefore development must occur outside the tribes' direct purview or influence. Tribal impediments to progress include jurisdictional uncertainty, instability of and interference in tribal government, underdeveloped support institutions, and an ethos of nepotism. Private and traditional efforts must therefore predominate. Yet clearly, with rare exceptions, the tribe cannot be completely shut out of the development process.

It is instructive to sort out the tribe's possible roles. These roles are essentially threefold: (1) the tribe as the principal actor in development efforts; (2) the tribe as catalyst or supporter of private efforts; and (3) the tribe as the regulator and monitor of a positive development environment. These roles are not necessarily mutually exclusive, but they do represent discrete lines of inquiry. What are some of the major features necessary for development to occur? They include social and physical infrastructure, economic institutions, productive or trainable labor, reliable and enforceable "rules of the game," and access to capital. Two of these, infrastructure and the "rules of the game," are completely within the areas of tribal authority and responsibility. The others are less so and often constitute the heart of private endeavor.

At a minimum, any meaningful development attempt must have tribal support to provide the physical infrastructure, such as roads, water, and energy supplies. This is not a serious problem on the reservations in South Dakota and throughout much of the West. The question of administrative infrastructure is more troublesome. Most tribes do not possess either the personnel or the institutional expertise to discharge the complex administrative functions that accompany technically complicated development projects. Also, they often lack the sophisticated legal apparatus necessary to decide and to enforce complex commercial transactions.[30] This shortcoming is frequently exacerbated by (federal) jurisdictional uncertainty over what the tribes' actual powers are. Administrative inefficiency is a delicate problem, but one that must be faced. Tribes must honestly confront their present shortcomings and develop accordingly, most likely in incremental fashion. Many tribes are increasingly improving their competency and efficiency in these areas.

Although it is easy to make sweeping pronouncements about what tribal governments must do to aid development, it is largely ineffective and pointless to do so. Blanket pronouncements have been made, but most are arrogant and utopian:

> Tribal business entities cannot be anything other than profit oriented organizations designed to further tribal economic goals. . . . Tribal codes must be revised to assure tribal courts jurisdiction over claims of non-member persons and entities, to assure competent professionalism in adjudication of commercial claims and to provide a range of remedies appropriate for enactment of judgments obtained in tribal courts, including means of appeal, garnishment, attachment, foreclosure sale, and the like.[31]

Such imperatives are very costly and require substantial institution building, personnel training, and political commitment. To think that such a transformation, although urged by an expert, is possible within less than a decade or two ignores tribal history, culture, and politics. Tribes must undertake to achieve what they are capable of, not the utopia imagined by experts. The experience of developing countries is instructive:

> A long standing complaint in developing countries has been the relative ease of getting "good" policy advice, but the subsequent difficulties in implementing the recommended policies. Separating policy analysis in this way from policy implementation is simply wrong. Policy analysis must evaluate the capacity to implement and manage the policy on a daily basis.[32]

Outside experts have a role, but only when they have their feet planted firmly on the ground and understand that development must begin from where the tribes currently are. The experts must be committed to the hard slog to make things work without recourse to mere theorizing.

When the tribe becomes involved in development projects, other considerations arise besides the normal ones of raising capital, gaining managerial expertise, and establishing sustainability. Other issues bedevil tribal development—for instance, political considerations in hiring, maximizing employment opportunities, and dealing with the inadequate segregation of governmental and proprietary functions. Tribes are under terrific pressure to alleviate unemployment. As a result, they often emphasize maximizing employment without sufficient concern for profitability and sustainability. This pressure is intensified because development projects present one of the few opportunities for political patronage and compliance with the cultural pattern of hiring members of one's extended family (or *tiyospaye*). Dealing with these forces mandates a careful analysis of tribal development efforts. Such problems are not grounds for writing off tribal projects as unworkable from the start, but when they occur, they must be adequately addressed to ensure success. For example, it is by no means impossible to design tribal development projects that seek to achieve optimal employment levels in accordance with economic principles of profitability and sustainability.[33] It is also possible, as many tribes have done, to adopt hiring and selection criteria that minimize nepotism.

Many tribal governments in the West, particularly in South Dakota, have only recently (that is, within the last twenty years) become directly involved in economic development. Therefore, they often lack experience in distinguishing their governmental from their proprietary functions. The blurring of this distinction often causes the tribe, acting in its governmental capacity, to intervene directly in and even legislatively terminate a particular project without understanding that the business venture is proprietary and must be regulated independently of direct control by the governing body. For those tribes that function with constitutions and corporate charters adopted pursuant to the Indian Reorganization Act,[34] a more exacting use and understanding of the function of these documents and processes would be extremely beneficial.

The tribe itself is the primary entity that determines the environment for development on the reservation. In this respect, the tribe must strive to reduce uncertainty about the laws that business ventures will encounter in tribal court and to guarantee that these ventures will be insulated from direct political interference. This is true for both tribally and nontribally controlled efforts. Tribes are also in a position to develop, as a matter of public policy, a program of incentives that would secure the willingness of indigenous and outside entities to engage in development efforts on the reservation. Such incentives could include technical assistance, tax advantages, abundant labor, a nonunionized workplace, and the opportunity to advance the aspirations of Native Americans. Note, however, that with the exception of the first and last items, the incentive package is identical to the aggressively and successfully marketed package of the state of South Dakota.[35] Development is, ultimately, competition over scarce resources, and tribes must carefully analyze where their competitive edge might lie.

The role of the tribe in development is, finally, a question of public policy. The tribe must identify the role that it regards as most fruitful in furthering development objectives and that accords with its current resources and capabilities. The discussion above suggests the range of options and a framework for evaluating their feasibility in a particular context. Everyone yearns for the moon; a deeper, more restrained wisdom settles on attainable but worthwhile goals. Having considered the possible roles of tribal government in the development process, we must address the overriding question: What are the specific objectives of development on the reservation? These objectives are most simply identified in the word "jobs." This is not surprising given the devastating unemployment that exists on many reservations. Yet such a narrow and often unexamined attitude is nearsighted. Reducing rampant unemployment must be a cornerstone concern, but ironically, a blind commitment to jobs alone will not significantly alter unemployment rates, especially in the long run. Attacking unemployment takes more than (short-lived) jobs.

Other underlying elements, such as the sustainability of the proposed venture, the wage and skill structure of the new jobs, and the nature of the unemployed population must be examined in order to gauge the true impact of any proposed project. The CETA program is a textbook example. It purported to be a comprehensive employment training program designed to help individuals already in the workforce to upgrade their skills and enhance their employability. This approach assumed that jobs were available and that the only thing many individuals needed was training. Yet on most reservations, particularly in South Dakota and throughout the West, this was not and is not the case. Jobs do not exist on the reservations, and "training" people makes no real sense unless the program also *creates* jobs. Job training per se cannot significantly reduce unemployment on the reservation.

The creation of new employment opportunities requires new economic endeavors and economic growth. These economic endeavors, however, must be sustainable; that is, they must reasonably address economic opportunity in such a way that they fulfill continuing needs and are completely and permanently integrated into the economy. For example, a local company starts up or an outside company is willing to locate on the reservation because it has a contract with the tribe to build forty houses and to employ qualified local people. What is the likelihood that the company will stay in business on the reservation after it completes the contract? Is there enough construction activity on or near the reservation so that the company can be competitive and continue to perform its services? If not, the opportunity will be a one-shot deal; it should not be rejected or scorned simply for that reason, but it should not be confused with true economic development.

The creation of jobs also raises questions about the wage and skill levels of the new jobs. Are the required skills, whether entry level or advanced, within the reach of an appropriate number of the unemployed? Is the proposed wage and wage structure sufficient incentive to attract enough qualified workers? In economic terms, what do the supply and demand curves and resulting equilibrium wage look like?

To create or to attract economic activity on the reservation, it is necessary to have an idea of the characteristics of the unemployed. It is not sufficient to know only that there are a lot of them. What are their characteristics in terms of gender, age, education, job experience, and job skills? What employment opportunities are best suited for this particular group or any subgroup of individuals? What cultural attitudes, if any, might affect receptivity or adaptability to particular kinds of employment? As a general rule, there is very little particularized information that describes these characteristics among the unemployed on the reservations. Such research, undertaken by the tribes or the community colleges on reservations, would greatly enhance the possibilities both of attracting development projects and of improving their chances for success. The tribe would be in a better position to identify opportunities that match the potential workforce: the better the "match," the more likely the success.

Development literature from the Third World places great emphasis on these issues. Development must involve substantial economic growth and a steadily increasing number of jobs. However, the issue of jobs, particularly in the rural countryside, is more easily focused on traditional agricultural pursuits and other off-farm employment. There is also concern about the often complex interrelationship between economic growth, employment, and the alleviation of poverty. Both economic growth and employment can yield skewed results that ultimately do little to eradicate poverty.[36] The benefits of development, even where tightly structured, are often captured by local elites,[37] are not equitably distributed, or are otherwise misallocated. As a result, employment opportunities go to those who are already marginally employed or to those who are in favor with the local power structure. The poorest of the poor, mostly women and other minorities, are ignored.

These factors point to the necessity of reviewing the nature and incidence of poverty on the reservation not in terms of raw numbers, which are readily available, but in terms of gender, blood quantum, and rural or town residence. Such a review will

ensure that development efforts do not leave out significant segments of the population. These choices are not easy to make, and
they raise questions of great moral and pragmatic difficulty: Who
should be helped and why? The answers are not always certain,
but the imperative to confront these disturbing questions is unavoidable.

The final element drawn from the Third World comparison is
that of population. Such discussions are often fraught with racial
and cultural biases. Experts who proclaim the necessity of sharp
reversals in personal, cultural, and philosophical beliefs are both
insensitive and ethnocentric. In the reservation context, population questions are seldom asked; the most relevant would seem
to be, What level of development will sustain current and future
generations in accordance with their material and cultural needs?

The braid of development has many strands: the rich interweaving of sustainable economic growth, increased numbers of
jobs, alleviation of poverty, and concern for population suggests
an innovative design that only the tribes and Indian people can
refine and complete.

WHAT IS THE STRATEGY OF DEVELOPMENT?

The capstone issue is, of course, how to identify the most effective strategy to achieve the goals of development once these goals
are clearly articulated and understood. It is not enough to assume
that laudable goals automatically lead to successful implementation. The rigorous formulation of goals is a necessary but not
sufficient condition for development to occur. There is no single,
magic strategy to pull the silver lining from the black clouds.
Nevertheless, there are some broad questions to examine in order
to devise the best possible strategy under a given set of conditions
and constraints.

Effective development requires efficient organizations capable
of performing the core tasks of choosing, allocating, motivating,
and linking all aspects of analysis and planning. The most accurate view of the process comes from the field of policy analysis,
which holds that an effective organization does not spring full-
blown from the brows of policymakers or analysts. Rather, it is

an organic entity, growing and developing over time. The development of an organization involves the obvious growth in infrastructure and administrative skills plus a less evident change in cultural values and expectations. The result is a complex, dynamic system of linkages which is only partially understood at any given time by the people it unites.[38] This overarching claim requires close analysis to determine its effective application within the development equation. The number of important variables that might be extracted from such an equation is quite large. This analysis chooses the following as most important: organization of the poor, attractiveness of benefits, harmony of objectives, and simplicity of means.[39]

Development schemes have traditionally been imposed on the poor, and the results have been negligible. There is no single creed of how to work with the poor, but there are some salient reminders of what not to do. The poor are not idly waiting to be organized; they are already organized, however imperfectly. No ideology about top-down or bottom-up approaches is particularly helpful. The key lies in greater sensitivity to the ongoing social realities in which the poor operate.

> Efforts to organize the rural poor are in reality efforts to reorganize, to create new patterns of linkage different from the old ones that already bind them. Effective policies for reorganization begin with a recognition of what the existing linkages are, and how they affect the well being of the poor.[40]

This observation is almost self-evident, but it is seldom followed in practice, particularly in the reservation setting. The ties of the poor are primarily personal and to family, *tiyospaye,* and community; the poor are often only very obliquely attached to the formal structure of the tribe itself. These more personal ties, which are the source of aid, protection, support, and reciprocity, are quite different from ties to contemporary organizations where the primary bond is based on common interests in specific goals. As noted in discussions of the developing world, interest group organization "involves different kinds of action, for different purposes, by people in different relationships with each other, from the kinds of action, purpose, and relationship enshrined in traditional cooperative society."[41] The poor are also too often characterized as "The People," although they actually have different and competing social and economic interests and personal loyalties. A primary task of the planner is to design local organizations that link rural people with one another and with the larger social system; the planner must also design support organizations to help them in their problem-solving efforts.[42]

The goal of organization is clear: to secure the necessary involvement and participation of the poor. The final question then becomes, Under what circumstances will there be the most productive participation? The most viable approach integrates three crucial variables: attractiveness of benefits, harmony of objectives, and simplicity of means. This integration depends on viewing the poor and unemployed as investors. Time, energy, and freedom from certain obligations are the resources the poor possess. The poor must be understood as rational decision makers: they invest their participation when they believe that doing so will secure them valuable benefits not otherwise available at comparable cost, time, and risk.[43]

In Indian country, the most deeply felt need is that of employment. There is little doubt about this desire, yet it should never be assumed in advance, and it must be identified anew in each situation. This need must become the basis for concerted action. In the employment area, the attractiveness of the jobs in terms of salary, skill level, permanency, working conditions, and meaningfulness will all strongly color the amount and quality of local participation.[44] It is also important to emphasize that reservation residents will perceive the attractiveness of a job opportunity not from an objective top-down view but from a more subjective (but not irrational) inside-out view. For example, the attractiveness of accepting some part-time employment is often overcome by the perception that such participation will result in the automatic loss of other benefits, such as welfare, Social Security, or Supplemental Security Income (SSI)[45] payments. Where this is true, either the law or the approach must be changed. The organizational goal must be to minimize the perception of risk and to maximize the perception of tangible rewards.

The concept of the harmony of objectives is deceptively simple. This is especially true on the reservation. Jobs are the primary objective, and there would not seem to be any potentially conflicting objectives. Yet in any condition of scarcity, the decision to do one thing means a decision *not* to do another thing. For example, what kind of job opportunities should be pursued, and should they be pursued at the expense of human services programs designed to treat health and social issues?[46] In addition, there is potential conflict in the design and promulgation of selection criteria for employment, unless they are fair and are equitably administered. What are the selection criteria to be, especially when the jobs do not have great skill requirements? How should age, gender, degree of poverty, blood quantum, and residence affect hiring? Should jobs be offered on a first-come, first-served basis? By lottery? Without equity and harmony in this area, the best-designed project could end in wrangling and bitter strife among the most needy.

The third element involves the simplicity of means. This simplicity focuses on the nature of the rules, structure, and pattern of decision making within the organization. It requires program designers to use a combination of techniques that match effectively with the size, communality, and other requirements of a particular local situation.[47] The organizational structure must have the best possible fit to existing social contours. The "fit" is more a matter of art than of science, more craft than computer. Simplicity is not always easy to attain, but it is a vital component of any successful strategy. Far too many worthwhile projects have been crushed under the weight of extensive but probably unnecessary bureaucratic paperwork and regulatory record-keeping.

Strategy must be a function of goals and circumstances—a problem-solving plan that grows organically from the people and their aspirations, their resources and limitations. No methodology or superstructure should be imported whole. Many organizational structures are available to tribes, groups, and individuals, including the appropriate legal structures ranging from joint ventures to nonprofit cooperatives. The key to implementing the proper structure is to creatively merge any generalized approach into a specific tribal context.

A necessary element of any successful strategy, beyond immediate goals such as generating income and employment, is the extension of individual and group capacity, thereby reducing dependency and advancing autonomy and self-determination.[48] For example, in order to increase tribal management and technical capabilities, tribes should not lease tribal natural resources or accept sweeping personal services contracts that do not permit the tribe to participate actively in the venture.

On most reservations information about the diverse development strategies devised and implemented by indigenous people around the world is simply not available. As a result, a deep sense of isolation often exists. Development efforts might therefore aim to increase the international exchange of development ideas and strategies, both new and old. For example, what are the rural people of Tanzania and the small business entrepreneurs of Taiwan doing to improve their situations, and how might these efforts relate to Indian country? What are the communal, culturally intact Hutterite communities of South Dakota doing? This kind of project would not be expensive and could be easily undertaken by community colleges or other educational institutions on the reservations.

Strategy is the final step in the development process, not the entire process. The focus here is on developing strategy once the material prerequisites for development have been achieved and the analysis of tribal conditions and goals is completed. Strategy is both an end and a beginning. Attempts to change *what* things are done must be accompanied by changes in *how* things are done.[49]

There is also a final cautionary note. One might conclude that development efforts are intended to replace or supersede social welfare programs and the consumption (as opposed to production) of human services. This is not the case. These programs, which include various health, nutrition, and social services activities, are a valuable, necessary complement to development efforts. They provide some jobs but, more important, they seek to advance the well-being of individuals. By improving the health and nutrition standards of tribal members, these programs increase individual ability to participate in the development process.

One of the most pernicious effects of poverty is that it debilitates some individuals physically and psychologically to such a degree that they are effectively foreclosed from participating in development efforts. Human services programs are a vital adjunct to economic development in limiting this debilitation and in ensuring that everyone has the opportunity to participate. Given the endemic shortage of resources, financial and otherwise, the challenge is to strike a balance between the mutually supportive and reinforcing efforts that involve both consumption and production programs.

INDIAN GAMING: A DEVELOPMENT CASE STUDY

In recent years, Indian gaming has become the single most powerful economic force in Indian country. It has generated significant income for many tribes, accentuated tribal-state tensions and interdependence, and posed new issues concerning wealth and power among the tribes themselves. All of this rapid development commenced with the U.S. Supreme Court's 1987 decision in *California v. Cabazon Band of Mission Indians.*[50]

In that case, the state of California attempted to prohibit the Cabazon Band of Mission Indians from holding high-stakes bingo and card games on the reservation. California claimed that since it was a Public Law 280[51] state and such activity was not generally legal elsewhere in the state, the tribes were bound by the state's general criminal prohibition. The Court disagreed, noting that California's ban on bingo was not absolute because the state permitted charitable and other organizations throughout the state to engage in bingo and certain other card games. Therefore, the state's statutory scheme was more "civil/regulatory" than "criminal/prohibitory" and therefore not subject to the jurisdictional strictures of Public Law 280. The Court also found "compelling federal and tribal interests" as an independent bar to state or local regulation of tribal gaming.[52]

In the aftermath of *Cabazon*, many states, particularly in the West, pressed Congress to exercise its (plenary) authority to regulate gaming in Indian country. The states claimed that such regulation was needed to avoid the specter of alleged tribal incompetence and the infiltration of organized crime on to many reservations (or, more likely, the loss of real or imagined local and state income). Many tribes, fearing even more draconian measures, supported the compromise legislation known as the Indian Gaming Regulatory Act (IGRA) of 1988.[53]

The statute created the National Indian Gaming Commission to monitor the implementation of and to supervise performance of gaming activities on the reservation. The statute also classifies gaming activities into three categories. Class I gaming includes social games for prizes of minimal value or traditional forms of Indian gaming engaged in as part of Indian ceremonies and celebrations; Class II includes all forms of bingo played for prizes and card games (excluding banking card games such as blackjack) played in conformity with state law; and Class III includes all other forms of gaming.

To undertake Class III activities, which are clearly the most lucrative, tribes have to enter into an appropriate compact with the state in which they are located, and the Class III activities have to be legal under both tribal *and* state law. These compacts must cover such items as the location of the gambling establishment, the types of gambling (and the number of devices, etc.) permitted, and matters of jurisdiction. The states are required to negotiate in good faith, and federal courts have jurisdiction to resolve disputes involving the requirements of the statute.

Not surprisingly, litigation has ensued. Although no case has yet reached the U.S. Supreme Court, the main issues have surfaced in the lower federal courts. Some states have claimed that the statute is unconstitutional under the Tenth Amendment,[54] while other states have claimed that they are immune from suit under the Eleventh Amendment.[55] These claims are usually asserted by the state when they have been sued by the tribes for such things as failure to negotiate in good faith or otherwise comply with the statute. The results to date are mixed.[56]

Economically, Indian gaming has been tremendously successful. More than one hundred and fifty tribes have entered into
gaming compacts with individual states and are actively engaged
in gaming activities; all nine tribes in South Dakota have entered
into such compacts. For the year 1993, it is estimated that Indian
gaming nationally grossed more than one billion dollars for
tribes.

This gaming revenue has enriched many tribal treasuries and
created more employment for tribal members than any other economic endeavor on most reservations. Yet as with any success, a
new crop of questions has been raised. Is gaming revenue only a
short-term solution to economic deprivation in Indian country?
Is market saturation inevitable? For example, can a small rural
state like South Dakota support gambling casinos on all nine reservations? What kinds of economic diversification, if any, are
tribes pursuing? What management training exists to ensure that
local people not only obtain entry-level employment but also
have opportunities for advancement to managerial positions?
Tribes *are* cognizant of these issues, and many have thoughtfully
developed (or are developing) plans to diversify their economy
and upgrade opportunities for their casino employees. For example, Marge Anderson, Chief Executive of the Mille Lacs Band of
Ojibwe, said, "Every cent of Indian gaming revenue goes right
back into services for tribal people. Two years ago," she continued, "unemployment for my 2,400 member tribe in Minnesota
was 45 percent and is now zero." [57]

Tribes are also finding that their success has sometimes given
them additional political clout within their states; in Minnesota,
for instance, they actively support and financially contribute to
state and federal candidates. In addition, Indian gaming is estimated to be the seventh-largest industry in Minnesota, creating
more than ten thousand jobs directly and twenty thousand indi-
rectly, according to a recent study by the Minnesota Indian Gaming Association.[58] Yet in other states, such as South Dakota,
tribes are whiplashed by success. They have often been criticized
by the state (and its non-Indian citizens) for their past economic
failures; now they are criticized for their success, as it is often

perceived to pose a threat to the state's own fragile gambling activities. Tribes often cannot win for losing.

Even at the national level, the Las Vegas gambling establishment and the Atlantic City impresario Donald Trump are critical of Indian gaming. Some claim that it encourages organized crime—something the Las Vegas gambling establishment should know something about! Mr. Trump, in his lawsuit against the federal government, alleges that Indian gambling establishments have an "unfair" advantage since they are free from the state regulations with which his establishments must comply.

As a recent editorial suggests:

> Indian casinos are a desperate remedy for a desperate situation [i.e., extensive poverty and high unemployment]. They well may be a flash in the pan, an unwise bargain with the devil. But that's a judgment for the tribes themselves to make. It's not a decision non-Indians should make for them—especially not the very state governments that are in direct competition with the tribe for gambling customers. . . .
>
> But to argue that Indians—having shown they can be spectacularly successful at a home-grown enterprise given the chance—have to be protected from their own success is just more of the same, tired old paternalism.[59]

This backlash has resulted in growing pressure on Congress to amend the IGRA of 1988. The proposed amendments seek to prohibit tribes from locating gaming establishments on trust land *off* the reservation (often the most lucrative sites) and to limit the range of Indian gaming to activities authorized and engaged in by private gaming establishments rather than those engaged in by the state itself. This second proposal is specifically designed to limit tribes to activities that are less lucrative and pose no (potential) economic competition to the states. The fate of such amendments will undoubtedly color the future economic potential of Indian gaming. The colonized are almost always overtly encouraged to succeed and pull their own weight, but there is often a covert subtext not to do it too well for fear they will undermine the privileged economic status of the colonizer. And such are the mixed messages one often hears in the context of discussions about Indian gaming.

Indian gaming has also created potential disparities within the national tribal community itself. The tribes that have been most successful economically, such as the Shakopee Mdewekantan in Minnesota and the Mashantucket Pequot Tribe in Connecticut, have tended to be smaller (sometimes recently recognized) tribes scattered in the Midwest or the East, while the larger tribes, such as the Navajo and the Oglala Sioux, still have little or nothing to show. The locations of these and other tribes in the most rural, and in some cases the most politically intransigent, areas of the West may prove problematical. It also remains to be seen whether the newfound wealth of some tribes will be a source of greater intertribal cooperation—whether it will bring more unity or less.

Some people have referred to the boom in Indian gaming as "the new buffalo economy." With gross revenues for 1993 approaching one billion dollars or more, such claims are not extravagant and yet it remains true that the precentage of Indian families in poverty grew from 30.0 percent in 1979 to 47.3 percent in 1989. The question remains how long the bonanza can last and what its legacy will be.[60]

DEVELOPMENT, CULTURE, AND MEANING: THE DEEPER QUESTIONS

No discussion on the matter of economic development is complete without a review of the deeper questions about the nature of exchange and the moral foundations of development and economic activity. Economic development of Indian country is often characterized as a necessity, with little attention paid to the implications for personal and cultural meaning.

Development activity is almost always completely premised on the assumed value of economic growth, increased income, and the cash nexus. Increased income augments purchasing power and the ability to get the material things one needs for oneself and one's family. This adds to the material well-being of both the individual and the community. Yet this kind of commodity exchange is not inevitable or exclusive, notwithstanding the overriding presumption to the contrary. It is this very presumption that disturbs many people in Indian country because it seems to mean a further walk down that non-Indian road that leads to assimilation and "civilization." In other words, to many Indians development is the road to cultural ruin.

Traditional Western ideas of economic transfer recognize that an exchange may create some kind of bond between the persons involved. Yet commodity exchange creates the most meager of connections. Traditional societies throughout the world have seen exchange in a much broader context, a context in which things are not bought and sold but are given as gifts according to special rules.[61] Bestowing these gifts creates not only economic bonds but also bonds of a psychological, social, and spiritual nature:

> If we take the synthetic power of gifts, which establish and maintain the bonds of affection between friends, lovers, and comrades, and if we add to these a circulation wider than a binary give-and-take, we shall soon derive society, or at least those societies—family, guild, fraternity, sorority, band, community—that cohere through faithfulness and gratitude. While gifts are marked by motion and momentum at the level of the individual, gift exchange at the level of the group offers equilibrium and coherence, a kind of anarchist stability. We can also say, to put the point conversely, that in a group that derives its cohesion from a circulation of gifts the conversion of gifts to commodities will have the effect of fragmenting the group, or even destroying it.[62]

This system, or the remnants thereof, offers cause to reflect on the nature of exchange implicit in economic development theories.

> Many tribal groups circulate a large portion of their material wealth as gifts. Tribesmen are typically enjoined from buying and selling food, for example; even though there may be a strong sense of "mine and thine," food is always given as a gift and the transaction is governed by the ethics of gift exchange, not those of barter or cash purchase. Not surprisingly, people live differently who treat a portion of their wealth as a gift. To begin with, unlike the sale of a commodity, the giving of a gift tends to establish a relationship between the parties involved. Furthermore, when gifts circulate within a group, their commerce leaves a series of interconnected relationships in its wake, and a kind of decentralized cohesion emerges.[63]

This model of exchange is relevant in Indian country, at least on the reservations in South Dakota and throughout the West.

Sharing of food characterizes all important events, such as traditional ceremonies, wakes, namings, powwows, and even visits of
an Indian law class to tribal court.[64]

This kind of exchange is further amplified by the traditional
Lakota "giveaway," which celebrates or commemorates births,
marriages, graduations, namings, and deaths by the distribution
of gifts such as horses, quilts, blankets, pots and pans, footlock-
ers, and tobacco to all present. The giveaway creates bonds that
are traceable to both exterior and invisible economies of the community and spirit.

The giveaway reflects a desire for cooperation and sharing to
permeate the economic sphere. Although it may not achieve this
goal completely on the reservation, its practice is more than mere
nostalgia. It illustrates a profound ambivalence about the ethos
of economic development that values only production and acqui-
sition. There is something significant to be said for both material-
istic and intangible economic systems. Planners will find no easy
answer to this dilemma, but it is important to acknowledge the
possibility of economic development that takes gift giving or
some variation of it as part of its model.

Such a development model must encounter the harsh realities
of poverty and dependence, but the exchange of complementary
efforts should enhance the chances for cross-fertilization and success in economic progress. Development need not proceed along
a monocultural path. So little is known about what actually
works in development that a well-conceived plan that draws on
the best of the old and the new, the indigenous and the imported,
offers the greatest chance for advancement and accomplishment.

Development discussions are often couched in technical jargon
from the fields of politics, economics, and technology, a jargon
that seems detached from the day-to-day lives of the people who
are to benefit. Development emphasizes economic growth and
income enhancement as worthy means to defeat poverty. If life
were that simple, it could be left at that. Unfortunately, individual and social life is not that tidy. Economic questions are inextricably entwined with social and moral questions. The organization of economic life in any society inevitably touches on the
fundamental issue of cultural meaning.[65] How does the pursuit

of development affect communities and individuals at this level
of meaning?

Much of this discussion is hidden in ideology. In the Third
World there is the ubiquitous clash between socialism and capitalism and their respective economic and political claims. In Indian country the clash is less pronounced. Although there is no
clear ideological opposition to the dominant theme of capitalist
development, an undertow of resistance is present all the same. It
is therefore instructive to examine some issues that development
raises beyond the question of improving economic performance.

Development means substantial change; as a general matter,
that change can be continuous or discontinuous with an individual's personal and social past. Part of this change is institutional,
but any change of such magnitude finally takes root in the individual at the level of consciousness and meaning. There is no
doubt that capitalist development pushes individuality, the profit
motive, and the accumulation of wealth. In contrast, traditional
Lakota values stress the importance of the group, noneconomic
bonds, and the sharing of wealth. This formulation suggests the
kind of tension that issues of development raise in Indian country. I do not mean to present this typology as a fixed reality but
rather as the end points of a continuum along which individuals
and communities are arrayed. It is not a simple question of one
or the other, but rather many shades and blends of both. This is
the complex reality that development must confront.

There is, as always, no easy answer to this problem, but there
are some signposts for guidance. Planners must concern themselves with a "calculus of meaning" and realize that "all material
development is, in the end, futile unless it serves to enhance the
meanings by which human beings live. This is why it is so important to be careful about riding roughshod over traditional values and institutions." [66] The calculus of meaning finds a necessary
complement in the notion of "cognitive respect": "a recognition
that no outsider, including the outsider who possesses power, is
in a position to 'know better' when it comes to the finalities of
other people's lives." [67] Economic planning and development can
be successful only if there is an authentic commitment to under-

stand history, culture, individuals, and communities at the grass-roots level.

Such an investment in time and dedication is generally not part of the cost-benefit analysis of development strategies, and it is also beyond what is provided by most experts and lending institutions. This shortcoming is rarely identified in the literature, which seldom concerns itself with deficits in the community of experts. Development requires reexamination and self-scrutiny by all participants in the development process, including those who do not engage regularly in professional soul-searching and who do not have to suffer the adverse consequences of their failure to do so.

The burdens of development may seem impossible to surmount, but they are not. Development *is* the paramount world issue in the latter part of the twentieth century, and this is no less true in Indian country than elsewhere. The questions of development often refer to complex historical, institutional, and cultural forces, but the *answers* lie with people:

> Ultimately, development is about neither numbers nor solutions; rather it is about people. Our bias for hope derives from our inclination to see people not only as the ends of development programs but also as the means for these programs' effective implementation. . . . [P]eople viewed as problem solving agents capable of acquiring increased competence and confidence, constitute a uniquely abundant and self-renewing resource. The very real prospect of exploiting this unique resource more broadly and effectively is among the most cogent and underrated justifications for hope.[68]

In economic development planning, it is necessary to be guided not by claims of theoretical perfection but by a deep commitment to do the best that can be done in actual tribal situations. This is a commitment that is wisely tempered by compassion and humility.

Conclusion:
A Geography of Hope

Law has played and will continue to play, for better or worse, a pervasive role in the lives of all people, but particularly Indian people, who live or do business on the reservation. This historical and quotidian reality has been largely characterized by federal dominance, substantial uncertainty, and fierce jurisdictional competition. Within this law-saturated context, two issues are paramount in this period of rapid change and development. The first is the ultimate distribution of (jurisdictional) power among the federal, tribal, and state sovereigns in Indian country; the second is the nature of the values embedded in the laws that govern on the reservation and their effect on the quality of contemporary tribal life.

Resolution of these issues plays out on many fronts and involves both looking forward and looking back. At the federal level, Congress and the federal courts have seldom demonstrated a consistent grasp of the theoretical and practical implications of tribal sovereignty. They need to improve their understanding and clarify their roles. At the congressional level, such clarification might include the passage of a statute that specifically and explicitly recognizes tribal sovereignty and reaffirms its centrality in Indian law jurisprudence. A corollary is the need for Congress to recognize the deleterious effect of the plenary power doctrine on

Indian tribes and to take appropriate action to curb its extravagant uses. Such congressional action is not likely to occur in the immediate future, but it needs to be kept in sight as an important goal that is based on continuing efforts to extend understanding and the webs of belief about tribal sovereignty. There can be little hope for enduring advances until there is a better understanding of the history and meaning of sovereignty within the halls of Congress.

In the federal courts, including the U.S. Supreme Court, there is the need to reanimate, especially on the civil side, the notion of tribal sovereignty found in such cases as *Worcester v. Georgia*,[1] *Williams v. Lee*,[2] and *White Mountain Apache Tribe v. Bracker*.[3] The *Montana*,[4] *Brendale*,[5] and *Bourland*[6] cases mark the almost complete erosion of sovereignty doctrine in which all that remains is a sterile subsoil of politics and expediency. This conceptual amnesia is specifically noted by Justice Blackmun in his concurring and dissenting opinion in *Brendale*:

> [T]o recognize that *Montana* strangely reversed the otherwise consistent presumption in favor of inherent tribal sovereignty over reservation lands is not to excise the decision from our jurisprudence. Despite the reversed presumption, the plain language of *Montana* itself expressly preserves substantial tribal authority over non-Indian activity on reservations, including fee lands, and, more particularly, may sensibly be read as recognizing inherent tribal authority to zone fee land.[7]

Reassertion of the sovereignty doctrine can be greatly augmented, in part, if the courts pay close attention to the articulation of tribal sovereignty as it emanates from tribal court jurisprudence. This emerging jurisprudence contributes significantly in advancing the tribal voice as part of the judicial dialogue on the parameters and contemporary meaning of tribal sovereignty.

These efforts in the legal arena should perhaps culminate in a specific constitutional amendment that recognizes the permanent and enduring nature of tribal sovereignty and its roots in treaties and in the government-to-government relationship of Indian tribes with the federal government. Such an amendment would be an appropriate capstone to the tribal struggle to preserve sovereignty and the (ultimate) majoritarian commitment to ensure the highest form of legal recognition and participation for Indian tribes within this republic. Constitutional recognition of tribal sovereignty through a constitutional amendment would enable tribal sovereignty to take a more central position within the national (and state) legal and political structures established by the Constitution; it would also provide needed certainty which has been sorely lacking in recent years.

This goal of furthering tribal sovereignty may also be advanced, odd as it may seem, by hearkening back to the judicial hermeneutics of Chief Justice Marshall in the seminal Indian law cases. Chief Justice Marshall's opinions (as discussed in chapter 2 and elsewhere) did assist in the process of colonization, for example, with their articulation of the doctrine of discovery and the guardian-ward relationship. In addition, these opinions voiced some of the most negative stereotypes of Indians as "un-Christian and uncivilized savages." However, these opinions are counterbalanced by strong, if somewhat paradoxical, progressive comments. Chief Justice Marshall is morally and ethically engaged in these opinions, and he often realizes that many of his assertions are extravagant and blatantly false. For example, he notes in *Worcester* the "existing pretensions" of the doctrine of discovery and the scurrilous attempt of the State of Georgia to dismantle and annul tribal rights of self-government. Chief Justice Marshall does recognize tribal sovereignty and the particular need for the federal government to protect these "domestic dependent nations" from jurisdictional encroachment by the states.

Chief Justice Marshall also knew that the Supreme Court was a young and fragile institution incapable of fully containing the congressional, executive, and public sentiment supporting ruthless expansion. Much of this inhospitable context to tribal sovereignty is captured by President Andrew Jackson's statement, in the aftermath of the *Worcester* case which held that Georgia's laws did not apply on the Cherokee Reservation, that "Chief Justice Marshall has made his decision; now let him enforce it."[8] Indeed, shortly after the *Worcester* decision Congress passed and the President signed the legislation that culminated in the infamous Trail of Tears, which relocated most of the Five Civilized Tribes from the southeastern part of the United States to lands west of the Mississippi River.

Given these powerful forces within the executive and legislative branches of the federal government and much of the public sector, it may be argued that Chief Justice Marshall's opinions did much to mediate a middle ground between the Constitution and the forces of an even more brutal colonization. For example, after the decision in the *Cherokee Nation* case, which held that the Cherokee Nation was not a foreign nation under Article III of the U.S. Constitution, Chief Justice Marshall encouraged Justices Thompson and Story to write a dissenting opinion recognizing the Cherokee Nation as a foreign nation in order to stem some of the jubilation within the executive circle of President Jackson.[9] This is hardly the work of someone thoroughly convinced of the legal and moral righteousness of colonization.

In fact, the willingness of the Marshall court to take the stand it did in *Cherokee Nation* and *Worcester* created a true constitutional crisis. The State of Georgia refused to appear at oral argument in either case, and President Jackson's initial refusal to honor the decision of *Worcester,* which reversed the state criminal conviction of two non-Indians preaching on the Cherokee Reservation without a state license (they did have tribal permission), clearly threatened constitutional integrity and viability within the young republic. President Jackson's subsequent softening of his opposition avoided a major constitutional debacle.[10]

The primary importance of Chief Justice Marshall's opinions is found in his willingness to engage in the arduous process of seeking to define and to understand both tribal sovereignty and nascent federalism and integrate them within national constitutional jurisprudence. This form of serious interpretation seems woefully absent from today's Supreme Court, which appears to be ever less engaged with understanding and determining the proper parameters of contemporary tribal sovereignty. This absence of authentic engagement has rendered the Court's pronouncements (with rare exceptions) steadily more affectless and incoherent. Today's Supreme Court (as well as lower federal and state courts) could learn much by going back to these seminal opinions of Chief Justice Marshall for their sense of intellectual and ethical concern.

Some of the pitfalls of Chief Justice Marshall's thinking can also be avoided in today's Indian law jurisprudence. The blatantly negative cultural stereotypes are no longer acceptable, and extensive scholarly writing describes the values and practices of Native Americans on their own terms without invidious comparison to dominant cultural values and practices. It remains true, however, that cultural parity and genuine pluralism are not automatic givens, as amply demonstrated by a quick review of the Supreme Court's decisions in the *Lyng*[11] and *Smith*[12] cases (on the matter of Native American First Amendment rights). Strong forces continue to exist, both on and off the Court, that are inimical to improved cultural and legal understanding. Yet better information is available to those ready to make the effort to understand and to move forward.

In addition, emerging tribal court jurisprudence serves as a valuable complementary force encompassing the indigenous perspective on tribal sovereignty and tribal values. This jurisprudence makes possible for the first time in the nation's history a true tribal-federal (judicial) dialogue on tribal sovereignty. If justice is a product of conversation rather than unilateral declaration, it is more likely to be achieved in the context of respectful dialogue rather than unilateral majoritarian conclusions about the "other." Native Americans need to be seen not as the "other," but at the same time they must not lose any of their cultural and historical uniqueness. Such is the promise of contemporary assessments of tribal sovereignty within the context of respect and meaningful judicial communication.

More specifically, it might be said that the two most important—indeed, complementary—projects in the field of contemporary Indian law are the decolonization of federal Indian law and the simultaneous construction of an indigenous version of tribal sovereignty and self-rule. This yoked endeavor also carries with it the need to extend the webs of belief about Indian law and tribal sovereignty within the state and national legal community as well as within the dominant society as a whole. In many ways tribal courts are ideally situated to serve as a bridge between local tribal culture and the dominant legal system.

Tribal courts and their emerging jurisprudence constitute primary forces on both sides of this process. The seminal U.S. Supreme Court decision in *National Farmers Union Insurance v. Crow Tribe of Indians*[13] and *Iowa Mutual Insurance v. Laplante*[14] have created significant "breathing space" for tribal courts to articulate their own version of tribal sovereignty, while at the same time reserving significant federal judicial authority to review much of that decision making.[15] It is therefore incumbent on tribal courts to ensure that their decision making can withstand the rigors of whatever federal review exists. Ultimately, however, the greater necessity is that such decision making craft a jurisprudence reflecting the aspiration and wisdom of traditional cultures seeking a future of liberation and self-realization in which age-old values may continue to flourish in contemporary circumstances. Much of this effort, if successful, will aid in both decolonizing federal Indian law and building an indigenous version of tribal sovereignty.

TRIBAL RENASCENCE

Development of Indian law at both the federal and especially the tribal levels needs to be seen in the context of a national (even international) tribal and indigenous renascence. Tribal nations are currently in a period of intense cultural renewal and spiritual rebirth. It takes only the briefest experience in Indian country to become aware of the keen concern for indigenous language, traditional cultural practices, and spiritual ceremonies such as the Sun Dance and *hamblecha* (vision quest), for example, among the Lakota people of the northern plains in South Dakota.

This renascence is also beginning to manifest itself in the area of law with the increased concern not only for defining tribal sovereignty but also for identifying the nature and scope of tribal traditional and customary law. This angle of vision is in many ways the crucial complement to the pursuit of tribal sovereignty. If sovereignty may be thought of as the legitimate ambit of tribal power, the critical countervailing question is how that power or authority will be used to realize important (tribal) values in the legal context. The law at both the federal and tribal levels is too often thought of solely in terms of the parameters of legal rules and too little in terms of the values that the rules embody and realize. Tribal sovereignty creates an arena of tribal choice in which to articulate legal values and establish normative tribal frames of reference. As a result of this development, tribal courts are more and more concerned with addressing the values and aspirations of tribal law within the normative space secured in the first instance by tribal sovereignty.

The values of a society are not only carried by its individual citizens but are even more deeply inscribed in the institutions of that society. This is especially true in our complex, modern world. As a result, it is only in tribal law and its judicial decisions that we can truly discern the configurations of justice and other significant values in the tribal context. Tribal sovereignty in and of itself is no guarantee that tribes will not simply reproduce the legal rules of the dominant society, a likely possibility in the context of decolonization. To avoid this pitfall, tribes need to excavate their past to discover materials from which they can forge a present and future tribal legal reality that reflects the best of both the federal and tribal worlds. All of this—in varying degrees—is, in fact, being actively pursued throughout Indian country even within the current situation, with its increasingly complex and less predictable federal judicial and congressional setting.

This tribal renascence in law is potentially subject to renewed federal assault, but that possibility ought not to dilute the commitment to move forward. The key pursuit here is not to institutionalize the false dichotomy of dominant versus indigenous but rather to synthesize the best of both worlds while actively seeking to achieve a sovereignty that realizes both the necessary federal deference and the normative space to make authentic and enduring tribal choices.

Tribal renascence is also potentially instructive and invigorating for the dominant society as well. It is instructive in the sense noted by the prairie reformer Wes Jackson:

"Thomas Wolfe wrote somewhere that the discovery of America lies before us. I think that's right. So far we've only colonized it. So what each of us has as our mission is to assist one another in seeing where we are, not only in the sweep of history but also in the history of the landscape. I don't think that we will have discovered America until we have some sense of the feelings of the natives that walked over this place. And the people that were the furthest from understanding the sense of the natives that walked over this place"—he thumps his desk like a tom-tom—"were the conquerors of those natives. As Wendell [Berry] said, we came through and plowed the prairies and we never knew what we were doing because we never knew what we were undoing. What we are about is the discovery of what we have undone, and then we can begin to talk about what to do." [16]

This powerful observation accurately captures how little the dominant society has learned about the landscape and its original inhabitants and how this failure has seriously hindered achieving any true sense of balance between Indians and non-Indians and their mutual relationship to the landscape. Tribal efforts in such areas as traditional and customary law may help to illuminate both the past and the present of a portion of that landscape so we might finally see it as if for the first time.

In addition, the exhausted, monocultural "manifest destiny" view of the history of the West needs correction:

Any effort to discover the historical realities of the West, historians now acknowledge, must begin with multiculturalism: that is, above all, by recognizing the West was not a *terra nullius* into which the whites marched; that it was a highly charged arena in which various cultures, the invading Anglo-American and the already resident Indian and Spanish, impacted on one another, never with simple results. Nor can the drama and complexity of the West be understood without seeing how persistent and resilient the values, beliefs and cultural forms of the "vanquished" still are, despite long efforts by the Anglo "victors" both to suppress them and to deny the suppression itself with the comfortable notion that they just faded away. [17]

Tribal renascence and tradition are potential dynamic sources for infusing new vitality and color into the history of the West:

Surprises crackle, like electric arcs, between the interfaces of culture. These interfaces are where history now seeks itself; they will be the historical sites of the future. You cannot remake the past in the name of affirmative action. But you can find narratives that haven't been written, histories of people or groups that have been distorted and ignored, and refresh history by bringing them in. . . . [Y]ou see a part of the world break its traditional silence—a silence not of its own choosing, but *imposed* on it by earlier imperial writers.[18]

None of this precludes the give-and-take of honest critique. In fact, such critique is essential. As noted by the African American scholar Cornel West:

> I want to know who did what under what conditions. I will not deny the monumental achievements, but I will be keeping my eye on the least of these and the blood that flows. That is how I look at the world.[19]

THE NEW WEST

As Indian tribes continue to (re)assert tribal sovereignty within the local reservation context, such efforts often come in tandem with complementary efforts in the regional context. As the Old West presses to reconfigure itself into the New West, Indian tribes are likely to play a prominent role in this process. Some of the central characteristics of the Old West include exploitation of natural resources without environmental concern, extensive federal dependence despite mythic rhetoric to the contrary, and racial animosity toward Native Americans and other minorities.

Ruthless economic pursuit and development threaten the natural landscape as never before. Native Americans who control a significant amount of land, water, and natural resources in the West are increasingly seen as major players in the region's economic and social reconfiguration. As a result, tribes are increasingly involved in the process of establishing a significant economic and ecological role in this period of fast-paced change. They increasingly look to strike a new (or even first-time) balance between economic development needs involving water and natural resources and respect for the integrity of landscape, often defined in traditional terms as the sacred source of a people's integrity and wisdom.

Such efforts necessarily involve forging new understandings and relationships with non-Indians, including corporations and state governments. These efforts require that all concerned confront racism, establish common ground (especially in light of exploitation of both Indians and non-Indians by outsiders), and develop a new ethic of mutuality and place. As in any period of rapid change, it is possible that the "new" may become more exploitative and racist rather than less. This is why these issues need to be faced and not avoided. They need to be examined with candor in order to avoid repetition and to ensure transformation.

There is still very much pristine physical space in the West, and it ought to serve as a valuable backdrop against which Indians and non-Indians, the tribes and the states, establish a new ethic of development, preservation, and mutual respect. There is no room to continue the harsh antagonisms of the past without diminishing the economic viability and cultural integrity of all involved. Yet it remains true that fierce competition over jurisdiction and natural resources will continue. This cycle too needs to be broken by the development of creative problem-solving strategies that establish win-win situations, rather than traditional litigation in which winner takes all.

The New West must approach Native Americans as players to be reckoned with not only because of their water and natural resources but also because of the ability of tribal cultures to contribute to the artistic and spiritual dimensions of life in the West. As noted throughout these pages, it is absolutely critical that the majoritarian society attempt to understand Native American thought and philosophy more fully. It is quite difficult to develop creative and workable relationships—whether economic, social, or political—if the parties are unable to establish an atmosphere of respect and reciprocity.

The Old West reality of ruthless exploitation, racial dominance, and disregard for the integrity of the landscape is coming under increasingly intense criticism for the destruction it has caused and may continue to wreak.[20] The resources and vision of Indian tribes are essential forces in this monumental effort to create new opportunities in the spacious terrain that has always promised so much for personal renewal and economic fulfillment but has often yielded so little of enduring merit. Attempts that do not recognize the key role of Indian tribes are inevitably doomed to repeat the shortcomings and inequalities of the past.

SOLIDARITY

Any hope for realizing the objectives envisioned within the scope of tribal sovereignty is inevitably founded on two kinds of solidarity. The first is what might be called indigenous or internal solidarity. This is the realization that the bedrock of tribal sovereignty is the existence of strong local institutions. In the area of law, this means the existence of mature, reliable tribal courts that render justice in such a way that litigants perceive that they are receiving their due and that the results comport with important tribal values. Indeed, the realization of such substantive values is premised on the availability of sufficient resources, procedural regularity, and individual competence. Tribal courts have made exceptional progress in these matters. This sphere of action provides tribes with the most opportunity for local development and control.

These local efforts are not, of course, immune from federal penetration and state infiltration, but they still offer the best means of resistance to such encroachment. In addition, strong local institutions establish the necessary institutional predicate to exercise any more wide-ranging powers that may come within the ambit of tribal authority via tribal sovereignty, federal delegation, or cooperative arrangements with the state. Such local institutional building many not seem as decisive or crucial as tribal appearances before Congress and in the federal courts, but it is. Local institutions such as tribal courts (potentially) embody the tribal vision in its most complete and developed form. This is the rock on which tribal sovereignty rests.

The second aspect of solidarity concerns the external effort by which the majoritarian society comes to respect the essential cultural and human reality that Native Americans inhabit. It is a view that does not flatten Native American human and cultural reality into some familiar assimilative ethos but rather makes an informed, essentially imaginative reach of understanding that preserves and honors a certain "pride" of difference. As the Lakota Chief Sitting Bull observed, "It is not necessary that eagles should be crows."

If we listen to each other, we will not necessarily erase difference; rather, we may use it to our mutual advantage. In fact,

Professor Martha Minow suggests that such an understanding is pivotal to resolving the difference dilemma:

> [T]he point is not to find the new, true perspective; the point is to strive for impartiality by admitting our partiality. The perspective of those who are labeled "different" may offer an important challenge to those who impose the label, *but it is a corrective lens,* another partial view, not the absolute truth. It is the complexity of our reciprocal realities and the conflict between the realities that constitute us which we need to understand.[21]

The ultimate goal is therefore not to undo difference but rather to create solidarity—a quality whose chief source is the imaginative ability "to see strange people as fellow sufferers."[22] Such efforts flow not from mere academic inquiry but from work of the heart and mind:

> Solidarity is not discovered by reflection but created. It is created by increasing our sensitivity to the particular details of the pain and humiliation of other, unfamiliar sorts of people. Such increased sensitivity makes it more difficult to marginalize people different from ourselves by thinking, "they do not feel as *we* would."[23]

This solidarity, itself grounded in imagination, forms in turn the bedrock of pluralism:

> In order to survive, a plurality of true communities would require not egalitarianism and tolerance but knowledge, and understanding of the necessity of local differences, and respect. Respect, I think, always implies imagination—the ability to see one another, across our inevitable differences, as living souls.[24]

Inevitably, the feather of Indian law jurisprudence will continue to be a prominent one in the braid of tribal life, complete with the potential to advance and enrich the quality of contemporary indigenous (and majoritarian) life. This potential future is, however, by no means assured, for we must still meet the challenges of history, national diversity, and the ideal of justice. Yet we may be guided by the geography of hope, with its coordinates of commitment, respect, imagination, and engagement.

Notes

1. Note that the term "Indian" (as opposed to the term "Native American") continues to predominate in the field of Indian law. See, for example, the titles of the two leading texts in the field, *Federal Indian Law* by Getches, Wilkinson, and Williams, and *American Indian Law* by Price, Clinton, and Newton, as well as the leading treatise, Felix Cohen's *Handbook of Federal Indian Law*. Volume 25 of the *United States Code Annotated* and volume 25 of the *Code of Federal Regulations* are captioned "Indians"; the term also appears in current federal legislation, such as the Indian Civil Rights Act of 1968, the Indian Child Welfare Act of 1978, and the Indian Gaming Regulatory Act (1990). Most tribes are largely known as "Indian" (e.g., Rosebud Sioux Indian Tribe). For these reasons, the term "Indian" is used throughout the text, although whenever possible local tribal or indigenous terms (e.g., Lakota) are used.

2. Vine Deloria, Jr., quoted in NATIVE AMERICAN TESTIMONY xviii (Peter Nabokov ed., 1992).

PART 1

1. *See, e.g.,* DAVID H. GETCHES, CHARLES F. WILKINSON, & ROBERT WILLIAMS, JR., FEDERAL INDIAN LAW 7–30 (3d ed. 1993).

2. 21 U.S. (8 Wheat.) 543 (1823).

3. 30 U.S. (5 Pet.) 1 (1831).

4. 31 U.S. (6 Pet.) 515 (1832). All three of these cases are discussed in detail in chapter 2.

CHAPTER 1. THE RESERVATION AS PLACE

1. *See, e.g.,* Benjamin Weiser, *Rosebud Sioux: Worst of Both Worlds,* WASHINGTON POST, Sept. 24, 1984, at 6–8; Schmickle & Buoen, *Indian Courts: Island of Injustice,* MINNEAPOLIS STAR AND TRIBUNE, Jan. 5, 1986, at 1A; Jan. 6, 1986, at 1A; Jan. 7, 1986, at 1A. Several reservation counties—such as Shannon County on the Pine Ridge Reservation, Buffalo County on the Crow Creek Reservation, Ziebach County on the Cheyenne River Reservation, and Todd County on the Rosebud Reservation—are among the poorest in the United States; indeed, the poorest county in the United States is Shannon County, the second poorest is Buffalo County, the fifth poorest is Ziebach County, and the eighth poorest is Todd County. BUREAU OF THE CENSUS, U.S. DEPARTMENT OF COMMERCE, PRD #9 CAPITAL, 1979 COUNTY PER CAPITA INCOME FIGURES RELEASED BY CENSUS BUREAU FROM THE 1980 CENSUS 2 (1983).

2. *See, e.g.,* Peter Nabokov, *Present Memories, Past History, in* THE AMERICAN INDIAN AND THE PROBLEM OF HISTORY 144 (C. Martin ed., 1987) for a thoughtful exegesis on the problem of being truthful to the "deeper riches" of native cultures without straying into falsehood and sentimentality. *See also* VINE DELORIA, JR., GOD IS RED (1973).

3. *See, e.g.,* NATIONAL LAWYERS GUILD COMM. ON NATIVE AMERICAN STRUGGLES, RETHINKING INDIAN LAW (1982).

4. *See, e.g.,* CHARLES F. WILKINSON, AMERICAN INDIANS, TIME, AND THE LAW (1987).

5. The word "Lakota" is the term traditionally used by the Teton Sioux people to describe themselves in their own language. The word "Sioux" is a French corruption of a Chippewa word which means "snake" or "adder" and which was used by the Chippewas in a derogatory fashion to describe their traditional enemy, the Lakota. For this reason, "Lakota" is the preferred term, although popular and legal usage has made the word "Sioux" a much more conventional and better known term. The terms are used interchangeably throughout the text.

The Teton Sioux make up one of the three main divisions of the Sioux people. The other two main divisions of the Sioux people are the Santee and Yanktonai. The Santee were basically woodland people who lived in Wisconsin and Minnesota. The Yanktonai were primarily riverine people who lived in Minnesota and eastern South Dakota. The Teton lived in the plains of the Dakotas. The Teton dialect emphasized the *l* sound (thus *Lakota*); the Yanktonai emphasized the *d* (*Dakota*) and the Santee the *n* (*Nakota*). *See, e.g.,* JAMES L. SATTERLEE AND VERNON D. MALAN, HISTORY AND ACCULTURATION OF THE DAKOTA INDIANS (Bulletin 613, S.D. State Univ. Rural Sociology Department, 1973).

In South Dakota, the Santee division of the Sioux people are found primarily on the Lake Traverse and Flandreau Santee Reservations; the

Yanktonai on the Yankton, Standing Rock, and Crow Creek Reservations; and the Tetons on the Rosebud, Pine Ridge, Lower Brule, Cheyenne River, and Standing Rock Sioux Reservations. It is reasonably accurate to state that today the strongest identification of Indians in South Dakota is with their reservation rather than with their major Sioux branch. *See, e.g.,* MICHAEL L. LAWSON, DAMMED INDIANS 31–32 (1982).

6. See, for example, the statement by the former state Attorney General, Roger Tellinghuisen, that "Indian reservations are a 'divisive system' of government that have outlived their usefulness" (quoted in Gale, *Divisive System,* SIOUX FALLS ARGUS LEADER, Feb. 15, 1989, at 1A).

In almost ironic juxtaposition, see the thoughtful proposals of Dr. Jim Wilson, an Oglala Sioux educator, to improve Indian-white relations in South Dakota; he suggests, for example, that the state legislature go on record with reassurance that its intention is not to wipe out the Indian tribes and that there be specific efforts to develop cooperation between the state and tribe. M. Cook, *Wilson "Knocking on Door" of Governor's Mansion with Indian/White Guidelines,* LAKOTA TIMES, Feb. 14, 1989, at 7.

7. *See, e.g.,* DeCoteau v. District County Court, 420 U.S. 425 (1975); Rosebud Sioux Tribe v. Kneip, 430 U.S. 584 (1977); United States *ex rel.* Cook v. Parkinson, 525 F.2d 120 (8th Cir. 1975); Wood v. Jameson, 130 N.W.2d 95 (S.D. 1964).

8. *See, e.g.,* State *ex rel.* Meierhenry v. Rippling Water Ranch, Inc., 531 F. Supp. 449 (D.S.D. 1982), which was an action brought by the State of South Dakota to adjudicate the water rights of all parties to the Missouri River and its tributaries. It was ultimately dismissed on the state's own motion, apparently because of problems related to financing the complex and massive litigation. At no time prior (or subsequent) to this litigation did the state attempt to meet with the tribes to discuss (much less negotiate) the important issues related to Indian and non-Indian water rights in South Dakota. This is not to say that the tribes would necessarily welcome or accede to such an invitation but only to emphasize that such discussion is apparently not seen as even helpful, much less fruitful. See also remarks made in 1977 by William Janklow, the former governor and then attorney general, about this same dilemma; Janklow stated, in part, "[I]f we don't act quickly, intelligently, and correctly . . . we may find ourselves up the proverbial creek, (and) not only will the tribes and Uncle Sam have all the paddles, there may not be any water to keep us afloat." William Janklow, *Can Indian Water Rights Effect* [sic] *South Dakota Development?,* STOCK-GROWER 12 (Dec. 1977).

9. Simply stated, all major elected state (e.g., governor, attorney general) and federal officials (both senators and congressman) are uni-

formly opposed to any kind of legislative redress to return federally held land in the Black Hills to the Sioux Nation. For a review of the legal history, *see* United States v. Sioux Nation of Indians, 448 U.S. 371 (1980), which awarded the Sioux Nation $17.1 million (plus interest) for the wrongful taking of 7.7 million treaty-protected acres in the Black Hills. Justice Blackmun, writing for the majority, adopted the characterization of the Court of Claims that "[a] more ripe and rank case of dishonorable dealing will never in all probability, be found in our history. . . ." *Id.* at 388. The initial proposed bill (S. 705, 100th Cong., 1st Sess. [1987]) was entitled the Sioux Nation Black Hills Act. There is currently no bill before Congress. See also a survey of articles on the various issues in THE WICAZO SA REVIEW, no. 1 (1988).

10. *See, e.g.,* State v. Onihan, 427 N.W.2d 365 (S.D. 1988), in which the South Dakota Supreme Court held that the state had criminal and civil jurisdiction over both Indians and non-Indians on highways on the reservations. This was the first time it had been held in South Dakota that the state had jurisdiction over Indians on the reservation. Note, however, that this case was effectively overruled by Rosebud Sioux Tribe v. South Dakota, 900 F.2d 1164 (8th Cir. 1990).

11. WALLACE STEGNER, ANGLE OF REPOSE (1971). This extraordinary novel traces the moral and *loving* investigation by the narrator, Lyman Ward, of the lives of his grandparents Oliver and Susan Ward in the West of the nineteenth century, as well as, finally, the narrator's own inner life as a modern twentieth-century westerner. The book has nothing to do with Native Americans or South Dakota, yet the title and introspection of the work seem especially resonant in the context of my work. "Angle of repose" is also an engineering term that refers to the angle between the horizontal and the plane of contact between two bodies when the upper body is just about to slide over the lower. MCGRAW HILL DICTIONARY OF SCIENTIFIC AND TECHNICAL TERMS 78 (S. Parker ed., 3d ed. 1984). "Repose" is referred to then in the sense of rest—rest not from the demands of mutual problem solving but from antagonism.

12. *See, e.g.,* FRANCIS JENNINGS, THE INVASION OF AMERICA 32–42 (1975).

13. *See, e.g.,* OLIVER SACKS, AWAKENINGS 202–10 (1983), for an insightful discussion that matters of health and well-being require the complementary concerns of both mechanical and metaphysical approaches to understanding.

14. This statement may seem seriously out of place in a scholarly work, yet it is one I want to make. As previously mentioned, I lived and worked on the Rosebud Sioux Reservation from 1973 to 1983 and presently serve as an Appellate Justice of both the Rosebud and Cheyenne River Sioux Tribal Courts of Appeal. These facts affect what I say.

The experience did not make me blind to problems on the reservation; instead, it has deepened my understanding of their etiology and increased my appreciation of the values and commitment embodied in Lakota history and culture.

The best statement of what I am trying to say comes from this description by the English writer John Berger of living with, and writing about, rural peasants and their villages in France:

> The fact that a stranger does not belong to the centre means that he is bound to remain a stranger. Yet provided the stranger's interests do not conflict with those of his neighbor—and such a conflict is likely immediately if he buys land or builds—and provided that he can recognize the portrait already in existence—and this involves more than recognizing names or faces—he too may contribute to it, modestly, but in a way that the making of this continuous communal portrait is not a vanity or a pastime: it is an organic part of the life of the village. Should it cease, the village would disintegrate. The stranger's contribution is small, but it is to something essential.
>
> Thus, in a double role as novices and independent witnesses, a certain reciprocity has been established.

JOHN BERGER, PIG EARTH 11 (1979).

15. *See, e.g.*, THE AMERICAN INDIAN AND THE PROBLEM OF HISTORY (C. Martin ed., 1987); VINE DELORIA, JR., & CLIFFORD LYTLE, THE NATIONS WITHIN (1984).

16. WILLIAM CRONON, CHANGES IN THE LAND 163–67 (1983).

17. *See, e.g.*, Leslie Silko, *Landscape, History, and the Pueblo Imagination, in* ON NATURE 83–94 (Dennis Halpern ed., 1987); BARRY LOPEZ, CROSSING OPEN GROUND 61–71 (1988).

18. *See, e.g.*, WENDELL BERRY, THE GIFT OF GOOD LAND 50–52 (1981) (discussing the Papago Indians of the Southwest, although his descriptions are equally pertinent in the Lakota context).

19. *See, e.g.*, JOHN NEIHARDT, BLACK ELK SPEAKS (1932) and LUTHER STANDING BEAR, THE LAND OF THE SPOTTED EAGLE (1933) for the most forceful descriptions of these observations.

20. FREDERICK TURNER, BEYOND GEOGRAPHY 238 (1980).

21. Frederick Turner, *Literature Lost in the Thickets,* NEW YORK TIMES BOOK REVIEW, Feb. 15, 1987, at 35. *See particularly* N. SCOTT MOMADAY, HOUSE MADE OF DAWN (1966); LESLIE SILKO, CEREMONY (1977); LESLIE SILKO, ALMANAC OF THE DEAD (1992); JAMES WELCH, WINTER IN THE BLOOD (1973); JAMES WELCH, FOOLS CROW (1986); LOUISE ERDRICH, LOVE MEDICINE (1985); LOUISE ERDRICH, TRACKS (1988); LOUISE ERDRICH, THE BINGO PALACE (1994).

22. Interview with Robert Logterman, Rosebud Sioux Reservation (May 1986).

23. This BIA policy was prominent during the period 1955–61, the latter part of the termination period (1945–61), when it was believed,

among other things, that the reservations were inhospitable anachronisms which should be dismantled; or, barring termination, that the inhabitants should be encouraged to leave.
See generally DONALD FIXICO, TERMINATION AND RELOCATION: FEDERAL INDIAN POLICY 1945–1960 (1986).

24. See, e.g., Keith Basso, *"Stalking with Stories": Names, Places, and Moral Narratives among the Western Apache, in* ON NATURE 95–116 (D. Halpern ed., 1987). Note also the observations of N. Scott Momaday (Kiowa) concerning the moral dimensions of Native American conceptions of the land:

> You cannot understand how the Indian thinks of himself in relation to the world around him unless you understand his conception of what is appropriate; particularly what is morally appropriate within the context of that relationship.
> The Native American ethic with respect to the physical world is a matter of reciprocal appropriation: appropriations in which man invests himself in the landscape, and at the same time incorporates the landscape into his own most fundamental experience. . . . This appropriation is primarily a matter of imagination which is moral in kind. I mean to say that we are all, I suppose, what we imagine ourselves to be. And that is certainly true of the American Indian. . . . [The Indian] is someone who thinks of himself in a particular way and his idea comprehends his relationship to the physical world. He imagines himself in terms of that relationship and others. And it is that act of imagination, that moral act of imagination, which constitutes his understanding of the physical world.

N. SCOTT MOMADAY, NATIVE AMERICAN ATTITUDES TO THE ENVIRONMENT, *quoted in* ON NATURE at 115.

25. For example, when the Sioux reservations were established in South Dakota, Sioux people were already living there. This was in vivid contrast to the removal policy which required many southeastern tribes, such as the Five Civilized Tribes, to remove to the Oklahoma Territory to settle on new "reservations" there. See generally GRANT FOREMAN, INDIAN REMOVAL (1932).

26. See, e.g., DAVID H. GETCHES & CHARLES F. WILKINSON, FEDERAL INDIAN LAW 98–99 (2d ed. 1986).

27. CHARLES F. WILKINSON, AMERICAN INDIANS, TIME, AND THE LAW 4 (1986).

28. It is important to note that the Lakota did not see the treaty as mere expedience and the power politics of the day, subject to future accommodation to other emerging national interests. Every treaty was settled with the smoking of the pipe. As insightfully noted by Father Peter John Powell, the well-known historian and anthropologist:

> Whites rarely, if ever, have understood the sacredness of the context in which treaties were concluded by the Lakota people. . . . "[T]he pipe never fails," my people, the Cheyennes, say, for the pipe is the great sacramental, the great sacred means that provides unity between the Creator and the peo-

ple. Any agreement that was signed was a sacred agreement because it was sealed by the smoking of the pipe. It was not signed by the chiefs and headmen before the pipe had been passed. Then the smoking of the pipe sealed the treaty, making the agreement holy and binding.

Thus, for the Lakota, the obligations sealed with the smoking of the pipe were sacred obligations.

PETER JOHN POWELL, THE SACRED TREATY, *quoted in* ROXANNE DUNBAR ORTIZ, THE GREAT SIOUX NATION 141–42 (1977).

Reservations were also established without treaties through acts of Congress and executive orders. *See, e.g.,* MONROE E. PRICE, ROBERT N. CLINTON, & NELL JESSUP NEWTON, AMERICAN INDIAN LAW 679–767 (3d ed. 1991).

29. *See, e.g.,* FELIX COHEN, HANDBOOK OF FEDERAL INDIAN LAW 220–28 (1982 ed.).

30. *See, e.g.,* Charles F. Wilkinson & John M. Volkman, *Judicial Review of Indian Treaty Abrogation: "As Long as Water Flows or Grass Grows Upon the Earth"—How Long a Time Is That?,* 63 CAL. L. REV. 601 (1975).

31. *Id.* at 611.

32. *Id.* at 609–10.

33. *See, e.g.,* Fort Laramie Treaty of April 29, 1868, 15 Stat. 635 (1868).

34. Treaty with Chippewas, Ottawas, and Potawatomies, 9 Stat. 853 (1846); Speech of Commissioner in Journal of Proceedings (Nov. 12, 1845).

35. *See, e.g.,* FRANCIS P. PRUCHA, AMERICAN INDIAN POLICY IN THE FORMATIVE YEARS: THE INDIAN TRADE AND INTERCOURSE ACTS 1790–1834 (1962).

36. *See, e.g.,* GETCHES & WILKINSON, *supra* note 26, at 98–99.

37. 15 Stat. 635 (1868).

38. *Id.* at Art. II.

39. *See, e.g.,* WILKINSON, *supra* note 27, at 14–19.

40. *Id.* at 19–23.

41. Act of Feb. 8, 1887, ch. 119, 24 Stat. 388 (1887) (codified as amended at 25 U.S.C. §§ 331–34, 339, 341–42, 348–49, 354, 381 [1983]).

42. STEVEN TYLER, A HISTORY OF INDIAN POLICY 104 (1973) (quoting President Theodore Roosevelt).

43. Act of May 8, 1906, ch. 2348, 34 Stat. 182 (1906).

44. *See generally* LeAnn LaFave, *South Dakota's Forced Fee Indian Land Claims: Will Landowners Be Liable for Government's Wrongdoing?,* 30 S.D. L. REV. 59 (1984).

45. 25 U.S.C. § 348 (1983).

46. WILKINSON, *supra* note 27, at 20.

47. FRANCIS P. PRUCHA, THE GREAT FATHER 896 (1984).

48. 25 U.S.C. §§ 461–78 (1983).

49. *See, e.g.*, WILKINSON, *supra* note 27, at 20; FRANK POMMER-
SHEIM, BROKEN GROUND AND FLOWING WATERS 69–71 (1979).

50. *See, e.g.*, WILKINSON, *supra* note 27, at 21; WILLIAM WASH-
BURN, RED MAN'S LAND/WHITE MAN'S LAW: A STUDY OF THE PAST
AND PRESENT STATUS OF THE AMERICAN INDIAN 75–76 (1971).

51. *See, e.g.*, D.W. Adams, *Fundamental Considerations: The Deep
Meaning of Native-American Schooling, 1880–1900, 58* HARV. ED.
REV. 1 (1988).

52. *See, e.g.*, Federal Agencies Task Force, American Religious Freedom Act Report, Pub. L. No. 95–341 1–17 (1979).

53. Interview with Albert White Hat, Rosebud Sioux Reservation
(May 1983).

54. D. OTIS, THE DAWES ACT AND THE ALLOTMENT OF INDIAN
LANDS 8 (1973).

55. *Id.*

56. 25 U.S.C. §§ 461–78 (1983).

57. *See, e.g.*, GETCHES & WILKINSON, *supra* note 26, at 128–29.

58. This discussion does not include the 7.7 million acres taken as
part of the Black Hills Act of 1877, Act of Feb. 28, 1877, 19 Stat. 254,
or the 9 million acres lost as part of the Great Sioux Agreement of 1889,
Act of March 2, 1889, 25 Stat. 889, which carved out the six West
River reservations (Pine Ridge, Rosebud, Cheyenne River, Standing
Rock, Lower Brule, and Crow Creek) from the Great Sioux Reservation
established as part of the Fort Laramie Treaty of 1868.

59. *See* the discussion in DeCoteau v. District County Court, 420
U.S. 425 (1975).

60. *See* the discussion in Wood v. Jameson, 130 N.W.2d 95 (S.D.
1964).

61. *See* the discussion in United States *ex rel.* Cook v. Parkinson,
525 F.2d 120 (8th Cir. 1975).

62. *See* the discussion in Rosebud Sioux Tribe v. Kneip, 430 U.S.
584 (1977).

63. *Id.* at 586.

64. *Id.* at 585–86. *See also* Lone Wolf v. Hitchcock, 187 U.S. 553
(1903), for a discussion of Congress's plenary authority in Indian affairs. *See also* the discussion in chapter 2.

65. 430 U.S. 584 (1977).

66. *Rosebud Sioux Tribe*, 430 U.S. at 629–30 (Marshall, J., dissenting).

67. 465 U.S. 463 (1984).

68. Act of May 29, 1908, ch. 218, 35 Stat. 460 (1908).

69. *Solem*, 465 U.S. 476.

70. *Id.* at 470.

71. *Id.*

72. *Id.* at 471.

73. *Id.*

74. *Id.* The Supreme Court recently revisited the issues of diminishment and, applying the *Solem* analysis, held that the Uintah Indian Reservation in Utah was diminished by an act of Congress in 1902. Hagen v. Utah, 114 S. Ct. 958 (1994).

75. *Supra* note 59.

76. *Supra* note 60.

77. *Supra* note 62.

78. *Supra* note 61.

79. *Rosebud Sioux Tribe,* 430 U.S. at 616.

80. MICHAEL LAWSON, DAMMED INDIANS xxi (1982).

81. *Id.* at 20.

82. *Id.* at 27.

83. *Id.* at 29.

84. *Id.*

85. *Id.* at 45.

86. *Id.* at 94–107.

87. Vine Deloria, Jr., *Foreword* to LAWSON, *supra* note 80, at xiv.

88. The title of this section derives from WALLACE STEGNER, THE AMERICAN WEST AS LIVING SPACE (1987).

89. The West is not always easily defined geographically. Wallace Stegner suggests:

> The most accepted definition states that it starts about the 98th meridian of west longitude and ends at the Pacific Ocean. Neither boundary has the Euclidean perfection of a fixed emerging line, for on the West the Pacific plate is restless, constantly shoving Los Angeles northward where it is not wanted, and on the east the boundary between the Middle West and West fluctuates a degree or two east depending on wet and dry cycles.
>
> Actually it is not the arbitrary 98th meridian that marks the West's beginning, but a perceptible line of real import that roughly coincides with it, reaching southward about a third of the way across the Dakotas, Nebraska, and Kansas, and then swerving more southwestward across Oklahoma and Texas. This is the isohyetal line of twenty inches normally necessary for unirrigated crops.

Id. at 5. For purposes of this book, I have included all of South Dakota in the West. Yet it is interesting to note that most of the Indian population and Indian land in South Dakota are in the western part of the state, and there is a clear east/west distinction marked by the Missouri River in South Dakota. East of the river it is more the traditional crop agriculture of the Midwest, while west of the river it is mostly cattle ranching and the literal province of "cowboys and Indians."

90. *Id.* at 80–81.

91. *Id.* at 8–9.

92. *Id.* at 15.

93. *See, e.g.,* OUR BROTHER'S KEEPER: THE INDIAN IN WHITE AMERICA (E. Cahn & D. Hearne eds., 1969). *But see also* the more balanced Indian view in VINE DELORIA, JR., CUSTER DIED FOR YOUR SINS 128–47 (1969).

94. STEGNER, *supra* note 88, at 14–15.

95. *Supra* note 29 and accompanying text. *See also* the discussion of the trust relationship in chapter 2.

96. WILLIAM KITTREDGE, *Redneck Secrets, in* OWNING IT ALL 88 (1987).

97. The congressional bill for return of the Black Hills (S. 705) could not find a sponsor in the South Dakota Congressional delegation. The original sponsor was Senator Bill Bradley (D.-N.J.), who conducted summer basketball clinics for the children of Pine Ridge, where he first heard about the Black Hills issue.

98. For example, note the views of Palestinian villagers exiled from their village in 1948 but allowed to return to the same village by the Israeli government in 1972:

> I ask my conversants how the return to their land affected them.
> "Everything changed," Abu Harb says. "We now live here among real people. The people who stayed behind in the Deheisha and in Jericho are miserable. They are going mad from sadness and longing for their land. They come and plead with us to give them a little garden plot. Just so they can regain a little self-respect. Something to live for. After all, it is not just land, it is everything. They are cut off everything there. They have ceased to be people. We have been planted anew. Not only in the land. This is only the beginning: we are planted in life as a whole. In normal relations with other people. In tradition. In all the right things. We are no longer strangers in the world."

DAVID GROSSMAN, THE YELLOW WIND 73–74 (1987). Note also the Israeli-Palestinian movement in 1994 found mutual accord on these issues.

99. STEGNER, *supra* note 88, at 52.

100. *Owning It All* in KITTREDGE, *supra* note 96, at 67–68. *See also* PATRICIA LIMERICK, THE LEGACY OF CONQUEST (1987).

101. STEGNER, *supra* note 88, at 22–23.

102. Charles Wilkinson, *Law and the American West: The Search for an Ethic of Place,* 59 U. COLO. L. REV. 401, 405 (1988).

103. *Id.* at 407.

104. STEGNER, *supra* note 88, at 43, 60. In this statement Stegner's own hope wavers. See also his splendid earlier observation:

> Angry as one may be at what careless people have done and still do to a noble habitat, it is hard to be pessimistic about the West. This is the native home of hope. When it fully learns that cooperation, not rugged individualism, is the pattern that most characterizes and preserves it, then it will have achieved itself and outlived its origins. Then it has a chance to create a society to match its scenery.

WALLACE STEGNER, THE SOUND OF MOUNTAIN WATER 38 (1980).

105. Each of these colleges has an enrollment of more than five hundred students with growth rates of about 5 percent or more annually. *See, e.g., New Enrollment High at OCC,* LAKOTA TIMES, Jan. 31, 1989, at 14. There are also smaller reservation-based colleges on the Cheyenne River, Standing Rock, Yankton, and Sisseton-Wahpeton Reservations in South Dakota. More than twenty such colleges are located throughout Indian country. The national organization is known as the American Indian Higher Education Consortium (AIHEC).

106. Both Sinte Gleska University and Oglala Lakota College are independently accredited by the North Central Association of Colleges and Schools to offer recognized A.A. (two-year) and B.S. (four-year) degrees in human services and elementary education. Sinte Gleska University also offers a master's degree in elementary education.

107. I held a faculty position there during the period 1973–80. I continue to teach courses and have close contact with staff and students.

108. As quoted in William Grieder, *The Heart of Everything That Is,* ROLLING STONE, May 7, 1987, at 62.

109. See, for example, the discussion between scholars William Cronon and Richard White, *Indians in the Land,* AM. HERITAGE, Aug.–Sept. 1986, at 19–25.

110. BERRY, *supra* note 18, at 71–72.

111. As quoted in Basso, *supra* note 24, at 95.

112. Interview with Stanley Red Bird, Rosebud Sioux Reservation (May 1986).

113. MICHAEL PERRY, MORALITY, POLITICS, AND LAW 137 (1988).

114. *Id.*

115. *Id.*

116. JAROSLAV PELIKAN, THE VINDICATION OF TRADITION 60 (1984).

117. *See, e.g.,* William Brennan, *The Constitution of the United States: Contemporary Ratification,* 27 S. TEX. L. REV. 433, 434 (1986), in which he notes that

the Constitution embodies the aspiration to social justice, brotherhood, and human dignity that brought this nation into being. . . . [W]e are an aspiring people, a people with faith in progress. Our amended Constitution is the lodestar of our aspirations.

CHAPTER 2. THE COLONIZED CONTEXT

1. STEVEN CORNELL, THE RETURN OF THE NATIVE 19 (1988).

2. *See, e.g.,* FRANCIS JENNINGS, THE INVASION OF AMERICA 39–42 (1975).

3. CORNELL, *supra* note 1, at 74.

4. *Id.* Such economic activity was fostered by a federal policy of nonintercourse. This policy was premised on a perception that non-Indians could not live harmoniously with Indians. The federal government early on regulated contact between Indians and non-Indians. Non-Indians (including the states) could not purchase land from individual Indians or tribes without approval of the federal government. Hence, the federal government also regulated trade, interdicted liquor, and punished criminal activity in Indian country. *See* the discussion in chap. 1. *See also* FRANCIS PAUL PRUCHA, AMERICAN INDIAN POLICY IN THE FORMATIVE YEARS: THE INDIAN TRADE AND INTERCOURSE ACTS, 1790–1834 (1962).

5. CORNELL, *supra* note 1, at 24. It is also significant to note that the ecological effects were devastating. Many fur-bearing and game populations were completely wiped out.

6. *Id.* at 32.

7. *Id.* at 53–54.

8. *See* the discussion in chap. 1. *See also* CHARLES F. WILKINSON, AMERICAN INDIANS, TIME, AND THE LAW 19–23 (1986). Between 1887 and 1934, the national Indian land estate was reduced from 138 million acres to 52 million acres. *See generally* FRANCIS PAUL PRUCHA, THE GREAT FATHER 890–900 (1984).

9. DAVID H. GETCHES & CHARLES F. WILKINSON, FEDERAL INDIAN LAW 37, 42 (2d ed. 1986).

10. *See, e.g.,* GETCHES & WILKINSON, *supra* note 9, at xxiii–xxx; FELIX COHEN, HANDBOOK OF INDIAN LAW vii–xi (1982 ed.).

11. U.S. CONST. art. I, § 2, cl. 3.

12. U.S. CONST. art. I, § 8, cl. 3. "The Congress shall have power . . . To regulate commerce with foreign nations, and among the several states, and with the Indian tribes."

13. U.S. CONST. art. II, § 2, cl. 2.(2).

14. U.S. CONST. amend. X.

15. As noted by Professor Judith Resnik:

[I]n the Preface to the First Edition of Henry M. Hart's and Herbert Wechsler's THE FEDERAL COURTS AND THE FEDERAL SYSTEM xi (Foundation, 1953), the authors described their subject matter as the exploration of a "legal system that derives from both the Nation and the states as separate sources of authority." Also reprinted in PAUL M. BATOR, PAUL J. MISHKIN, DANIEL J. METZER, AND DAVID L. SHAPIRO, HART AND WECHSLER'S THE FEDERAL COURTS AND THE FEDERAL SYSTEM XXVII (Foundation, 3rd ed. 1988). The opening epigram in FELIX FRANKFURTER'S AND WILBER G. KATZ'S CASES AND OTHER AUTHORITIES ON FEDERAL JURISDICTION AND PROCEDURE (Nat'l Casebook Series, 1931) is from Benjamin R. Curtis. The comment, written in 1864, reads: Let it be remembered, also,—for just now we may be in some danger of forgetting it,—that questions of jurisdiction were questions of power as between the United States and the several states.

Judith Resnik, *Dependent Sovereigns: Indian Tribes, States, and the Federal Courts*, 56 U. CHI. L. REV. 671, 675 n.16 (1989).

16. *Id.* at 687–90.

17. *See, e.g.*, WILKINSON, *supra* note 8, at 117.

18. *See, e.g.*, GETCHES & WILKINSON, *supra* note 9, at xxiv–xxv, 61–66, 332–36; COHEN, *supra* note 10, at 62–108. Note also that from the tribal perspective (of many, if not all, tribes), treaties are the cornerstone of tribal sovereignty and legal identity. *See generally* Frank Pommersheim, *The Reservation as Place: A South Dakota Essay*, 34 S.D. L. REV. 246, 252–55 (1989); Frank Pommersheim, *The Black Hills Case: On the Cusp of History*, 4 WICAZO SA REV. 18, 19 (1988).

19. *See, e.g.*, GETCHES & WILKINSON, *supra* note 9, at xxvi, 217–68 (with an occasional nod to the Indian Commerce Clause of the Constitution); COHEN, *supra* note 10, at 220–28. Some commentators take sharp exception to the legal validity of the trust relationship. *See, e.g.*, Milner S. Ball, *Constitution, Court, Indian Tribes*, 1987 AM. B. FOUND. RES. J. 1, 61–66.

20. *See, e.g.*, United States v. Kagama, 118 U.S. 375, 454 (1886). The Court stated:

> The power of the general government over these remnants of a race once powerful, now weak and diminished in numbers, is necessary to their protection, as well as to the safety of those among whom they dwell. It must exist in that government, because it never existed anywhere else because the theatre of its exercise is within the geographical limits of the United States, because it has never been denied, and because it alone can enforce its laws on all the tribes.

See also Lone Wolf v. Hitchcock, 187 U.S. 553, 565 (1903) (noting that "[p]lenary authority over the tribal relations of the Indians has been exercised by Congress from the beginning, and the power has always been deemed a political one, not subject to be controlled by the judicial department of the government").

21. 21 U.S. (8 Wheat.) 503 (1823).

22. 30 U.S. (5 Pet.) 1 (1831).

23. 31 U.S. (6 Pet.) 515 (1832).

24. *See, e.g.*, GETCHES & WILKINSON, *supra* note 9, at 195; COHEN, *supra* note 10, at 212–16; Charles F. Wilkinson & John M. Volkman, *Judicial Review of Indian Treaty Abrogation: "As Long as Water Flows, or Grass Grows Upon Earth"—How Long a Time Is That?*, 63 CAL. L. REV. 601 (1975).

25. *See infra* notes 63–73 and accompanying text. For slight modifications of the doctrine relevant to judicial review and the application of the "rational basis" test to Congress's legislative authority in Indian affairs, *see* Delaware Tribal Business Committee v. Weeks, 430 U.S. 73

(1977). *But see* United States v. Sioux Nation of Indians, 448 U.S. 371 413 n.28 (1980).

The plenary power doctrine is the subject of extensive scholarly criticism and commentary. Professor Judith Resnik cites the following authorities:

> *See* Ball, 1987 AM. B. FOUND. RES. J. at 46–59 . . . ; Nell Jessup Newton, *Federal Power over Indians: Its Sources, Scope, and Limitations*, 132 U. PA. L. REV. 195, 197–98, 207–28, 236 ("plenary power" doctrine has been narrowed since the 1930s, but limits on congressional power still unclear); Comment, *Inherent Indian Sovereignty*, 4 AM. INDIAN L. REV. 311, 316–20 (1976) (by Jessie D. Green and Susan Work). For debate about the utility for Indian tribes of Congressional "plenary power," *see* Robert Laurence, *Learning to Live with the Plenary Power of Congress over the Indian Nations*, 30 ARIZ. L. REV. 413 (1988) (replying to Williams, *The Algebra of Federal Indian Law: The Hard Trail of Decolonizing and Americanizing the White Man's Indian Jurisprudence*, 1986 WIS. L. REV. 219); Robert A. Williams, Jr., *Learning Not to Live with Eurocentric Myopia: A Reply to Professor Laurence*, 30 ARIZ. L. REV. 439 (1988); Robert Laurence, *On Eurocentric Myopia, the Designated Hitter Rule and "The Actual State of Things,"* 30 ARIZ. L. REV. 459 (1988).

RESNIK, *supra* note 15, at 693 n.99. *See also* the critique and sources cited by Robert Clinton, *Tribal Courts and the Federal Union*, 26 WILLAMETTE L. REV. 841, 847 (1990), and *infra* note 78.

The significance of this doctrine in either a positive or negative sense in the actual fabric of the present and future day-to-day life on the reservation needs to be considered, lest the discussion be mired in simple academic tedium. *See* the discussion in chap. 1.

26. *See, e.g.,* Lone Wolf v. Hitchcock, discussed *supra* at note 20 and accompanying text.

27. *See, e.g.,* JENNINGS, *supra* note 2, at 32–42.

28. U.S. CONST. art. VI, cl. 2 (providing that "all treaties made . . . shall be the Supreme Law of the Land.")

29. *See generally,* WILKINSON, *supra* note 8, at 14–19.

30. *See supra* notes 21–23 and accompanying text. *Cherokee Nation v. Georgia* contained separate concurring opinions by Justices Johnson and Baldwin and a dissent by Justice Thompson. Cherokee Nation v. Georgia, 30 U.S. (5 Pet.) 1 (1831). *Worcester v. Georgia* contained a concurring opinion by Justice McLean and a dissent by Justice Baldwin. Worcester v. Georgia, 31 U.S. (6 Pet.) 515 (1832).

31. 21 U.S. (8 Wheat.) 503 (1923).

32. 30 U.S. (5 Pet.) 1 (1931).

33. 31 U.S. (16 Pet.) 515 (1832).

34. *Johnson,* 21 U.S. at 504–523. The doctrine of discovery holds that "discovery" of new lands by European nations confers title to the "discoverer" because of its superior civilization and Christian heritage. Indigenous people retain a limited right of use and occupancy. Title is

in the "discoverer" supposedly as trustee for the benefit of the dependent tribes. The rights of the beneficiary tribe can be changed only through purchase or a "just" war. The reality of the dominant society's power did not always make for compliance with these requirements. The doctrine is therefore often blatantly racist and self-serving in practice.

35. *Cherokee Nation,* 30 U.S. at 17.

36. *Id.*

37. *Worcester,* 31 U.S. at 559.

38. *See, e.g.,* Seminole Nation v. United States, 316 U.S. 286 (1942) (holding that a breach of the federal government's fiduciary obligation occurred in entrusting tribal funds to tribal representatives who acted improperly). *See generally* Reid Chambers, *Judicial Enforcement of the Federal Trust Responsibility to Indians,* 27 STAN. L. REV. 1213 (1975). Note also that there is sharp criticism of the trust relationship doctrine as including so much blatant federal power—in other words, a new way of shuffling the old deck. *See* Ball, *supra* note 19, at 61–66, for the appropriate sources and discussion. *See also* the discussion in chap. 1 for a cautionary note not about doctrine, right or wrong, but about a place called "home."

39. *Seminole Nation,* 316 U.S. at 296–97; Chambers, *supra* note 38, at 1247.

40. Indian tribes are mentioned only once in the Constitution, and that is in the Commerce Clause, which states that Congress shall have the power to "regulate Commerce with foreign Nations, and among the several States, and with the Indian tribes." By its terms, the Indian Commerce Clause does two things. First, it recognizes, but does not define, tribal sovereignty except to note by the language employed that it is on a par with, but not identical to, the sovereignty of foreign nations or states. In fact, this is the distinction seized on by Chief Justice Marshall in *Cherokee Nation* to recognize tribal sovereignty but to indicate that Indian tribes were neither foreign nations nor states.

Second, the Indian Commerce Clause recognizes a specific but limited congressional authority to regulate "commerce" with Indian tribes. Yet this limitation was swallowed whole with the emergence of the plenary power doctrine articulated in *Kagama* and *Lone Wolf.* This federal gluttony has never abated despite certain assertions to the contrary in some modern cases. For example, the language in McClanahan v. Arizona State Tax Commission, 44 U.S. 164, 172 n.7 (1973)—that "[t]he source of federal authority over Indian matters has been the subject of some confusion, but it is now generally recognized that the power derives from federal responsibility for regulating commerce with Indian tribes and from treaty making"—seems clearly erroneous as it pertains to the Indian Commerce Clause.

41. *Worcester,* 31 U.S. at 559–63.

42. *Id.* at 561.

43. *See, e.g.,* GETCHES & WILKINSON, *supra* note 9, at 269–336, 416–547 (see cases and discussions).

44. *Johnson,* 21 U.S. at 573.

45. *Id.* at 590.

46. *Id.* at 591.

47. *Id.* at 591–92.

48. *Cherokee Nation,* 30 U.S. at 15.

49. G. EDWARD WHITE, THE MARSHALL COURT & CULTURAL CHANGE, 1815–1835, at 729 (abridged ed. 1991).

50. *Id.* Professor White demonstrates that in these early cases Indians are consistently treated as the "other" not entitled to the "natural rights" of full human beings. *Id.* at 703–40.

51. See, for example, the insightful work of Robert A. Williams, Jr., in THE AMERICAN INDIAN IN WESTERN LEGAL THOUGHT 233–328 (1989).

52. *See, e.g., Kagama,* 118 U.S. 375; and especially *Lone Wolf,* 187 U.S. 553.

53. *Seminole Nation,* 316 U.S. at 296–97, CHAMBERS, *supra* note 38, at 1247.

54. CHAMBERS, *supra* note 38, at 1234–42.

55. In the reported words of Vine Deloria, Jr.:

> "Indian law doesn't really exist as a theoretical discipline. [Deloria] said that the study of different disciplines such as culture, religion, education, economics, history, language and logic all have important lessons for a lawyer looking for new strategies to practice law. . . ." In his address, Deloria urged attorneys to look forward from the field of law to what is happening in other areas of human experience to find new ways to articulate Indian law.

NATIVE AM. RTS. FUND LEGAL REV. 3–4 (Summer 1990). And more specifically the question arises as to how tribes and Indian people—the *objects* (not often the *subjects*) of the trust relationship—conceive of the trust relationship's validity and goals.

56. *See, e.g.,* Fort Laramie Treaty of 1868, art. 13, between the United States and the Sioux Nation, 14 Stat. 635, 640 (1868):

> The United States hereby agrees to furnish annually to the Indians the physician, teachers, carpenter, miller, engineer, farmer, and blacksmiths as herein contemplated, and that such appropriations shall be made from time to time, on the estimates of the Secretary of the Interior, as will be sufficient to employ such persons.

57. *Id.*

58. *Id.* at art. 10, 15 Stat. 635, 638 (clothes and an annual beneficial appropriation of ten dollars for each person who "roam[s] and hunt[s]" and twenty dollars for each person who "engages in farming" for a period of thirty years).

59. During the notorious "termination period," which encompassed the 1950s, the U.S. Congress terminated the legal existence of more than one hundred tribes. *See, e.g.,* Charles F. Wilkinson & Eric R. Biggs, *The Evolution of the Termination Policy,* 5 AM. INDIAN L. REV. 139 (1977).

60. 88 Stat. 2203 (codified at 25 U.S.C. § 450a and elsewhere). These services include, for example, police, judicial, and social services and land operations.

61. See, for example, the potential constitutional crisis narrowly avoided in the Cherokee Nation cases discussed in Joseph C. Burke, *The Cherokee Cases: A Study in Law, Politics, and Plurality,* 21 STAN. L. REV. 500 (1969)

62. *See e.g.,* Philip P. Frickey, *Marshalling Past and Present: Colonialism, Constitutionalism, and Interpretation in Federal Indian Law,* 107 HARV. L. REV. 381 (1993).

63. *See, e.g., supra* notes 20 and 25, for the cases and sources cited. *But see* COHEN, *supra* note 10, at 217–20, for a more limited and benign view of plenary power.

64. Nell Newton, *Federal Power over Indians: Its Sources, Scope, and Limitations,* 132 U. PA. L. REV. 195, 199 (1984).

65. 187 U.S. 553 (1903); *see also Lone Wolf*'s immediate precursor, *Kagama,* 118 U.S. 375.

66. *Lone Wolf,* 187 U.S. at 564.

67. *Id.* at 565 (emphasis added).

68. *See, e.g.,* United States v. Sioux Nation, 448 U.S. 371 (1980), especially 411 n.27; United States v. Dion, 476 U.S. 734 (1986) (abrogation of treaty-based hunting rights by congressional scheme).

69. For a general discussion of the "termination period," see COHEN, *supra* note 10, at 152–80. *See also* Wilkinson & Biggs, *supra* note 59.

70. 430 U.S. 73 (1977).

71. 448 U.S. 371 (1980).

72. *Delaware Tribal Business Committee,* 430 U.S. at 73 (holding that rational basis test is used for reviewing congressional decisions about the distribution of tribal funds). "The general rule emerging from our decisions ordinarily requires the judiciary to defer to congressional determination of what is the best of most efficient use for which tribal funds should be employed." *Id.* at 84. But see *Sioux Nation,* which states:

> [C]ases, which establish a standard of review for judging the constitutionality of Indian legislation under the Due Process Clause of the Fifth Amendment [a rational basis test], do not provide an apt analogy for resolution of the issue presented here—whether Congress' disposition of tribal property was an exercise of its power of eminent domain or its power of guardianship.

Sioux Nation, 448 U.S. at 413 n.28. Neither of these cases found a violation of the rational basis test.

73. Choate v. Trapp, 224 U.S. 665 (1912) (holding that a 1908 federal statute which purported to remove restrictions on alienation and taxation of certain allotments made to members of the Five Civilized Tribes without the payment of just compensation violated the Fifth Amendment); Hodel v. Irving, 481 U.S. 704 (1987) (holding that a federal statute which provided for escheatment of individual Indian fractional land interest to the tribe without the payment of just compensation violated the Fifth Amendment). My good friend Robert Clinton informs me also of Muskrat v. United States, 219 U.S. 346 (1910) (holding a 1907 Act of Congress that purported to create a special cause of action in the Court of Claims for certain Cherokee citizens to test the validity of several allotment statutes unconstitutional as violation the "cases" and "controversies" requirements of Article III, Section 2 of the U.S. Constitution) and of several lower federal court decisions.

74. Clinton, *supra* note 25, at 847.

75. 30 U.S. (5 Pet.) 1 (1831). *See supra* notes 22, 32, 48 and accompanying text.

76. 31 U.S. (6 Pet.) 515 (1832). *See supra* notes 23, 33, and accompanying text.

77. 118 U.S. 375. *See supra* note 64 and accompanying text.

78. 187 U.S. 553, 565. *See supra* notes 25–26 and 63–66 and accompanying text. ("Plenary authority over the tribal relations of Indians has been exercised by Congress from the beginning, and the power has always been deemed a political one, not subject to be controlled by the judicial department of the government.") The sweeping scholarly criticism of the doctrine collected by Professor Clinton retorts:

> The legitimacy of federal assertions of such sweeping unilateral authority frequently is proclaimed in Indian country. Indeed, scholars consistently have questioned the purported doctrine of plenary federal authority over Indians because of the lack of any textual roots for the doctrine in the Constitution, the breadth of its implications, and the lack of any tribal consent to such broad federal authority. Therefore, many commentators have sought out limits on that authority. *E.g.*, Milner S. Ball, *Constitution, Court, Indian Tribes*, 1987 AM. B. FOUND. RES. J. 1 (suggesting lack of textual authority for plenary powers); R. BARSH & J. HENDERSON, THE ROAD: INDIAN TRIBES AND POLITICAL LIBERTY 257–69 (1980) (suggesting limitations derived from article I and the ninth amendment); Robert Clinton, *Isolated in Their Own Country: A Defense of Federal Protection of Indian Autonomy and Self-Government*, 33 STAN. L. REV. 979, 996–1001 (1981) (suggesting inherent limits in the reach of the Indian commerce clause); Richard B. Collins, *Indian Consent to American Government*, 31 ARIZ. L. REV. 365 (1989) (arguing for Indian consent as a limitation on federal authority); Robert T. Coulter, *The Denial of Legal Remedies to Indian Nations under U.S. Law*, *in* RE-THINKING INDIAN LAW 103, 106 (National Lawyers Guild Committee on Native American Struggles ed., 1982) ([T]here is not textual support in the Constitution for the proposition that Congress has plenary authority over Indian nations.); Nell Jessup Newton, *Federal Power over Indians: Its*

Sources Scope and Limitations, 132 U. Pa. L. Rev. 195, 261–67 (1984) (suggesting due process and takings limitations).

Clinton, *supra* note 25, at 856 n.21.

79. These developments followed close on the heels of the General Allotment Act, ch. 119, 24 Stat. 388 (1887) (codified as amended at 25 U.S.C. §§ 461–79 [1988]), which sought to "break up the tribal mass" and incorporate tribal members into both the American economy and polity. Clinton, *supra* note 25, at 853–54.

80. 435 U.S. 313, 323 (1978).

81. *See, e.g.,* Steven Burton, An Introduction to Law and Legal Reasoning 107–10 (1985).

82. U.S. Const. amend. X. *See also supra* notes 24–28 and accompanying text.

83. *See, e.g.,* Garcia v. San Antonio Metro. Transit Auth., 469 U.S. 528 (1985). *See supra* notes 14–15 and accompanying text.

84. *See, e.g.,* Albert Memmi, The Colonizer and the Colonized (1965); Frantz Fanon, The Wretched of Earth (1963).

85. 471 U.S. 845 (1985).

86. 480 U.S. 9 (1987).

87. *Iowa Mutual,* 480 U.S. at 14–15.

88. In fact, there is much current debate about how much federal review of tribal court decision making exists or ought to exist and more generally an inquiry about the exact nature of the relationship of the tribal judiciary to the federal judiciary. *See* the in-depth discussion in chap. 3.

89. *See, e.g.,* Phillip P. Frickey, *Congressional Intent, Practical Reasoning, and the Dynamic Nature of Federal Indian Law,* 78 Cal. L. Rev. 1137 (1990).

90. Getches & Wilkinson, *supra* note 9, at xxx (quoting Felix Cohen).

91. Felix Cohen, Handbook of Federal Indian Law 122–23 (1942 ed.).

92. *See, e.g., supra* notes 74–78 and accompanying text.

93. 118 U.S. 375. *See supra* notes 63–78 and accompanying text.

94. 187 U.S. 553. *See supra* notes 63–78 and accompanying text.

95. 104 U.S. 621 (1882) (states retain jurisdiction over non-Indian versus non-Indian crimes committed in Indian country).

96. Getches & Wilkinson, *supra* note 9, at 279.

97. 109 U.S. 556 (1883) (tribes retain jurisdiction over Indian versus Indian homicides in Indian country). This result was effectively overruled by Congress's enactment of the Major Crimes Act, 18 U.S.C. § 1153 (1885).

98. 163 U.S. 376 (1896). (The U.S. Constitution—particularly the Bill of Rights—does not apply to tribes when exercising powers that predate the U.S. Constitution.)

99. COHEN, *supra* note 91, at 367–82.

100. U.S. v. Wheeler, 435 U.S. 313 (1978).

101. WILKINSON, *supra* note 8, at 118–22.

102. *Id.* at 121.

103. See discussion of treaties, *supra* notes 24–28 and accompanying text.

104. WILKINSON, *supra* note 8, at 104.

105. *Id.* at 105.

106. Oliphant v. Suquamish Indian Tribe, 435 U.S. 191 (1978) (holding that tribes have no criminal jurisdiction over non-Indians).

107. Montana v. United States, 450 U.S. 544 (1981) (holding that tribes do not have civil regulatory jurisdiction over non-Indians on fee land unless there is a consensual relationship or non-Indian conduct "threatens or has some direct effect on the political integrity, the economic security or the health or welfare of the tribe"). *See also* the discussion in chap. 3.

108. Brendale v. Confederated Tribes and Bands of Yakima Indian Nation, 409 U.S. 163 (1989) (holding that a tribe is unlikely to have zoning authority over non-Indian fee land on the reservation). *See also* the discussion in chap. 5.

PART 2

1. 471 U.S. 845 (1985) (holding that whether a tribal court has exceeded the lawful limits of its jurisdiction is a question that must be answered by reference to federal law, including federal common law, but that a federal court proceeding is proper only upon exhaustion of tribal court remedies).

2. 480 U.S. 9 (1987) (holding that regardless of the basis of federal jurisdiction, the federal policy supporting tribal self-government directs a federal court to stay its hand in order to give the tribal court a full opportunity to determine its own jurisdiction).

3. *Id.* at 14–15.

CHAPTER 3. THE CRUCIBLE OF SOVEREIGNTY

1. 25 U.S.C. §§ 461–62, 464–79 (1983); 25 U.S.C. § 463 (Supp. 1987).

2. All tribes possessed, at some time, traditional methods for adjudicating disputes. See, for example, Karl Llewellyn and E. Adamson Hoebel's classic study THE CHEYENNE WAY: CONFLICT AND CASE LAW IN PRIMITIVE JURISPRUDENCE (1941). For more recent attempts in this vein, see, for example, James W. Zion, *The Navaho Peacemaker Court: Deference to the Old and Accommodation to the New*, 11 AM. INDIAN L. REV. 89 (1983).

3. WILLIAM HAGAN, INDIAN POLICE AND JUDGES 104–07 (1966).
4. *Id.* at 104.
5. *Id.*
6. *Id.* at 107.
7. *Id.* at 109.
8. *Id.*
9. *Id.* at 110.
10. *Id.*
11. *Id.*
12. *See, e.g.,* Snyder Act, 25 U.S.C. § 13 (1983); 25 U.S.C. §§ 13(b)–13(e) (1986).
13. HAGAN, *supra* note 3 at 145.
14. *See, e.g.,* United States v. Clapox, 35 F. 575 (D.C. Or. 1888). *Clapox* has been cited with approval in every subsequent case upholding the legality of Courts of Indian Offenses. *See, e.g.,* Settler v. Yakima Tribal Court, 419 F.2d 486, 489 (9th Cir. 1969); Colliflower v. Garland, 342 F.2d 369, 373 (9th Cir. 1965); Iron Crow v. Oglala Sioux Tribe, 231 F.2d 89, 95 (8th Cir. 1956).
15. This process began with the Dawes Severalty Act, 25 U.S.C. § 331 *et seq.* (1983), which was also known as the General Allotment Act of 1887 and had as its principal goal the breakup of the tribal tradition of communal ownership through the means of providing individual Indians with specific allotments ranging from 80 to 160 acres. The objective was to convert Indians into individual farmers and ranchers and thereby make them readily assimilable into the surrounding non-Indian farming and ranching communities. The policy failed dismally, resulting mainly in the reduction of the nationwide Indian land base from 138 million acres in 1887 to 48 million acres in 1934. For an expanded description, *see generally* D. S. OTIS, THE DAWES ACT AND ALLOTMENT OF INDIAN LANDS (1973). *See also* the discussion in chap. 1.
16. The Allotment Act also gave the Secretary of the Interior authority to negotiate with any tribe whose members had all been allotted or, where the president believed it to be in the tribe's best interest, to purchase the unallotted or "surplus" lands within the reservation. 25 U.S.C. § 348 (1983). These lands were subsequently made available for non-Indians to homestead.
17. The persistent questions involving the dilemma of who has jurisdiction—that is, whether the federal, tribal, or state government may claim bona fide authority over any given matter in Indian country—is an enduring and significant theme that permeates Indian law. *See generally* FELIX COHEN, HANDBOOK OF FEDERAL INDIAN LAW 281–386 (1982 ed.); DAVID H. GETCHES & CHARLES F. WILKINSON, FEDERAL INDIAN LAW 416–78 (2d ed. 1986); and MONROE E. PRICE, ROBERT N. CLINTON, & NELL JESSUP NEWTON, AMERICAN INDIAN LAW 181–666 (3d ed. 1991).

18. HAGAN, *supra* note 3, at 120.

19. *See, e.g.,* GETCHES & WILKINSON, *supra* note 17, at 111–22. For expanded treatment, *see* FRANCIS PRUCHA, THE GREAT FATHER, THE UNITED STATES GOVERNMENT AND THE AMERICAN INDIANS 609–757 (1984); HENRY FRITZ, THE MOVEMENT FOR INDIAN ASSIMILATION, 1860–1890 (1963).

20. HAGAN, *supra* note 3, at 109.

21. *Id.*

22. Acting Commissioner R. B. Belt as quoted in HAGAN, *supra* note 3, at 109.

23. Comment, *Tribal Self-Government and the Indian Reorganization Act of 1934,* 70 MICH. L. REV. 955, 955–61 (1972); HAGAN, *supra* note 3, at 150.

24. INSTITUTE FOR GOV'T. RESEARCH, STUDIES IN ADMINISTRATION, THE PROBLEM OF INDIAN ADMINISTRATION (1928).

25. HAGAN, *supra* note 3, at 150.

26. 25 U.S.C. §§ 461–62, 464–79 (1983); 25 U.S.C. § 463 (Supp. 1986).

27. VINE DELORIA, JR., & CLIFFORD LYTLE, THE NATIONS WITHIN 76–79 (1984).

28. *Id.* at 76.

29. *See, e.g.,* ROSEBUD SIOUX TRIBAL CONST. art. IV, § 1(k) (1935).

30. DELORIA & LYTLE, *supra* note 27, at 77.

31. *Id.*

32. *Id.*

33. *Id. See also* GETCHES & WILKINSON, *supra* note 17, at 128–29; FRANK POMMERSHEIM, BROKEN GROUND AND FLOWING WATERS 13–14 (1979).

34. DELORIA & LYTLE, *supra* note 27, at 77.

35. *Id.* at 78.

36. The notion of "things not going well" on the reservation reflects only the perception of the non-Indian, dominant society, wholly unhinged from the local perspective of the tribe and its members.

37. For a more recent example, there is the controversy involving the adoption and implementation of the Indian Civil Rights Act of 1968, 25 U.S.C. §§ 1301–03 (1983). *See* Coulter, *Federal Law and Indian Tribal Law: The Right to Civil Counsel and the 1968 Indian Bill of Rights,* 3 COLUM. SURVEY OF HUMAN RIGHTS LAW 49, 50 (1971).

38. DELORIA & LYTLE, *supra* note 27, at 78.

39. *Id.*

40. *Readjustment of Indian Affairs: Hearings on H.R. No. 7902,* 73d Cong., 2d Sess. (1934).

41. DELORIA & LYTLE, *supra* note 27, at 140–53.

42. 25 U.S.C. § 476 (1983).

43. DELORIA & LYTLE, *supra* note 27, at 173. *See generally* GRA-HAM D. TAYLOR, THE NEW DEAL AND AMERICAN INDIAN TRIBALISM: THE ADMINISTRATION OF THE INDIAN REORGANIZATION ACT, 1934–45 (1980).

44. *See, e.g.,* NATIONAL AMERICAN INDIAN COURT JUDGES ASSOCI-ATION, INDIAN COURTS AND THE FUTURE 7–13 (David Getches ed., 1978).

45. ROSEBUD SIOUX TRIBAL CONST. art. IV, § 1(k) (1935).

46. Kerr-McGee Corp. v. Navajo Tribe of Indians, 471 U.S. 195 (1985). Such BIA approval was *not* required by the Indian Reorganiza-tion Act itself.

47. *See, e.g.,* ROSEBUD SIOUX TRIBAL CONST. former art. IV, § 2 (1935), repealed at art. IV, § 1 (1985). This requirement did not, and does not, generally arise in a non-IRA tribal constitution. *See, e.g., Kerr-McGee,* 471 U.S. 195.

48. *See, e.g.,* Talton v. Mayes, 163 U.S. 376 (1896).

49. STEVEN BURTON, AN INTRODUCTION TO LAW AND LEGAL REA-SONING 169 (1985). This section draws substantially on the analytical framework set forth in this appealing work.

50. *Id.* at 187–88.

51. *Id.* at 199.

52. *Id.* at 199–200.

53. *See, e.g.,* Frank Pommersheim and Terry Pechota, *Tribal Immu-nity, Tribal Courts, and the Federal System: Emerging Contours and Frontiers,* 31 S.D. L. REV. 553, 564–67 (1986). This problem has de-creased sharply in recent years with the growing competence and re-spect tribal courts have achieved.

54. BURTON, *supra* note 49, at 202.

55. *Id.* at 187–88.

56. *See, e.g., National Farmers Union,* 471 U.S. 845, and *Iowa Mu-tual,* 480 U.S. 9.

57. Visits with my Indian law class to the Rosebud Sioux Tribal Court in October 1986 and October 1991.

58. The roots of this dispute are more cultural than financial. The plaintiff indicated that she had brought this action not so much for the alleged money owed but to seek redress for the (cultural) wrong she suffered. As an elder and grandmother she felt an important cultural rule was violated when her daughter came and simply removed her chil-dren who were staying with the grandmother without obtaining the grandmother's endorsement and consent for their return. The nature of the dispute raises significant questions about whether there is or should be some other nonlegal but culturally consonant way to mediate such conflict.

59. BURTON, *supra* note 49, at 230.

60. Such a tribal bar examination is currently administered on the Navajo Reservation. It is in the final planning stages on both the Rosebud Sioux and Pine Reservations in South Dakota.

61. Few if any tribes put on their own CLE programs. There is some training (principally for tribal judges) provided by such national tribal groups as the National American Indian Court Judges Association (NAICJA). Local training for tribal judges and tribal court advocates is often provided by Indian legal services programs such as the DNA–People's Legal Services program in Navajo country and Dakota Plains Legal Services program in the Dakotas. States occasionally have CLE programs on Indian law topics. However, no CLE program effectively brings together the full spectrum of tribal practitioners including judges, attorneys, and tribal advocates.

62. Some tribes do have tribal code provisions delineating broad criteria for suspension or dismissal. *See, e.g.,* ROSEBUD SIOUX TRIBAL CODE tit. 9, ch. 2, §§ 8–9 (1985) (suspension for contempt or acting in an unethical or improper manner); SISSETON-WAHPETON SIOUX TRIBAL CODE ch. 32, § 5 (1982) (disbarment or suspension for false swearing, conviction of a felony, disbarred by a federal or state court, conduct unbecoming an officer of the court, and failure to act as counsel for a defendant upon assignment by the court). Few codes identify a detailed administrative procedure to be followed.

63. BURTON, *supra* note 49, at 212. For an interesting example concerning the occupation of Wounded Knee on the Pine Ridge Indian Reservation, *see* DELORIA & LYTLE, *supra* note 27, at 213–14.

64. 25 U.S.C. §§ 1301–03, 1321–26, 1341 (1983).

65. *See, e.g.,* COULTER, *supra* note 37, at 49–50.

66. *Id.*

67. 436 U.S. 49 (1978).

68. *See, e.g.,* Tom v. Sutton, 533 F.2d 1101 (9th Cir. 1976); Wounded Head v. Tribal Council of Oglala Sioux Tribe of Pine Ridge Reservation, 507 F.2d 1079 (8th Cir. 1975); McCurdy v. Steele, 506 F.2d 653 (10th Cir. 1974); Conroy v. Frizzell, 429 F. Supp. 918 (D.C.S.D. 1977).

69. See, for example, the cases and discussions in Douglas B. L. Endreson, *Selected Tribal Court Decisions on Sovereign Immunity and Related Issues Reported in the Indian Law Reporter 1988–92,* Address at the Eighteenth Annual Federal Bar Association Indian Law Conference (1993) 314–34.

70. No IRA tribal constitutions and very few, if any, non-IRA tribal constitutions provide for separation of powers. This seems to reflect a major oversight by the federal drafters from the Bureau of Indian Affairs and the Justice Department whose handiwork dominates most tribal constitutions. *See also Kerr-McGee,* 471 U.S. 195.

71. This observation is based on personal experiences with tribal courts in South Dakota and interviews with (former) Judge Sambroak of the Rosebud Sioux Tribal Court, Judge Marshall of the Rosebud Sioux Tribal Court, (former) Judge Rousseau of the Sisseton-Wahpeton Tribal Court, and (former) Judge Greaves of the Cheyenne River Sioux Tribal Court.

72. *See, e.g.,* CHEYENNE RIVER SIOUX TRIBAL CONST. art. IV, § 1(k) (1992) ("Decisions of tribal courts may be appealed to tribal appellate courts, but shall not be subject to review by the Tribal Council").

73. BURTON, *supra* note 49, at 232.

74. *See, e.g.,* STANLEY FISH, IS THERE A TEXT IN THIS CLASS? (1980).

75. BURTON, *supra* note 49, at 209.

76. *Id.* at 96.

77. *See, e.g.,* VINE DELORIA, JR., & CLIFFORD LYTLE, AMERICAN INDIANS, AMERICAN JUSTICE 193–202 (1983).

78. BURTON, *supra* note 49, at 209.

79. *See, e.g.,* BURTON, *supra* note 49, at 101–237.

80. The Intertribal Court of Appeals was established in 1982 and currently involves the following tribes: the Lower Brule, Crow Creek, Sisseton-Wahpeton, and Flandreau tribes of South Dakota; the Omaha and Winnebago tribes of Nebraska; and the Three Affiliated Tribes of North Dakota. It has been renamed the Northern Plains Intertribal Court of Appeals.

81. Intertribal Court of Appeals Court Rule 17 (1982).

82. *Id.*

83. 18 U.S.C. § 1151. The term "Indian country" is defined as "(a) all land within the limits of any Indian reservation under the jurisdiction of the United States Government, notwithstanding the issuance of any patent, and, including rights-of-way running through the reservation, (b) all dependent Indian communities within the borders of the United States whether within the original or subsequently acquired territory thereof, and whether within or without the limits of a state, and (c) all Indian Allotments, the Indian titles to which have not been extinguished, including rights-of-way running through the same."

84. 18 U.S.C. § 1152 (1984). This statute is supplemented by the Assimilative Crimes Act, 18 U.S.C. § 13 (1984). *See infra* note 89 and accompanying text.

85. 18 U.S.C. § 1153 (1984), as amended by Pub. L. No. 99-646 § 87(e)(5), 100 Stat. 3603 (1986).

86. The statute specifically provides:

Except as otherwise expressly provided by law, the general laws of the United States as to the punishment of offenses committed in any place within the sole and exclusive jurisdiction of the United States, except the District of Columbia, shall extend to Indian country.

This section shall not extend to offenses committed by one Indian against the person or property of another Indian, nor to any Indian committing any offense in Indian country who has been punished by the local law of the tribe, or to any case where, by treaty stipulation, the exclusive jurisdiction over such offenses is or may be secured to the Indian tribes respectively.

18 U.S.C. § 1152 (1984).

87. *See, e.g.,* David Vollman, *Criminal Jurisdiction in Indian Country: Tribal Sovereignty and Defendants' Rights in Conflict,* 22 KAN. L. REV. 387, 391–92 (1974).

88. 104 U.S. 621 (1882) (state has jurisdiction over a homicide committed by one non-Indian against another non-Indian on the Ute Reservation in Colorado).

89. 18 U.S.C. § 13 (1984).

90. *See* GETCHES & WILKINSON, *supra* note 17, at 406–07.

91. 109 U.S. 556 (1883).

92. The statute reads:

(a) Any Indian who commits against the person or property of another Indian or other person any of the following offenses, namely, murder, manslaughter, kidnapping, maiming, a felony under chapter 109A, incest, assault with intent to commit murder, assault with a dangerous weapon, assault resulting in serious bodily injury, arson, burglary, robbery, and a felony under § 661 of this title within the Indian country, shall be subject to the same law and penalties as all other persons committing any of the above offenses, within the exclusive jurisdiction of the United States.

(b) Any offense referred to in subsection (a) of this section that is not defined and punished by Federal law in force within the exclusive jurisdiction of the United States shall be defined and punished in accordance with the laws of the state in which such offense was committed as are in force at the time of such offense.

18 U.S.C. § 1153 *as amended by* Pub. L. No. 100-690, Title VII, § 7027, 100 Stat. 4397 (1988).

93. *Id.*

94. *Id.*

95. *See, e.g.,* GETCHES & WILKINSON, *supra* note 17, at 401–02.

96. The penalty that may be imposed in tribal court is limited by the Indian Civil Rights Act of 1968, 25 U.S.C. § 1302, *as amended by* Pub. L. No. 99-570, § 4217 (1986), to a maximum of one year in jail and a $5,000 fine or both.

97. Oliphant v. Suquamish Indian Tribe, 435 U.S. 191 (1978). See, for example, Justice Rehnquist's broad assertion:

By submitting to the overriding sovereignty of the United States, Indian tribes necessarily gave up their power to try non-Indian citizens of the United States except in a manner acceptable to Congress. This principle would have been obvious a century ago when most Indian tribes were characterized by a "want of fixed laws [and] of competent tribunals of justice. . . . " It should be no less obvious today, even though present-day Indian tribal courts embody dramatic advances over their historical antecedents.

Id. at 210.

98. Examples include adultery, gambling, and prostitution. *See, e.g.,* Robert Clinton, *Criminal Jurisdiction over Indian Lands: A Journey Through a Jurisdictional Maze,* 18 ARIZ. L. REV. 503, 535–36 (1976).

99. *See, e.g.,* United States v. Marcyes, 537 F.2d 1361 (9th Cir. 1977) (upholding the applicability of Washington State's fireworks law on the Puyallup Indian Reservation).

100. *See, e.g.,* Duro v. Reina, 495 U.S. 676 (1990), holding that tribal courts do *not* have criminal jurisdiction over nonmember Indians (i.e., Indians who are *not* enrolled members of the tribe on whose reservation the offense takes place). This result was set aside by Congress, Act of Oct. 28, 1991, Pub. L. No. 102-137, 102d Cong., 1st Sess.

101. As noted by the Supreme Court, "Although the criminal jurisdiction of the tribal courts is subject to substantial federal limitation, . . . their civil jurisdiction is not similarly restricted." *Iowa Mutual,* 480 U.S. at 15.

102. *National Farmers Union,* 471 U.S. at 855.

103. *Iowa Mutual,* 480 U.S. at 18.

104. There is also the corollary issue of when the states may have legislative and/or judicial jurisdiction on the reservation. The leading case analyzing the reach of state authority on a reservation is White Mountain Apache Tribe v. Bracker, 448 U.S. 136 (1980). State authority does not generally apply to Indians or their property on the reservation unless there is special federal legislation such as the Act of August 15, 1953, Pub. L. No. 280, 67 Stat. 588 [hereinafter Public Law 280]. *See also* the discussion in chap. 5.

105. *Iowa Mutual,* 480 U.S. at 12.

106. *Id.* at 19, 20.

107. See, for example, the cases cited and discussed in Timothy W. Joranko, *Exhaustion of Tribal Remedies in the Lower Courts after National Farmers Union and Iowa Mutual: Toward a Consistent Treatment of Tribal Courts by the Federal Judicial System,* 78 MINN. L. REV. 259 (1993).

See particularly Duncan Energy Co. v. Three Affiliated Tribes, 27 F.3d 1294 (8th Cir. 1994), which reasserts the importance of the *Montana* proviso in evaluating tribal legislative authority over non-Indians on fee lands and specifically reiterates the importance of exhausting tribal judicial remedies in *all* reservation-based civil causes of action including those that arise on fee land. The Eighth Circuit Court notes that only after such exhaustion may a federal district court review actions of the tribal court and such review must comport with particular standards of review. The federal district court may review the tribal court's determination of its own jurisdiction *de novo* because it is a question of federal law, but it must also apply a deferential, clearly erroneous standard to the tribal court's findings of fact and conclusions of (tribal) law. *See also F.M.C. v. Shoshone Bannock Tribes*, 905 F.2d 1311 (9th Cir. 1990).

108. FELIX COHEN, HANDBOOK OF FEDERAL INDIAN LAW 122–23 (1942). *See also* the discussion and critique of this doctrine in chapter 2.

109. *See, e.g.*, GETCHES & WILKINSON, *supra* note 17, at 278–80.

110. 109 U.S. 556 (1883) (the tribe has jurisdiction over a homicide committed by one Indian against another Indian on the reservation).

111. 163 U.S. 376 (1896) (tribal powers predate the U.S. Constitution and therefore are not directly subject to its requirements).

112. 118 U.S. 375 (1886) (tribes are wards of the United States and subject to its superior power).

113. 187 U.S. 553 (1903) (tribes are subject to the "plenary power" of Congress over their affairs).

114. 104 U.S. 621 (1882) (tribal courts do *not* have criminal jurisdiction over offenses committed by one non-Indian against another non-Indian in Indian country).

115. GETCHES & WILKINSON, *supra* note 17, at 279.

116. 435 U.S. 191 (1978).

117. *Id.* (judicial or legislative jurisdiction, although the opinion itself does not make that distinction).

118. *See, e.g., Iowa Mutual*, 480 U.S. at 18 (quoting *Merrion*, 455 U.S. 149 n.14).

119. SISSETON-WAHPETON TRIBAL CODE ch. 33, § 1 (1982). The tribal code specifically provides that

[c]ivil matters shall be governed by the laws, customs and usage of the tribe not prohibited by the laws of the United States, applicable federal laws and regulations and decisions of the Department of Interior. The laws of the State of South Dakota may be employed as a guide. Where doubt arises as to the customs and usage of the Tribe, the court shall request the address of tribal elders familiar with tribal customs and usages. Where appropriate, the laws of the State of South Dakota may be employed to determine civil matters. The laws of the State of South Dakota shall not be used as a substitute for existing tribal law.

120. Federal law also preempts any contrary state law. *See, e.g., White Mountain Apache Tribe*, 448 U.S. 136; Warren Trading Post v. Arizona Tax Comm'n, 380 U.S. 685 (1965).

121. *See, e.g.*, Shantz v. White Lightning, 231 N.W.2d 812, 814

(N.D. 1975) (the Standing Rock Sioux Tribal Code limited relief not to exceed $300.00).

122. *See, e.g.,* ROSEBUD SIOUX TRIBAL CODE tit. 4-1-57 (1986), which bars any claim for declaratory relief. This section was subsequently amended to permit such relief in 1991.

123. ROSEBUD SIOUX TRIBAL CODE ch. 2, § 1 (1979), *as amended by* tit. 4-2-6 (1986).

124. Of course, in a non-Indian versus non-Indian situation there is state court jurisdiction because there is no infringement of tribal law. *See, e.g.,* Williams v. Lee, 358 U.S. 217 (1959).

125. CHEYENNE RIVER SIOUX TRIBE BYLAWS art. V, § 1(c) (1935). Despite this organic limitation, the Cheyenne River Sioux Tribal Code asserts jurisdiction over all actions where the persons are present or residing within the reservation. Cheyenne River Sioux Tribal Code § 1-4-3 (1978). There is also a tribal appellate decision in which the Cheyenne River Court found that the signing of a contract between an Indian and a non-Indian provided the necessary "consent." Duchenaux v. First Fed. Sav. & Loan Ass'n of Rapid City, No. 85-002-A (1986). But see the 1992 amendment, which simply states that "the tribal courts shall have jurisdiction over claims and disputes arising on the reservation."

126. OGLALA SIOUX TRIBAL CONST. art. V, § 2 (1935).

127. *See, e.g.,* Santa Clara Pueblo v. Martinez, 436 U.S. 49 (1978) (in construing the Indian Civil Rights Act of 1968, 25 U.S.C. §§ 1301–03, the Court found congressional intent to protect sovereign immunity and the right to tribal self-government).

128. All tribal constitutions contain amendment provisions. Most IRA constitutions contain a provision like the representative provisions of Article IX of the Cheyenne River Sioux Tribe Constitution (1935):

> Sec. 1. This constitution and the appended by-laws may be amended by a majority of qualified voters of the tribe voting at an election called for that purpose by the Secretary of the Interior provided that at least 30 per cent of those entitled to vote shall vote in such elections; but no amendment shall become effective until it shall have been approved by the Secretary of the Interior.
>
> Sec. 2. It shall be the duty of the Secretary of the Interior, upon presentation of a petition signed by at least two hundred (200) legal voters of the tribe, and upon request by the council, to call an election on any proposed amendment.

See also the amended Article IX of the Constitution of the Rosebud Sioux Tribe (1985) which provides for a potential tribal constitutional convention:

Article IX—Amendments

Section 1. This constitution and by-laws may be amended by a majority vote of the qualified voters of the Rosebud Sioux Tribe voting at an election called for that purpose by the Secretary of the Interior, provided that at least thirty (30) per cent of those entitled to vote shall vote in such election; but no amendment shall become effective until it shall have been approved by the Secretary of the Interior. It shall be the duty of the Secretary of the Interior to call an election on any proposed amendment, upon receipt of a written resolution signed by at least three-fourths (3/4) of the membership of the council.

Sec. 2. Upon receipt of a petition that contains the signatures of at least thirty (30) per cent of the voters in the last tribal election, the Tribal Secretary shall refer this petition to the next Tribal Council meeting which shall call a Tribal Constitution convention to commence within thirty (30) days and to appoint a seven-member Tribal Constitutional Task Force, consisting of tribal members outside the Tribal Council, to conduct this Convention for the purpose of hearing proposed amendments and to approve those of which shall be referred to the Secretary of the Interior, and upon receipt of them, it shall be the duty of the Secretary of the Interior to set an election as described in Section 1 above.

129. 25 U.S.C. §§ 1301–03 (1982 & Supp. 1987).

130. See, for example, Article X of the Rosebud Sioux Tribe Constitution, which added a Bill of Rights amendment in 1966:

Article X—Bill of Rights

Section 1. All members of the tribe and all Indians on the reservation shall enjoy without hindrance freedom of religion, speech, press, assembly, conscience and association.

Sec. 2. Any Indian on the reservation accused of any offense shall have the right to a speedy and public trial and to be informed of the nature and cause of the accusation, and to be confronted with witnesses against him. Any Indian accused of any offense shall have the right to the assistance of counsel and to demand trial by jury. Excessive bail should not be required, nor excessive fines imposed, nor cruel and unusual punishments inflicted.

Sec. 3. No person shall be subject for the same offense to be twice put in jeopardy; nor be compelled in any criminal case to be a witness against himself; nor be deprived of life, liberty, or property, without due process of law; nor be denied equal protection of law.

131. The same problem arises when there is an Indian retailer and a defaulting non-Indian consumer.

132. Such "consent to suit" provisions are generally not replicated in federal or state statutes or constitutions.

133. For example, it is hard to fathom why the BIA put these provisions in some tribal constitutions and not in others. Timidity, ineptitude, or unique tribal circumstances are all plausible if not totally justifiable reasons.

134. 13 Indian L. Rep. 6030 (Rosebud Sioux Tribal Court 1986).

135. 326 U.S. 310 (1945).

136. *Rosebud Hous. Auth.*, 13 Indian L. Rep. at 6032. The tribal court stated:

> The defendant admits in its answer continuous and systematic activity on the Rosebud Reservation. In addition the defendant enjoys and benefits from the protection of tribal law while on the reservation. The alleged breach of the oral contract sued upon here arises out of defendant's activities within the reservation. The defendant has had more than minimum contacts on the reservation to constitute a "presence" so that assertion of personal jurisdiction over it by this court will not violate due process or the Constitution. The term "resident" as included in the former tribal code includes foreign corporations who have "presence" on the reservation, *i.e.*, those corporations who have engaged in sufficient activity to meet the "minimum contacts" requirement of *International Shoe*. The defendant in this case clearly meets the test, and therefore, the court holds that it has personal jurisdiction over it.

137. The tribal court found personal jurisdiction could be asserted, both under the tribal law and within the "minimum contacts" confines of *International Shoe. Id.* at 6031. *See, e.g.,* Talton v. Mayes, 163 U.S. 376 (1896) (holding that since Indian tribes exercise powers that predate [and have no source in] the U.S. Constitution, federal constitutional limitations and guarantees do not apply to the exercise of tribal authority, despite the fact that the tribal actions are subject to the supreme legislative authority of the United States).

138. *See, e.g.,* FED. R. CIV. P. 4(e). For an extensive analysis of service of process in Indian country, see Laurence, *Service of Process and Execution of Judgment on Indian Reservations,* 10 AM. INDIAN L. REV. 257 (1982).

139. U.S. CONST. art. IV, § 1, cl. 1.

140. *Id.* This clause is addressed in Comment, *Recognition of Tribal Decisions in State Courts,* 37 STAN. L. REV. 1397 (1985).

141. U.S. CONST. art. IV, § 1, cl. 1. The full text of the Full Faith and Credit Clause reads as follows and does not mention Indian tribes: "Full Faith and Credit shall be given in each State to the Public Acts, Records, and Judicial Proceedings of every other State." Congress extended the Full Faith and Credit Clause to all territories and possessions of the United States. 28 U.S.C. § 1738 (1982).

142. For example, New Mexico, as a result of Jim v. CIT Financial Services Corp., 87 N.M. 362, 533 P.2d 751 (1975); and Washington, as a result of *In re* Buehl, 87 Wash. 2d 649, 555 P.2d 1334 (1976). The U.S. Supreme Court has not directly addressed the issue but has stated that "judgments of tribal courts, as to matters properly within their jurisdiction, have been regarded in some circumstances as entitled to full faith and credit in other courts." *Santa Clara Pueblo,* 436 U.S. at 65 n.21.

143. South Dakota provides comity to tribal court judgments which meet the following statutory requirements:

When order or judgment of tribal court may be recognized in state courts.
No order or judgment of a tribal court in the state of South Dakota may be
recognized as a matter of comity in the state courts of South Dakota, except
under the following terms and conditions:

(1) Before a state court may consider recognizing a tribal court order or
judgment the party seeking recognition shall establish by clear and convinc-
ing evidence that:

   (a) The tribal court had Jurisdiction over both the subject matter and the
   parties;

   (b) The order or judgment was not fraudulently obtained;

   (c) The order or judgment was obtained by a process that assures the
   requisites of an impartial administration of justice including but not limited to due notice and hearing;

   (d) The order or judgment complies with the laws, ordinances and regulations of the jurisdiction from which it was obtained; and

   (e) The order or judgment does not contravene the public policy of the
   state of South Dakota.

(2) If a court is satisfied that all of the foregoing conditions exist, the court
may recognize the tribal court order or judgment in any of the following
circumstances:

   (a) In any child custody or domestic relations case; or

   (b) In any case in which the jurisdiction issuing the order or judgment
   also grants comity to orders and judgments of the South Dakota courts;
   or

   (c) In other cases if exceptional circumstances warrant it; or

   (d) Any order required or authorized to be recognized pursuant to 25
   USC § 1911(d) or 25 USC § 1919.

S.D. CODIFIED LAWS § 1-1-25 (1986).

   144. *See, e.g.,* FRANK POMMERSHEIM, SOUTH DAKOTA TRIBAL
COURT HANDBOOK (rev. ed. 1993). Tribal code silence does not, however, prevent tribal courts from determining as a matter of tribal common law to apply the principle of comity in particular situations.

   145. 25 U.S.C. §§ 1901–63 (1982).

   146. 25 U.S.C. § 1911(d) (1982). Note also that the Secretary of
the Interior must give full faith and credit to tribal actions under tribal
ordinances limiting descent and distribution of trust or restricted or
controlled lands. 25 U.S.C. § 2207 (1982).

   147. A determination of diminishment is often made by the federal
judiciary through a determination of congressional intent. See, for example, the Rosebud Sioux Reservation, in Rosebud Sioux Tribe v.
Kneip, 430 U.S. 584 (1977); the Sisseton-Wahpeton Reservation, in De-
Coteau v. District County Court, 420 U.S. 425 (1975); and the Red
Lake Reservation, in Red Lake Band of Chippewa Indians v. Minnesota, 614 F.2d 1161 (8th Cir. 1980). *See also* the discussion in chap. 1.

   148. As a result of the ravages of the allotment process and the sale
of "surplus" land after allotment, much land within the original bound-

aries of many reservations is held by non-Indians as well as individual Indians and the tribe. If diminishment of any reservation resulted from such congressional action (and the judicial ratification thereof), some tribal land and individual Indian allotments would then be located outside the diminished reservation's boundaries. For example, as a result of the decision in *Rosebud Sioux Tribe*, 430 U.S. 584, over 350,000 acres of tribal and individual trust land (and approximately two thousand tribal members) are located outside the boundaries of the diminished Rosebud Sioux Reservation but within the boundaries of the original reservation.

149. "Dependent Indian community" is defined as part of "Indian country" at 18 U.S.C. § 1151 (1984) as follows:

> Except as otherwise provided in sections 1154 and 1156 of this title, the term "Indian country", as used in this chapter, means (a) all land within the limits of any Indian reservation under the jurisdiction of the United States Government, notwithstanding the issuance of any patent, and, including rights-of-way running through the reservation, (b) all dependent Indian communities within the borders of the United States whether within the original or subsequently acquired territory thereof, and whether within or without the limits of a state, and (c) all Indian allotments, the Indian titles to which have not been extinguished, including rights-of-way running through the same.

150. *Id.*

151. *DeCoteau*, 420 U.S. at 427 n.2.

152. *Id.* at 446 (the Court noted that "[i]n such a situation [*i.e.*, diminishment] exclusive tribal and federal jurisdiction is limited to the retained allotments").

153. 358 U.S. 217 (1959).

154. *Id.* at 223.

155. *See supra* notes 114–54 and accompanying text.

156. 450 U.S. 544 (1981). *See also* Brendale v. Confederated Tribes and Bands of Yakima Indian Nation, 492 U.S. 408 (1989), which is discussed in more detail in chapter 5. This is a plurality case involving three separate complex and inconsistent opinions.

157. *Id.* at 557.

158. *Id.*

159. *Id.*

160. *Id.* at 564–65.

161. *Id.* at 564.

162. *Oliphant*, 435 U.S. at 195.

163. *Montana*, 450 U.S. at 565.

164. *Id.* at 565–66. Justice Stewart specifically stated:

> To be sure, Indian tribes retain inherent sovereign power to exercise some forms of civil jurisdiction over non-Indians on their reservations, even on non-Indian fee lands. A tribe may regulate, through taxation, licensing, or

other means, the activities of nonmembers who enter consensual relationships with the tribe or its members though commercial dealing, contracts,
leases, or other arrangements. A tribe may also retain inherent power to
exercise civil authority over the conduct of non-Indians on fee lands within
its reservation when that conduct threatens or has some direct effect on the
political integrity, the economic security, or the health or welfare of the tribe.
[Citations omitted.]

165. *Id.* at 556.

166. *Id.* at 566.

167. *Id.* at 567.

168. *See supra* notes 102–27 and accompanying text. *See also* the
discussion in chap. 2.

169. *Montana,* 450 U.S. at 565.

170. *National Farmers Union,* 471 U.S. at 855.

171. Knight v. Shoshone and Arapahoe Indian Tribes, 670 F.2d 900
(1st Cir. 1982).

172. Cardin v. DeLaCruz, 671 F.2d 363 (9th Cir. 1982).

173. Confederated Salish and Kootenai Tribes v. Namen, 665 F.2d
951 (9th Cir. 1982).

174. Superior Oil Co. v. United States, 605 F. Supp. 675 (D. Utah
1985).

175. Sandoval v. Tinian, 13 Indian L. Rep. 6041 (Nav. D. Crown
Point 1986).

176. *Rosebud Hous. Auth.,* 13 Indian L. Rep. at 6033.

177. Sage v. Lodge Grass School Dist. No. 27, 13 Indian L. Rep.
6035 (Crow Ct. App. 1986).

178. 419 U.S. 544 (1975). The statutory delegation is found in the
Act of Aug. 15, 1953, Pub. L. No. 277, 67 Stat. 586 (1953) (codified at
18 U.S.C. § 1161 [1983]).

179. *See, e.g., Kerr-McGee,* 471 U.S. 195.

180. *See, e.g.,* Rosebud Sioux Tribe Const. art. IV, §§ 1(h), (i),
(k), and (q) (1935), which, prior to a 1985 amendment, required all
ordinances enacted by the tribe pursuant to these sections to be approved by the Secretary of the Interior.

181. Washington v. Confederated Tribes of Colville Indian Reservation, 447 U.S. 134 (1980).

182. *Id.*

183. A property tax and income tax directly raise the problem of
double taxation in areas where it has never existed. Such taxes also
reach areas that states regard as intimately related to their sovereignty.
Broad political and legal conflict would be inevitable, and it may yet
come as tribes actively pursue the limits of their sovereignty.

184. *See also* Pommersheim and Pechota, *supra* note 53, at 590–92.

185. 436 U.S. 49 (1978).

186. 71 U.S. 845 (1985).

187. 480 U.S. 9 (1987).

188. *See supra* notes 102–07 and accompanying text.

189. 25 U.S.C. § 1303 (1982).

190. *See, e.g.,* Smith v. Confederated Tribes of the Warm Springs Reservation, 783 F.2d 1409 (9th Cir. 1986) (the procedures that tribal courts choose to adopt are not necessarily the same procedures that the federal courts follow); Tom v. Sutton, 533 F.2d 1101 (9th Cir. 1976) (due process and equal protection under the Indian Civil Rights Act of 1968 are not necessarily defined in the same way as they are under the Fourteenth Amendment).

191. *See, e.g., Lone Wolf,* 187 U.S. 553.

192. Robert Williams, *The Discourses of Sovereignty in Indian Country,* 11 INDIAN LAW SUPPORT CENTER REP. 9 (Sept. 1988).

193. POMMERSHEIM, *supra* note 144 at 58.

CHAPTER 4. LIBERATION, DREAMS, AND HARD WORK

1. This section draws extensively on the rich and innovative work of MARTHA MINOW, MAKING ALL THE DIFFERENCE (1990).

2. *See, e.g.,* Robert Clinton, *Tribal Courts and the Federal Union,* 26 WILLAMETTE L. REV. 841, 860 (1990): "Colonization usually results in substantial influx of the new occupants from the colonizing society, redistributes substantial property in favor of the colonizing authority, destroys or impairs some of the cultures of the colonized peoples, and restructures the production and trade relationships within the colonized area in ways that defy immediate or long-term restoration of the *status quo ante.* Even after colonization ends, its residual effects remain and create new realities that must be recognized and addressed by the legal system."

3. *See, e.g., supra* chapter 1, text accompanying note 16, where I comment that "tribal members have been committed to remaining indelibly Indian, proudly defining themselves as a people apart and resisting full incorporation into the dominant society around them."

4. Judith Resnik, *Dependent Sovereigns: Indian Tribes, States, and the Federal Courts,* 56 U. CHI. L. REV. 671, 749 (1989).

5. *Id.*

6. *Id.* at 750.

7. *Id.* at 751. Of course, this likely richness cannot avoid the problem of potential error or wrongdoing within a community-based separate sovereign such as the tribe. In essence, there is a necessity "to try to understand what animates federal decisions to sustain the power of the other, what prompts decisions to diminish that power, and what criteria should lead us to praise or criticize such decisions" *Id.* at 753.

8. MINOW, *supra* note 1, at 21–22.

9. *Id.* at 11.

10. *See, e.g.,* JOHN NIEHARDT, BLACK ELK SPEAKS (1932). *See also* the discussion in chapter 1.

11. MINOW, *supra* note 1, at 20.

12. *Id.* This dilemma is dramatically played out in how faculty members "treat" Native American law students. In treating them just like any other students, there is a risk of exaggerating difference by pretending that there isn't any difference, while treating them differently (e.g., not calling on them in the class) also risks exacerbating differences. There is also the question of how any given Native American law student prefers to be treated. Needless to say, there is no consistency or confidence in any particular approach, at least not at the law school at which I teach.

13. *Id.* at 20–21.

14. Vaclav Havel, *Words on Words,* NEW YORK REV. OF BOOKS, Jan. 18, 1990, at 11.

15. ROBERT SCHOLES, PROTOCOLS OF READING 7 (1989).

16. Some of this undoubtedly sounds like the controversy involving originalist and nonoriginalist interpretation in constitutional law. It is, of course, partly about that, but it is meant to suggest something broader and more pervasive at the same time.

17. HAVEL, *supra* note 14, at 19.

18. Vine Deloria, Jr., *Laws Founded in Justice and Humanity: Reflections on the Content and Character of Federal Indian Law,* 31 ARIZ. L. REV. 203, 204 (1989).

This point is also tellingly illustrated in a reading from the Gospel of John. Mary goes to the tomb of Jesus. He addresses her, "Woman, what is it you want?" She does not know Him. He says, "Mary, what do you seek?" Mary now recognizes Him, because in speaking her *name* He honors her particularity and sacred personhood. See John 20:15–16, NEW OXFORD ANNOTATED BIBLE (Revised Standard Version, 1977).

With the right words, light splits the rock.

19. Vine Deloria, Jr., *NARF Celebrates Its Twentieth Anniversary,* 15 NATIVE AM. RTS. FUND LEGAL REV. 3 (Summer 1990). It has also been observed, for example, that "when we make a classification scheme to sort the kaleidoscope variety of human culture into a related, understandable pattern, we may end up earnestly talking about the classification scheme when we think we are still talking about human cultures." JIM CORBETT, GOATWALKING 8 (1991).

20. Deloria, *supra* note 18, at 205.

21. *See, e.g.,* GUSTAVO GUTIERREZ, LIBERATION THEOLOGY (1973).

22. For example, the Lakota (Sioux) word *wolakota* expresses the deep unity and harmony of all living things.

23. NORTHROP FRYE, WORDS WITH POWER 28 (1991).

24. Adrienne Rich, *An Interview by David Montenego,* AMERICAN POETRY REV., Jan.–Feb. 1991, at 7.

25. *Id.*

26. Linda Hogan, *What Holds the Water, What Holds the Light,* PARABOLA, Winter 1990, at 16.

27. N. Scott Momaday, *The Native Voice in American Literature, in* COLUMBIA LITERARY HISTORY OF THE UNITED STATES 6 (Emory Elliott ed., 1988).

28. *Id.* at 7.

29. *See, e.g.,* Frank Pommersheim, *Constitutional Decisionmaking in Tribal Courts: An Opportunity for Transformation,* 27 GONZ. L. REV. 393 (1992).

30. *See, e.g.,* the discussion in chapter 2.

31. *See, e.g.,* the discussion in chapter 2.

32. Richard Delgado, *Storytelling for Oppositionists and Others: A Plea for Narrative,* 87 MICH. L. REV. 2411, 2412 (1987).

33. *See, e.g.,* Cherokee Nation v. Georgia, 30 U.S. (5 Pet.) 1 (1831), analogizing the relationship of the Indian to the federal government like that of a "ward to his guardian."

34. DELGADO, *supra* note 32, at 2413.

35. *Id.*

36. Thorstenson v. Cudmore, 18 Indian L. Rep. 6051 (1991). Please note that I sit as a member of this court and am the primary author of the court's opinion in this case.

37. The specific provision conditions civil jurisdiction in a lawsuit between Indians and non-Indians by requiring a stipulation of the parties. CHEYENNE RIVER SIOUX TRIBE BY-LAWS art. V, § 1(c) (1935). This provision has since been amended by the Cheyenne River Sioux Tribe. No stipulation is presently required. CHEYENNE RIVER SIOUX TRIBE BY-LAWS art. V, § 1(c) (1992).

38. *Thorstenson,* 18 Indian L. Rep. at 6053.

39. Note that the portion of the *Thorstenson* opinion quoted *supra* at note 38 has recently been cited in Harris v. Young, 473 N.W.2d 141 (S.D. 1991), for its "detailed analysis" and "scathing criticism" of the provision at issue.

40. MOMADAY, *supra* note 27, at 7.

41. DELGADO, *supra* note 32, at 2414.

42. PAULA GUNN ALLEN, ED., SPIDER WOMAN'S GRANDDAUGHTERS 2 (1989).

43. TIM O'BRIEN, THE THINGS THEY CARRIED 40 (1990).

44. THOMAS L. FRIEDMAN, FROM BEIRUT TO JERUSALEM 325 (1989).

45. *Id.* at 326. *See also* the observation that "[i]f as Arabs we say correctly that we are different from the West, as well as different from

its image of Arabs, we have to be persuasive on this point. That takes a lot of work, and cannot be accomplished by a resort to cliches or myths. . . . The competitive, coercive guidelines that have prevailed are simply no good anymore. To argue and persuade rather than boast, preach, and destroy, *that* is the change to be made." Edward W. Said, *Ignorant Armies Clash by Night,* THE NATION, Feb. 11, 1991, at 163.

46. FRIEDMAN, *supra* note 44, at 340.

47. BARRY LOPEZ, CROW AND WEASEL 48 (1990).

48. Ronald Goodman, Wild Plants and Remembering to Remember 2 (1990) (unpublished manuscript on file with the author). The quotation is from Stanley Red Bird (1917–87) of the Rosebud Sioux Tribe.

49. Robert M. Cover, *The Folktales of Justice: Tales of Jurisdiction,* 14 CAP. U. L. REV. 179, 182 (1985).

50. Robin West, *The Supreme Court 1989 Term Foreword: Taking Freedom Seriously,* 104 HARV. L. REV. 43, 104 (1990).

51. *Id.* at 105.

52. FRIEDMAN, *supra* note 44, at 380.

53. WENDELL BERRY, WHAT ARE PEOPLE FOR? 169 (1990) (addressing the issue of reviving rural communities).

54. JAMES BOYD WHITE, JUSTICE AS TRANSLATION xiii (1990).

55. *Id.* This view is often associated with a school of thought known as Critical Legal Studies. *See, e.g.,* MARK KELMAN, A GUIDE TO CRITICAL LEGAL STUDIES (1987).

56. WHITE, *supra* note 54, at xiv.

57. *Id.* at 137.

58. *See, e.g.,* Pommersheim, *supra* note 29 and accompanying text.

59. WHITE, *supra* note 54, at 233.

60. *See, e.g.,* JOSEPH EPES BROWN, THE SPIRITUAL LEGACY OF THE AMERICAN INDIAN (1989).

61. WHITE, *supra* note 54, at 152.

62. *Id.* at xvii. *See also* discussions of the "other" *supra,* notes 4–7 and accompanying text.

63. MINOW, *supra* note 1, at 149–52.

64. *Id.* at 152.

65. U.S. CONST. amends. I–X.

66. 25 U.S.C. §§ 1301–03 (1984). Note, however, that the youth, fragility, and cultural differences of many tribal governments may require more modest substantive remedies. *See, e.g.,* Tom v. Sutton, 533 F.2d 1101 (9th Cir. 1976) (due process and equal protection under the ICRA are not necessarily defined the same as under the Fourteenth Amendment); Smith v. Confederated Tribes of the Warm Springs Reservation, 783 F.2d 1169 (9th Cir. 1986) (the procedures that tribal courts choose to adopt are not necessarily the same procedures that federal courts follow).

In addition, there is, of course, the ongoing discussion of whether the federal government ought to have infringed on tribal sovereignty by implementing this statute without tribal consent. *See, e.g.,* Coulter, *Federal Law and Indian Tribal Law: The Right to Civil Counsel and the 1968 Indian Bill of Rights,* 3 COLUM. SURVEY OF HUMAN RIGHTS LAW 49 (1971).

67. *See, e.g.,* ROSEBUD SIOUX TRIBAL CONST. art. X (1966).

68. *Tiyospaye* is the Lakota (Sioux) word for "extended family."

69. MINOW, *supra* note 1, at 311.

70. *Id.* at 85.

71. *Id.* at 84. The example of the hearing-impaired child also comes from Professor Minow, *supra* note 1, at 82–84.

72. *See supra* note 66 and accompanying text.

73. Note, for example, this helpful observation:

> It is only contradictory to defend both rights and relational strategies in a conceptual framework that poses either/or solutions and reads any focus on interconnection as a retreat from liberalism to feudalism. We are more inventive than that. It is a mistake to infer that relational strategies are inconsistent with rights. An emphasis on connections between people, as well as between theory and practice, can synthesize what is important in rights with what rights miss. Especially when located as a historical response to patterns of assigned status, rights represent an important cultural tool to challenge persistent relationships of unequal power.

MINOW, *supra* note 1, at 382–83.

74. As quoted in ALLEN, *supra* note 42, at 9.

75. *Id.* In other words:

> try telling yourself
> you are not accountable
> to the life of your tribe
> the breath of your planet

ADRIENNE RICH, *North American Time, in* YOUR NATIVE LAND, YOUR LIFE 34 (1986).

76. *See, e.g.,* Frank Pommersheim, *Economic Development in Indian Country: What Are the Questions?,* 12 AM. INDIAN L. REV. 195 (1984), and the discussion in chapter 6.

77. Note, however, that the concept of "natural resources" is actually a misnomer. A natural "resource" cannot exist without some intervening *human* agency to define it. WILLIAM CRONON, CHANGES IN THE LAND 165 (1983).

78. This theme has been developed under the rubrics of "moral monism" and "moral pluralism" in the work of CHRISTOPHER STONE, EARTH AND OTHER ETHICS (1987).

79. RICHARD NELSON, THE ISLAND WITHIN 13 (1989).

80. See, for example, the general discussion in chapter 2. *See also* Escondido Mut. Water Co. v. LaJolla Band of Mission Indians, 466 U.S. 765, 788 n.30 (1984) ("All aspects of Indian sovereignty are subject to defeasance by Congress") as well as the scholarly discussion in Milner S. Ball, *Constitution, Court, Indian Tribes,* 1987 Am. B. Found. Res. J. 3, 49; Robert Williams, *Learning Not to Live with Eurocentric Myopia: A Reply to Professor Laurence's Learning to Live with the Plenary Power of Congress over the Indian Nations,* 30 Ariz. L. Rev. 439, 446 n.31 (1988).

81. *See* the discussion in chapter 2.

82. "Congress shall have the power . . . to regulate commerce with foreign nations, and among the several states, and with the Indian tribes." U.S. Const. art. I, § 8. *See* the discussions of this doctrine in chapter 2.

83. More than 109 tribes and bands were terminated during the notorious termination era of the 1950s and early 1960s. The effects of termination were extensive and wide-ranging. For example, "termination ended the special federal-tribal relationship almost completely and transferred almost all responsibilities for, and powers over, affected Indians from the federal government to the states. The historic special Indian status came to an abrupt end for terminated individual Indians and tribes." Charles F. Wilkinson and Eric R. Biggs, *The Evolution of the Termination Policy,* 5 Am. Indian L. Rev. 139, 151–54 (1977).

84. *See also* the discussion on the importance of treaties in chapter 2 (discussing treaties as the cornerstone of tribal-federal and tribal-state relations). *See also* Pommersheim, *supra* note 29 (discussing treaties as an important organic source of tribal sovereignty in the context of tribal constitutional adjudication).

85. *See, e.g.,* Robert Williams, *The Discourses of Sovereignty in Indian Country,* 11 Indian Law Support Center Rep. 1 (Sept. 1988). I believe most people in the field of Indian law, but particularly at the state and federal level, have little understanding or "feel" for the real threat—used often enough in history in such things as termination and P.L. 280 era legislation—that plenary power holds for Indian people and tribes.

86. President Clinton as quoted in B.I.A. Indian News Week-in-Review, May 13, 1994, at 1.

87. U.S. Const. art. VI.

88. Federal Power Commission v. Tuscarora Indian Nation, 362 U.S. 99, 142 (1976) (Black, J., dissenting).

89. Charles F. Wilkinson, American Indians, Time, and the Law 4 (1986). To fulfill this commitment, there may even be the need to adopt a constitutional amendment to formally assemble and contemporize tribal sovereignty and bring it from the margin to the center of our constitution text and faith. See also the call for constitutional re-

form to achieve economic democracy and security. Savoy, *Time for a Second Bill of Rights,* THE NATION, June 17, 1991, at 1.

90. Robert A. Williams, Jr., *Encounters on the Frontiers of International Human Rights Law: Redefining the Terms of Indigenous Peoples' Survival in the World,* 1990 DUKE L. J. 660, 672. Much of this section of the chapter draws on Professor Williams's fine work. *See also* S. James Anaya, *The Rights of Indigenous People and International Law in Historical and Contemporary Perspective,* 1989 HARV. INDIAN L. SYMP. 191 (1990).

91. 21 U.S. (8 Wheat) 543 (1823).

92. *Id.* at 587.

93. Williams, *supra* note 90, at 673–74.

94. *Id.* at 675. Note also the echo of the language from Cherokee Nation v. Georgia, 30 U.S. (5 Pet.) 1 (1831), which described Indians as being "in a state of pupilage. This relation to the United States resembles that of a ward to his guardian."

95. Williams, *supra* note 90, at 675.

96. *Id.* at 676. This process is described in more detail at pp. 676–82.

97. *Id.* at 683. *See* the *Report of the Working Group on Indigenous Populations on Its Fifth Session,* at 3–5, U.N. Doc. E/CN.4/Sub. 2/1987, Annex II. The Working Group's original draft principles respecting indigenous peoples' rights recognize the following:

1. The right to the full and effective enjoyment of the fundamental rights and freedoms universally recognized in existing international instruments, particularly in the Charter of the United Nations and the International Bill of Human Rights.
2. The right to be free and equal to all other human beings in dignity and rights, and to be free from discrimination of any kind.
3. The collective right to exist and to be protected against genocide, as well as the individual right to life, physical integrity, liberty, and security of person.
4. The collective right to maintain and develop their ethnic characteristics and identity.
5. The collective right to protection against any act which has the aim or effect of depriving them of their ethnic characteristics or identity. This protection shall include prevention of any form of forced assimilation, any propaganda directed against them, etc.
6. The collective right to participate fully in the economic, political and social life and to have their specific character reflected in the legal system and in the political institutions of their country.
7. The duty of the territorial State to grant—within the resources available—the necessary assistance for the maintenance of their identity and their development.
8. The right to special State measures for the immediate, effective and continuing improvement of their social and economic conditions, with their consent, that reflect their own priorities.

9. The right to be secure in the enjoyment of their own traditional means of subsistence, and to engage freely in their traditional and other economic activities, without adverse discrimination.
10. The right to determine, plan and implement all health, housing and other social and economic programs affecting them.
11. The right to manifest, teach, practice and observe their own religious traditions and ceremonies, and to maintain, protect, and have access to sites for these purposes.
12. The right to all forms of education, including the right to have access to education in their own languages, and to establish their own educational institutions.
13. The right to preserve their cultural identity and traditions, and to pursue their own cultural development.
14. The right to promote intercultural information and education, recognizing the dignity and diversity of their cultures.

98. Williams, *supra* note 90, at 683.

99. *Id.* at 684–85.

100. *See, e.g.,* Robert Clinton, *The Rights of Indigenous Peoples as Collective Group Rights,* 32 ARIZ. L. REV. 739 (1990).

101. "Ethnocide" may be defined as including "any act which has the aim or effect of depriving them [indigenous people] of their ethnic characteristics or cultural identity [or] any form of forced assimilation or integration, [such as the] imposition of foreign life-styles." Williams, *supra* note 90, at 688, quoting from *Discrimination Against Indigenous Peoples: First Revised Text of the Draft Universal Declaration on Rights of Indigenous People,* U.N. Doc. E/CN.4/Sub. 2/1989/33 (1989) at 6, para. 5 [hereinafter *W.G. Draft*].

102. Frank Pommersheim, *When It Comes to Indians, the West Is Ignorant,* HIGH COUNTRY NEWS, May 21, 1990, at 15, col. 1 (note that the speaker of the quotation in the article, Elizabeth Garriott, now goes by her maiden name, Elizabeth Little Elk).

103. *See,* for example, the discussion in chapter 1.

104. *See, e.g.,* the discussion *supra* at note 83 and accompanying text.

105. "Diminishment" refers to the congressional practice of unilaterally reducing the size of reservations. *See, e.g.,* Solem v. Bartlett, 465 U.S. 463 (1984), and the discussion in chapter 1.

106. Williams, *supra* note 90, at 689–90, quoting *W.G. Draft, supra* note 101, at 6, paras. 12, 13. According to the wording of the draft, indigenous peoples possess the following:

12. The right of *collective and individual* ownership, possession and use of the lands or resources where they have traditionally occupied or used. The lands may only be taken away from them with their free and informed consent or released by a treaty or agreement.
13. The right to recognition of their land-tenure systems for the protection and promotion of the use, enjoyment, and occupancy of the land.

107. *See, e.g.,* DAVID H. GETCHES & CHARLES F. WILKINSON, FEDERAL INDIAN LAW 151–60 (2d ed. 1986).

108. Williams, *supra* note 90, at 694–95.

109. *Id.* at 695.

110. *Id.* at 698, quoting W.G. *Draft, supra* note 101, at 8, para. 28.

111. Williams, *supra* note 90, at 699.

112. *See, e.g.,* the discussion in chapter 3.

113. All of this requires a caveat. These developments have yet to achieve the status of fully recognized international law. They supplement, but do not supplant, the other sources of tribal court jurisprudence discussed in this work. And for those so inclined, there is the raw skepticism of Professor Laurence's declaration that he has "little faith in the ability of public international law to protect any valuable rights. I have no faith in the ability of public international law to put bread on American Indian tables." Laurence, *Learning to Live with the Plenary Power of Congress over the Indian Nations,* 30 ARIZ. L. REV. 413, 428 (1988).

114. As a member of both the Rosebud Sioux Tribal Court of Appeals and the Cheyenne River Sioux Tribal Court of Appeals and as a person with wide tribal court contacts throughout the state, I can personally attest to the high level of commitment and pride that is evident in the Indian people—both professional and nonprofessional—who work in tribal courts. See also the comments of South Dakota Circuit Judge Merton Tice, *infra* note 119 and accompanying text.

115. Attendance survey distributed at the South Dakota Tribal-State Judicial Conference (May 1991). Note also that the number of Native American law school graduates has risen from 44 in 1960 to 999 in 1980. Michael Taylor, *Modern Practice in Indian Courts,* 10 U. PUGET SOUND L. REV. 231, 236 n.21 (1987).

116. See, for example, the plans of the Northern Cheyenne Constitutional Revision Project for wide-ranging change, including the separation of powers, in Woody Kipp, *Northern Cheyenne Work on Constitutional Changes,* LAKOTA TIMES, Aug. 7, 1991, at A10; as well as the plans of eight Indian reservations in Wyoming and Montana to form an Indian supreme court in order to "strengthen sovereignty." *Eight Tribes Form Indian Supreme Court,* LAKOTA TIMES, July 10, 1991, at A1.

117. The amendment specifically provides that

[u]pon receipt of a petition that contains the signatures of at least thirty (30) percent of the voters in the last tribal election, the Tribal Secretary shall refer this petition to the next Tribal Council meeting which shall call a Tribal Constitution convention to commence within thirty (30) days and to appoint a seven-member Tribal Constitutional Task Force, consisting of tribal members outside the Tribal Council, to conduct this Convention for the purpose of hearing proposed amendments and to approve those of which shall be

referred to the Secretary of the Interior, and upon receipt of them, it shall be the duty of the Secretary of the Interior to set an election as described in Section 1 above.

ROSEBUD SIOUX TRIBE CONST. amend. XIX (1985).

118. *See, e.g.,* James W. Zion, *The Navaho Peacemaker Court: Deference to the Old and Accommodation to the New,* 11 AM. INDIAN L. REV. 89 (1983). *See also* the discussion and cases collected in Kathryn W. Pieplow, "This Pride of Difference": Reflections on the Use of Precedent in Indian Common Law (1993) (student paper, on file with the University of South Dakota School of Law Library).

119. *See, e.g.,* the recent testimony (June 12, 1991) of the Chief Deputy Attorney General of the State of South Dakota before the U.S. Senate Select Committee on Indian Affairs that claimed, in part, that "[a]buses in tribal government and court argue against extension of tribal jurisdiction." This testimony was offered in opposition to S. 962 and S. 963, which would make permanent the interim congressional suspension of the result of Duro v. Reina, 110 S. Ct. 2053 (1990) (holding that tribes did not have criminal jurisdiction over nonmember Indians). This testimony was provided even in the face of a South Dakota legislative resolution explicitly endorsing S. 962 and S. 963.

Despite this executive antagonism, there appears to be much more cooperation and mutual respect at the judicial level evinced by such things as the successful national conference entitled Civil Jurisdiction of Tribal and State Courts: From Conflict to Common Ground (June 30–July 2, 1991, Seattle) as well as the equally successful Tribal-State Judicial Conference called by Chief Justice Robert Miller of the South Dakota Supreme Court (May 1, 1991). Note also the comments of South Dakota Circuit Judge Merton Tice after conducting a state civil trial in a tribal courtroom on the Pine Ridge Reservation:

> The Oglala Sioux Tribe should be proud of the high standards and quality displayed during the course of this trial by their Tribal Police. . . .
> The cooperation, professionalism, and the warmth I felt from literally everyone with whom I came into contact during the trial leave me with a very special appreciation of Pine Ridge and the Oglala Sioux Tribe.

Tice Compliments OST Court System, LAKOTA TIMES, May 29, 1991, at A5.

120. This lack of research capability is a serious problem and needs to be addressed. See, for example, the discussion of the Indian Tribal Judicial Act, *infra* at notes 124–27 and accompanying text.

121. In my experience as an associate justice on both the Rosebud Sioux Tribal Court of Appeals and the Cheyenne River Sioux Tribal Court of Appeals, I have often seen practitioners exhibit a lack of familiarity with the precedent of the very court they are practicing before. This problem is often exacerbated by irregular publication of opinions

in the *Indian Law Reporter*. It is also to be noted that the absence of tribal legislation (including treaties and the tribal constitution) or a tribal court precedent on point does *not* exhaust the possible sources of dispositive law. Another vital source is that body of law known as tradition and custom and which is part of the oral tradition. A given tribal code may or may not direct one to this source. *See, e.g.,* SISSETON-WAHPETON TRIBAL CODE ch. 33, § 1 (1982), which specifically provides that

> civil matters shall be governed by the laws, customs and usage of the tribe not prohibited by the laws of the United States, applicable federal laws and regulations and decisions of the Department of Interior. The laws of the State of South Dakota may be employed as a guide. Where doubt arises as to the customs and usage of the tribe, the court shall request the address of tribal elders familiar with tribal customs and usages. Where appropriate, the laws of the State of South Dakota may be employed to determine civil matters. The laws of the State of South Dakota shall not be used as a substitute for existing tribal law.
>
> Note also the directory role given to state law in this tribal code.

See also the discussion in chapter 3.

122. This subscription service is published and updated monthly by the American Indian Lawyer Training Program, located in Oakland, California.

123. Most contemporary tribal courts were not established until the 1930s after the adoption of written tribal constitutions pursuant to the authorization contained in the Indian Reorganization Act, 25 U.S.C. § 476 (1990). Most tribal courts have dealt with serious, voluminous, and complex litigation for approximately thirty years. *See also* the discussion in chap. 3.

124. Pub. L. No. 103-176, 107 Stat. 2004 (1993)

125. 137 CONG. REC. S3400–01 (daily ed., Mar. 14, 1991) (statement of Sen. McCain).

126. Pub. L. No. 103-176, *supra* note 124, § 103(a).

127. *Id.* § 2(5).

128. *See, e.g.,* Deloria, *supra* note 19. Deloria observes that because federal courts seem to be operating on an ad hoc basis, Indian law doesn't really exist as a theoretical discipline. The study of different disciplines such as culture, religion, education, economics, history, language, and logic all have important lessons for a lawyer looking for new strategies to practice law.

129. *See, e.g.,* Cover, *supra* note 49, at 4–11.

130. ROBERT N. BELLAH ET AL., THE GOOD SOCIETY 5 (1991). The authors also point out that "[i]n surveying our present institutions we need to discern what is healthy in them and what needs to be altered, particularly where we have begun to destroy the non-renewable natural

and nearly non-renewable human resources upon which all our institutions depend." *Id.*

131. For example, no scholarly article in the past five years discusses tribal sovereignty in the context of local institution building.

132. *See* the discussion in chapter 3.

133. Chief Judge Marshall is a bilingual, bicultural member of the Rosebud Sioux Tribe. He is also a 1984 graduate of the University of South Dakota School of Law and a member of the South Dakota Bar.

134. Interview with Sherman Marshall, Chief Judge of the Rosebud Sioux Tribal Court, Rosebud Sioux Indian Reservation (July 1990).

135. Additional plans include the administration of a tribal bar examination. A bar association and bar examination already exist on the Navajo Reservation and the Colville Reservation in the state of Washington.

136. *See, e.g.,* Resnik, *supra* note 4.

137. WILKINSON, SUPRA note 89, at 14–19.

138. *See, e.g.,* Justice Stewart's declaration that "the sovereignty that the Indian tribes retain is of a unique and limited character. It exists only at the sufferance of Congress and is subject to complete defeasance." United States v. Wheeler, 435 U.S. 313, 323 (1978).

139. "Modern" tribal institutions, such as tribal courts, particularly those that have their origins in the Indian Reorganization Act of 1934, face the problem of being seen as "the imposition of white man's law and standards." *See also* the discussion in chap. 2.

140. Love undoubtedly seems like a strange, if not inappropriate, word to use in legal scholarship. But maybe not. Love, after all, is the foundation from which to speak truth to power. *See, e.g.,* Anthony E. Cook, *Beyond Critical Legal Studies: The Reconstructive Theology of Dr. Martin Luther King, Jr.,* 103 HARV. L. REV. 985 (1990).

Love is also the life force that weds one to the life and landscape of others. "Every place, like every person, is elevated by the love and respect shown toward it, and by the way its bounty is received." NELSON, *supra* note 79, at xii. It is also an "expression of an intense spiritual affinity with the mystery that is 'to be sharing life with another life.' " Barry Lopez quoted in RICHARD NELSON, *supra* note 79, at frontispiece.

And as wisely observed by a leading neurologist:

> This sense of affection is neither sentimental nor extraneous. In studying these patients one comes to love them; and in loving them, one comes to understand them: the study, the love, the understanding are all one. . . . Neurologists scarcely dare *admit* to emotion—and yet emotion, warmth of feeling, shines through all genuine work.

OLIVER SACKS, AWAKENINGS 254 (1983).

141. Gabriel García Marquez, *The Solitude of Latin America,* NEW YORK TIMES, Feb. 6, 1983, at EY 19.

142. RICH, *supra* note 75, at back cover (paperback edition).

143. Bloomberg v. Dreamer, Oglala Sioux Civ. Ap. 90-348 at 5–6 (1991) (holding that due process requires a hearing before attempting to remove anyone from the Pine Ridge Reservation).

144. The phrase comes from the South African writer Nadine Gordimer.

CHAPTER 5. TRIBAL-STATE RELATIONS

1. Indian tribes are mentioned only once in the Constitution, and that is in the Commerce Clause, which states that Congress shall have the power to "regulate Commerce with foreign Nations, and among the several States, and with the Indian Tribes." U.S. CONST. art. I, § 8, cl. 3. Indian tribes are implicit subjects of the treaty-making power at U.S. CONST. art. II, § 2. Individual Indians are mentioned as "Indians not taxed" at U.S. CONST. art. I, § 2. *See also* the discussion in chapter 2.

2. The Tenth Amendment states, in relevant part, that "the powers not delegated to the United States by the Constitution, nor prohibited by it to the States, are reserved to the States respectively, as to the people."

3. For example, the South Dakota Constitution contains no provisions that deal with tribal-state relations except to repeat the "disclaimer clause" language of the Enabling Act, Act of February 22, 1989, ch. 180, 25 Stat. 676, 677 (1989). This language states: "we forever disclaim all right and title to . . . all lands lying within said limits used or held by any Indian on Indian tribes . . . and said Indian lands shall remain under the absolute jurisdiction and control of the Congress of the United States. . . ." S.D. CONST. art. XXVI, § 18.

4. For example, no tribal constitution of the nine tribes in South Dakota contains any provisions that deal with tribal-state relations.

5. *See, e.g.,* Gale, *Divisive System,* SIOUX FALLS ARGUS LEADER, Feb. 15, 1989, at A1 (reporting former South Dakota Attorney General Roger Tellinghuisen's statement that "Indian reservations are a 'divisive system' of government that have outlived their usefulness").

6. 31 U.S. (6 Pet.) 515 (1832). *See also* the discussion in chapter 2.

7. *Worcester,* 31 U.S. at 557.

8. *Id.* at 561.

9. 118 U.S. 375 (1886).

10. *Id.* at 376.

11. *Id.* at 383–84 (emphasis in original).

12. McClanahan v. Arizona State Tax Comm., 411 U.S. 164, 172 (1973).

13. *Id.*

14. White Mountain Apache Tribe v. Bracker, 448 U.S. 136, 144–45 (1980).

15. *See* the South Dakota Enabling Act, which provides: "[S]aid proposed states do agree and declare that they forever disclaim all right and title . . . to all lands lying within said limits owned or held by any Indian or Indian tribes . . . and said lands shall remain under the absolute jurisdiction and control of the Congress of the United States." Act of February 22, 1989, ch. 180, § 4, 25 Stat. 676–77 (this act covers North Dakota, South Dakota, Montana, and Washington). *See also* Enabling Act of June 16, 1906, ch. 3335, § 3, 34 Stat. 267, 269 (1905–1907) (Oklahoma); Enabling Act of June 20, 1910, ch. 310 § 2, 20, 36 Stat. 557, 558–59, 569 (1900–1911)(New Mexico and Arizona); Enabling Act of July 7, 1958, P.L. No. 85–508 § 4, 72 Stat. 339, 339 (1958) (Alaska). Idaho and Wyoming, which were both admitted to statehood in 1890 without prior enabling acts, nevertheless inserted disclaimers in their state constitutions. *See* IDAHO CONST. art 21, § 19; WYO. CONST. art. 21, § 26.

16. "[T]he presence or absence of specific jurisdictional disclaimers has rarely been dispositive in our consideration of state jurisdiction over Indian affairs or activities on Indian lands." Arizona v. San Carlos Apache Tribe of Arizona, 463 U.S. 545, 562 (1983).

17. During the period 1887–1934, 90 million acres of land in Indian country went from tribal to non-Indian ownership. *See also* the discussion in chapter 1.

18. 31 U.S. 515 (1832).

19. *See, e.g., White Mountain Apache Tribe,* 448 U.S. 136.

20. 450 U.S. 544 (1981).

21. 490 U.S. 163 (1989).

22. 492 U.S. 408, 109 S. Ct. 2994 (1989).

23. 113 S. Ct. 2309 (1993).

24. *Worcester,* 31 U.S. at 557, 559.

25. 358 U.S. 217 (1959).

26. *Id.* at 217–18.

27. *Id.* at 219.

28. *Id.* at 220.

29. *Id.* at 223.

30. 380 U.S. 685 (1965).

31. *Id.* at 685–86.

32. *Id.* at 691.

33. *Id.* at 690.

34. *Id.* at 686; *Williams,* 358 U.S. at 221.

35. 411 U.S. 164 (1973).

36. *Id.* at 165.

37. *Id.* at 171.

38. *Id.* at 172.

39. 448 U.S. 136 (1980).

40. *Id.* at 137–38.

41. *Id.* at 142–43, 145 (citations omitted); *see also supra* notes 12–14 and accompanying text.

42. 450 U.S. 544 (1981). *See also* discussion in chapter 3.

43. 109 S. Ct. 2994.

44. 113 S. Ct. 2309.

45. *Cotton Petroleum,* 490 U.S. at 184.

46. *Id.* at 163.

47. 455 U.S. 130 (1982) (tribe has the right to assert severance tax against non-Indian corporation engaged in oil and gas extraction on the reservation).

48. *Cotton Petroleum,* 490 U.S. at 168.

49. *Id.* at 173.

50. *Id.* at 175–77 (citations omitted).

51. 471 U.S. 759 (1985).

52. *Cotton Petroleum,* 490 U.S. at 179.

53. *Id.* at 186.

54. *Id.* at 180–81.

55. *Id.* at 204 (Blackmun, J., dissenting).

56. *Id.* (emphasis in original) (citations omitted).

57. *Montana,* 450 U.S. at 547.

58. *Id.*

59. *Id.* at 566–67.

60. Second Treaty of Fort Laramie, May 7, 1868, art. II, 15 Stat. 650; *Montana,* 450 U.S. at 553.

61. *Montana,* 450 U.S. at 561.

62. *Id.* at 564.

63. *Id.* at 565–67 (citations omitted).

64. *Brendale,* 109 S. Ct. 2996–97.

65. *Id.* at 2999, 3009, 3017. *Brendale* consolidated two cases which addressed the question of who possessed the authority to zone non-member fee land within the boundaries of the Yakima Reservation. *Id.* at 3002–03. During the course of the litigation, the parties treated the reservation as having two parts. First, there was the "closed area," so named because it had been closed to the public since 1972, consisting of over 800,000 acres of which only 25,000 were fee land. Second, there was the "open area" that had no restrictions concerning the general public and consisted of approximately 50 percent fee land. *Id.* at 3000.

Zoning power over the two pieces of land was in question. *Id.* at 3001. No clear majority could be reached on either land parcel. Justice White, joined by the Chief Justice, Justice Scalia, and Justice Kennedy, announced the judgment of the Court concerning the land within the "open area." *Id.* at 2999. Justice Stevens, joined by Justice O'Connor, announced the judgment of the Court concerning the land in the "closed area" and concurred with Justice White's judgment concerning the "open area." *Id.* at 3009. Justice Blackmun, joined by Justices Brennan and Marshall, concurred in the Court's judgment of the "closed area" and dissented from the judgment of the "open area." *Id.* at 3017.

66. *Id.* at 3006–07.

67. *Id.* at 3008.

68. *Id.* at 3014.

69. *Id.*

70. *Id.* at 3015.

71. *Id.* at 3017.

72. *Id.* at 3015.

73. *Id.* at 3018.

74. *Id.* at 3021.

75. *Id.* at 3022.

76. *Id.* at 3022–23.

77. *Id.* at 3024.

78. *Id.*

79. *Id.*

80. This line of cases is even more paradoxical (if not actually schizophrenic) when compared to the seminal cases of National Farmers Union Insurance Co. v. Crow Tribe of Indians, 471 U.S. 845 (1985), and Iowa Mutual Insurance Co. v. LaPlante, 480 U.S. 9 (1987), which ringingly endorse tribal courts as the primary forums to resolve civil disputes that arise on the reservation. *See generally* Frank Pommersheim, *The Crucible of Sovereignty: Analyzing Issues of Tribal Jurisdiction,* 31 ARIZ. L. REV. 331 (1989). *See also* the discussion in chapter 3.

81. Tribes retain authority over non-Indians (on fee land) who enter consensual relationships with the tribe or its members or whose activities otherwise directly affect the political integrity, the economic security, or the health or welfare of the tribe. Montana v. United States, 450 U.S. 544, 565–66 (1981).

82. 113 S. Ct. 2309 (1993).

83. *Id.* at 2313. The project also acquired eighteen thousand acres on the Cheyenne River Sioux Reservation that were owned in fee by non-Indians. *Id.* at 2314.

84. Flood Control Act of 1944, ch. 665, 58 Stat. 887 (1944) (codified at 33 U.S.C. § 701-1.

85. Cheyenne River Act of 1954, ch. 1260, 68 Stat. 1191 (1954).

86. *Bourland,* 113 S.Ct. at 2321 (Blackmun, J., dissenting). Specifically:

> The United States did not take this land with the purpose of destroying tribal government or even with the purpose of limiting tribal authority. It simply wished to build a dam. The Tribe's authority to regulate hunting and fishing on the taken acres is consistent with the uses to which Congress has put the land, and, in my view, that authority must be understood to continue until Congress clearly decides to end it.

87. *See supra* note 5 (a recent South Dakota Attorney General's statement that "Indian reservations are a 'divisive system' of government that have outlived their usefulness." To the best of my knowledge, this statement was never retracted nor criticized by any high-ranking South Dakota elected state or federal official).

88. *See, e.g.,* Centennial Accord, Aug. 4, 1989, Federally Recognized Indian Tribes in Washington State and the State of Washington [hereinafter Centennial Accord] (on file with the South Dakota Law Review).

89. See the text of the Governor's Proclamation, which provides in full that

WHEREAS, As the State of South Dakota celebrates the beginning of its second century, we must also remember that statehood was a very sad time for the Native American; and

WHEREAS, Two tragic events, the killing of Sitting Bull, on December 15, 1890, and the Wounded Knee massacre on December 29, 1890, occurred just 13 months after South Dakota became a state; and,

WHEREAS, The anniversary of these tragic conflicts, as well as the celebration of 100 years of statehood, offer an opportunity for South Dakotans to learn more about the life and culture of the Dakota-Lakota people; and,

WHEREAS, Any improvement in cultural understanding in the past can be attributed to the work of the Indian and non-Indian people of South Dakota who have striven to understand our differences and to educate those of us who have grown up together but who have never made the effort to bridge the cultural gap; and,

WHEREAS, That mutuality of interest provides a sound basis for constructive change, given a shared commitment to achieving our goals of equal opportunity, social justice and economic prosperity; and,

WHEREAS, by celebrating our cultural differences and drawing on those differences for the betterment of all, we can create a new respect among our citizens;

NOW, THEREFORE, I GEORGE MICKELSON, Governor of the State of South Dakota, do hereby proclaim, with the advice and consent of the state's tribal leaders, 1990 as a

YEAR OF
RECONCILIATION

in South Dakota, and call on our citizens, both Indian and non-Indian, to look for every opportunity to lay aside our fears and mistrust, to build friendships, to join together and take part in shared cultural activities, to learn about one another, to have fun with one another, and to begin a process of mutual respect and understanding that will continue to grow into South Dakota's second hundred years.

90. Centennial Accord, *supra* note 88, art. 1, at 1.

91. Such a commission was in place in South Dakota before. *See, e.g.,* SOUTH DAKOTA TASK FORCE ON INDIAN-STATE GOVERNMENT RELATIONS, 1974 REPORT (1974). The task force, created in 1973 to study tribal-state governmental relations, was appropriated $100,000 for fiscal year 1973 and an additional $40,000 for fiscal year 1974. *Id.* at 1–2. Comprising eighteen members, nine of these appointed by the tribes, the task force sought to establish mutual governmental programs. *Id.* at 2–3. In so doing, the task force reviewed staff reports on issues, took testimony, and examined the legal relationship between the parties. *Id.* at 5–12. It then proposed solutions to the legislature. *Id.* at 43–58.

92. Frank Pommersheim, Attorneys General Survey 2–3 (letter from South Dakota Attorney General on file with author). *See generally* Frank Pommersheim, *Tribal-State Relations: Hope for the Future?,* 36 S.D. L. REV. 239, 261–68 (1991).

93. Centennial Accord, *supra* note 88, at art. IV.

94. *Id.*

95. Frank Pommersheim, *When It Comes to Indians, the West Is Ignorant,* HIGH COUNTRY NEWS, May 21, 1990, at 15, col. 1.

96. *See supra* notes 5 and 87 and accompanying text.

97. Avis Little Eagle, *Democrats Give Tribes Support,* INDIAN COUNTRY TODAY, July 7, 1994, at B1–B2.

98. The Western Governors' Association was established in 1984. Its membership includes Alaska, American Samoa, Arizona, California, Colorado, Guam, Hawaii, Idaho, Kansas, Minnesota, Montana, Nebraska, Nevada, North Dakota, Northern Mariana Islands, Oregon, South Dakota, Utah, Washington, and Wyoming. The Western Governors' Association was established to respond to policy issues identified by the western governors. Within the association, the issue of tribal-state relations has seen increased examination. The association has determined that, especially in rural areas, many problems faced by the states and tribes are the same. 1990 ANNUAL REPORT TO THE WESTERN GOVERNORS' ASSOCIATION, A NEW ERA FOR STATE-TRIBAL RELATIONS 14 (1990). Therefore, the association has begun projects between state governors, tribal chairs, and interested groups to promote these mutual concerns. *Id.* at 15–18.

99. The Council of Energy Resources Tribes is a group based in Denver, Colorado, representing tribal interests in energy matters. CERT has worked with the Western Governors' Association and is developing environmental management projects. *Id.* at 15–16.

100. *See, e.g.,* F. SANDER, B. PAULSON, L. RAY, G. KESSLER, & G. GRIENER, ALTERNATIVE DISPUTE RESOLUTION: AN ADR PRIMER

(1989) (description of these processes, which include mediation, negotiation, arbitration, private judging, neutral fact finding, and the use of an ombudsman); see also Charles Abourezk, Alternative Dispute Resolution in South Dakota's Tribal-State Conflict: Obstacles and Possibilities (1990) (University of South Dakota School of Law's McKusick Law Library collection of student papers) (a thoughtful and insightful review of the history and prospects of alternative dispute resolution in South Dakota and throughout the West).

101. Abourezk, supra note 100, at 20–21.

102. Id.

103. H. Ted Rubin, Tribal Court and State Courts: Disputed Civil Jurisdiction Concerns and Steps Toward Resolution, 14 STATE DIV. J. 9, (1991).

104. For example, witness the desire of outsiders to use South Dakota and its reservations as "dumping grounds" in the Lonetree (Edgemont, S.D.) and the Connecticut-based RSW, Inc. (Rosebud Sioux Reservation), waste disposal controversies. The metaphor is glaring. "Dances with Garbage"—a headline and story in the Christian Science Monitor—graphically captures this problem. This headline plays on the beautiful and successful Kevin Costner movie Dances with Wolves, made and set in South Dakota. Tom Daschle, Dances with Garbage, CHRISTIAN SCIENCE MONITOR, Feb. 14, 1991.

105. See, e.g., Tribal-State Relations: Hope for the Future (1990) (symposium sponsored by the University of South Dakota School of Law, the Native American Law Student Association, and the Indian Law Committee of the South Dakota Bar Association). This event encouraged and sparked this chapter in the first instance.

CHAPTER 6. ECONOMIC DEVELOPMENT
IN INDIAN COUNTRY

1. More specifically, the poorest county in the United States is Shannon County, the second poorest is Buffalo County, the fifth poorest is Ziebach County, and the eighth poorest is Todd County. BUREAU OF THE CENSUS, U.S. DEP'T OF COMMERCE, PRD #9 CAPITAL, 1979 COUNTY PER CAPITA INCOME FIGURES RELEASED BY CENSUS BUREAU FROM THE 1980 CENSUS 2 (1983). See also the discussion in chapter 1.

2. BUREAU OF THE CENSUS, U.S. DEP'T OF COMMERCE, PUB. NO. PC80-1-C43, 1980 CENSUS OF THE POPULATION (GENERAL SOCIAL AND ECONOMIC CHARACTERISTICS, SOUTH DAKOTA) 269 (1983).

3. Id.

4. BUREAU OF THE CENSUS, U.S. DEP'T OF COMMERCE, PUB. NO. PC80-1-C43, 1980 CENSUS OF THE POPULATION (DETAILED POPULATION STATISTICS, SOUTH DAKOTA) 318, 336 (1983). See also FRANK

POMMERSHEIM & ANNA REMEROWSKI, RESERVATION STREET LAW 98 (1979).

5. THE WORLD ALMANAC AND BOOK OF FACTS 1991, at 394 (1991).

6. "Underdeveloped" is most often used in the economic sense and is equated with extensive poverty and low productivity. "Development," by contrast, is most often defined as a process whereby an economy's real national income increases over a long period of time. More apt, perhaps, is the formulation by the economist John Kenneth Galbraith, who defines development as the process of providing people a release from the acculturation of poverty and providing them with some opportunity for upward mobility. Also note Professor Galbraith's own cautionary observation that one of the most compelling errors in social perception is the mistake in "believing that the advanced industrial countries, socialist and capitalist, are a guide and model for economic and social development of the new countries of the world." Galbraith, *Ideology and Agriculture,* HARPER'S MAGAZINE, Feb. 1985, at 15.

7. *See* Dennis Ickes, *Tribal Economic Independence—The Means to Achieve True Tribal Self-Determination,* 26 S.D. L. REV. 494 (1981).

8. *See* STEVEN HABERFELD ET AL., A SELF-HELP MANUAL FOR TRIBAL ECONOMIC DEVELOPMENT (1982).

9. *See* BRUCE JOHANSEN & ROBERTO MAESTAS, WASI'CHU: THE CONTINUING INDIAN WARS (1979).

10. BRUCE JOHNSTON & WILLIAM C. CLARK, REDESIGNING RURAL DEVELOPMENT 11 (1982). *See also* STEVEN CORNELL & JOSEPH P. KALT, WHAT CAN TRIBES DO? (1992).

11. JOHNSTON & CLARK, *supra* note 10, at 11.

12. *Id.* at 12.

13. Comprehensive Employment and Training Act of 1973, repealed at 29 U.S.C. §§ 801–999 (1984)

14. 25 U.S.C. § 13 (1983), 25 C.F.R. § 26.1–26.8 (1984).

15. Economic Opportunity Act of 1964, as amended and partially repealed at 42 U.S.C. §§ 2701–2995d (1984).

16. S.D. CODIFIED LAWS ch. 13–39 (1982).

17. JOHNSTON & CLARK, *supra* note 10, at 30.

18. *Id.* at 31.

19. *Id.* at 31–32.

20. *Id.* at 32.

21. *Id.* at 35.

22. PETER BERGER, PYRAMIDS OF SACRIFICE 47–49 (1974).

23. *See* C. PETER TIMMER ET AL., FOOD POLICY ANALYSIS 1–13 (1984).

24. HABERFELD ET AL., *supra* note 8, at 1-1.

25. *Id.* at 1-2.

26. These state tax agreements represent a cooperative effort by the

tribes and the state to administer, collect, and share sales tax revenues rather than to impose separate sales taxes and raise the difficult legal questions of their applicability to Indians and non-Indians and the administrative complexity of collection and accounting. In the case of the Rosebud Sioux Tribe, the agreement calls for 75 percent of the revenue to be provided to the tribe and 25 percent to the state. In the case of the Oglala Sioux Tribe, the agreement calls for 83 percent of the revenue to be provided to the tribe and 17 percent to the state. In the case of the Cheyenne River Sioux Tribe, the agreement calls for a 50-50 split. These different figures are based on estimates of the percentage of commercial trade volume engaged in by each segment of the population. The state also charges 1 percent for administrative costs. For the period July 1983 to June 1984, these agreements yielded $404,662 in revenue for the Rosebud Sioux Tribe, $238,817 for the Oglala Sioux Tribe, and $398,672 for the Cheyenne River Sioux Tribe. Interview with Don Lewis, Acting Director, University of South Dakota Research Bureau, University of South Dakota (Jan. 10, 1985).

27. For example, the 1993 budget of the Rosebud Sioux Tribe provides for a total budget in excess of $5 million, with less than $700,000 in nonfederal revenue. Telephone interview with Charles White Pipe, Treasurer, Rosebud Sioux Tribe (Aug. 15, 1993).

28. All BIA and other federal agency funding must be spent in strict accordance with applicable federal regulations. Under no circumstances may such monies be deposited in a tribe's unrestricted account or general fund. *Id.*

29. *See generally* HABERFELD ET AL., *supra* note 8.

30. For example, tribal courts in South Dakota have almost no long-established civil law governing complex commercial transactions or disputes. As a result, there is little experience or established tribal precedent in this area. Yet this too is changing as several South Dakota tribes have adopted their own version of the Uniform Commercial Code in recent years and are currently prepared to deal with litigation involving this complex area of law.

31. Ickes, *supra* note 7, at 516.

32. TIMMER ET AL., *supra* note 23, at 270.

33. "Optimal" is used here in the economic sense that means to allow for the most efficient use of resources, including labor, in order to achieve the profit necessary to sustain the venture. Since labor is a primary tribal resource, it must be considered accordingly in the planning and implementation phase.

34. 25 U.S.C. §§ 461–79 (1982). *See also* Frank Pommersheim & Terry Pechota, *Tribal Immunity, Tribal Courts, and the Federal System: Emerging Contours and Frontiers,* 31 S.D. L. REV. 553 (1986).

35. *See* Bill Richards, *Gov. Janklow Exhibits Strange Personal Style, But He Means Business,* WALL ST. J., Mar. 29, 1984, at 1, col. 1.

36. This is true even in developed countries like the United States. *See, Who Is Better Off Under Reagan—and Who Isn't*, BUSINESS WEEK, Oct. 22, 1984, at 14.

37. JOHNSTON & CLARK, *supra* note 10, at 167.

38. *Id.* at 160–61.

39. *Id.* at 173–82.

40. *Id.* at 166.

41. *Id.*

42. *Id.* at 168–69.

43. *Id.* at 172.

44. For a description, see *supra,* notes 35–38 and accompanying text.

45. 42 U.S.C. §§ 1381–94 (1982).

46. *See* Tim Giago, *Notes from Indian County,* LAKOTA TIMES, Nov. 21, 1984, at 2, col. 2.

47. JOHNSTON & CLARK, *supra* note 10, at 182.

48. HABERFELD ET AL., *supra* note 8, at 11-1, 11-2.

49. JOHNSTON & CLARK, *supra* note 10, at 155.

50. 480 U.S. 202 (1987).

51. Public Law 280 is a 1953 federal statute which transferred certain (tribal) criminal and civil (but *not* regulatory) jurisdiction to certain states in mandatory fashion while making such transfer optional in others. California was one of the six mandatory states. 67 Stat. 588, as amended, 18 U.S.C. § 1162, 28 U.S.C. § 1360 (1982 ed.).

52. *Cabazon,* 480 U.S. at 222.

53. 25 U.S.C. §§ 2701–21 (1993).

54. Cheyenne River Sioux Tribe v. South Dakota, F.3d 273 (8th Cir. 1993).

55. *Id. See also* Seminole Tribe of Florida v. Florida, 11 F.3d 1016 (11th Cir. 1994).

56. In *Cheyenne River Sioux Tribe v. South Dakota,* the Eighth Circuit rejected both the Tenth and Eleventh Amendment arguments. In *Seminole Tribe of Florida v. Florida,* the Eleventh Circuit upheld the Eleventh Amendment argument and dismissed the tribe's lawsuit. While this holding might appear to potentially moot IGRA, the Court of Appeals pointed out that once a suit is dismissed on Eleventh Amendment grounds, the tribe may, pursuant to 25 U.S.C. § 2701 d(7)(B)(vii), notify the Secretary of the Interior of its failure to negotiate a compact with the state. The Secretary may then prescribe regulations governing Class III gaming on the tribe's lands.

57. Bunty Anquoe, *Trump Hires Big Guns to Fight Indian Gaming,* INDIAN COUNTRY TODAY, Aug. 25, 1993, at A6.

58. *Id.*

59. *State Gaming Fears Emit "Stench of Hypocrisy,"* INDIAN COUN-
TRY TODAY, Aug. 11, 1993, at A5 (Reprint of *Seattle Post-Intelligence*
editorial).

60. Dirk Johnson, *Economies Come to Life on Indian Reservations,*
NEW YORK TIMES, July 3, 1994, at 1, 10–11.

61. *See generally* MARCEL MAUSS, THE GIFT (1967).

62. LEWIS HYDE, THE GIFT 74–75 (1983).

63. *Id.* at xiv.

64. Each fall from 1984 to 1993, I took my Indian law class to visit
the Rosebud Sioux Tribal Court. The court staff provided a special meal
for the class at the courthouse. The vice president of the tribe often welcomed the class and said a traditional prayer over the meal. Many of the
students found this an unexpected and powerful experience.

65. PETER BERGER, *supra* note 22, at 246–47.

66. *Id.* at 244.

67. *Id.* at 247–48.

68. JOHNSTON & CLARK, *supra* note 10, at 270.

CONCLUSION

1. 31 U.S. (6 Pet.) 515 (1832). *See* the detailed discussion in chapter 2 and elsewhere. Some of the thoughts expressed in this section were
developed in conversation with my good friend Phil Frickey. *See* Professor Frickey's own views in his *Marshalling Past and Present: Colonialism, Constitutionalism, and Interpretation in Federal Indian Law,* 107
HARV. L. REV. 381 (1993). *See also* the less optimistic vision of Robert A. Williams, Jr., *Columbus's Legacy: Law as an Instrument of Racial Discrimination Against Indigenous Peoples' Rights of Self-Determination,* 8 ARIZ. J. INT'L & COMP. LAW 51, 70–74 (1991).

2. 358 U.S. 217 (1959). *See* the detailed discussion in chapter 5.

3. 448 U.S. 136 (1980). *See* the detailed discussion in chapter 5.

4. 450 U.S. 544 (1981). *See* the detailed discussions in chapters 3
and 5.

5. 492 U.S. 408 (1989). *See* the detailed discussion in chapter 5.

6. 113 S. Ct. 2309 (1993). *See* the detailed discussion in chapter 5.

7. *Brendale,* 492 U.S. at 456.

8. *See* HORACE GREELEY, AMERICAN CONFLICT 106 (1864). Other
scholars doubt that he actually said it. *See, e.g.,* M. JAMES, THE LIFE
OF ANDREW JACKSON 603–04 (1938).

9. DAVID H. GETCHES & CHARLES F. WILKINSON, FEDERAL IN-
DIAN LAW 50–51 (2d ed. 1986).

10. CHARLES WARREN, THE SUPREME COURT IN UNITED STATES
HISTORY 189 (1923).

11. Lyng v. Northwest Indian Cemetery Protective Association, 485 U.S. 439 (1988) (holding that the U.S. government may build a highway to expand logging activities on federal land even if it violates the integrity of tribal sacred places also located in the public domain).

12. Employment Division, Dep't of Human Resources of Oregon v. Smith, 494 U.S. 872 (1990) (holding that the state of Oregon may properly criminalize the use of peyote by anyone, including members of the Native American Church). Overturning the result of this decision is one objective of the proposed Native American Free Exercise of Religion Act, S. 1021, 103d Cong., 1st Sess. (1993).

13. 471 U.S. 845 (1985). *See* the detailed discussions in chapters 3 and 4.

14. 480 U.S. 9 (1987). *See* the detailed discussions in chapters 3 and 4.

15. This "breathing space" permits, but does not necessarily endorse, the results of tribal court analysis of the extent of its jurisdiction. In addition, there is some congressional concern about the scope of federal review of tribal court decision making on the *merits* as opposed to basic questions of jurisdiction. This is particularly true in the context of Santa Clara Pueblo v. Martinez, 436 U.S. 49 (1978), and the Indian Civil Rights Act of 1968, 25 U.S.C. §§ 1301–03 (1984). *See, e.g.,* S. 517, 101st Cong., 1st Sess. (1990), which proposes to extend federal judicial review of tribal court decision making in this area.

16. Evan Eisenberg, *Back to Eden,* The Atlantic, Nov. 1989, at 89 (quoting Wes Jackson).

17. Robert Hughes, The Culture of Complaint 124 (1993).

18. *Id.* at 121.

19. Cornel West, *Critique and Mercy in the Cross of Christ,* The Other Side, July–August 1993, at 11.

20. *See, e.g.,* Patricia Limerick, The Legacy of Conquest (1989); Richard White, "It's Your Misfortune and None of My Own": A History of the American West (1991); Trails: Toward a New Western History (Patricia Limerick, Clyde Milner II, & Charles Rankin eds., 1991); Under an Open Sky: Rethinking America's Western Past (William Cronon, George Miles, & J. Gitlin eds., 1992).

21. Martha Minow, Making All the Difference 376 (1990).

22. Richard Rorty, Contingency, Irony, and Solidarity xvi (1984).

23. *Id.*

24. Wendell Berry, Sex, Economy, Freedom, and Community 173 (1993). Note also the observation of the Native American writer Sherman Alexie that survival on the reservation is a product of anger and imagination. Alexie, Tonto and the Lone Ranger Fistfight in Heaven (1993).

Index

Composition:	Maple-Vail
Text:	10/13 Sabon
Display:	Sabon
Printing and binding:	**IBT**